BROKE THROUGH BRITAIN

One Man's Penniless Odyssey

Peter Mortimer

MAINSTREAM
PUBLISHING

BROKE THROUGH BRITAIN

Peter Mortimer is a poet, playwright and editor. Born in Nottingham, he has been resident since 1975 in the wind-blown north-east coastal village of Cullercoats, where he protects his battered Remington typewriter against the ravages of modern technology. He has written 15 plays, for most of the region's main adult and children's theatre companies and for BBC Radio 4, and has also published various poetry books for both adults and children. For several years he was the region's drama critic for *The Guardian* and he is the founder/editor of IRON Press, which since 1973 has published an active list of new poetry, fiction and drama. His only precedent for such an incautious foray as *Broke through Britain* was in 1987, when he wrote the book *The Last of the Hunters* after spending six months at sea working with North Shields fishermen.

Peter Mortimer also works regularly as a Writer in Schools in a vainglorious attempt to subvert the education system.

BROKE THROUGH BRITAIN

One Man's Penniless Odyssey

Peter Mortimer

MAINSTREAM
PUBLISHING

EDINBURGH AND LONDON

First published in Great Britain in 1999 by
MAINSTREAM PUBLISHING COMPANY (EDINBURGH) LTD
7 Albany Street
Edinburgh EH1 3UG

Reprinted 1999, 2000, 2001

ISBN 1 84018 163 X

A catalogue record for this book is available from the British Library

Typeset in Garamond
Printed and bound in Great Britain by Cox & Wyman Ltd, Reading, Barkshire

For Kitty
who always keeps me going

Acknowledgements

Firstly, I'd like to thank the many dozens of people who were willing to feed and house me during my odyssey. Without their trusting nature it would have been impossible. I must also thank Sarah Davidson for trusting Sam into my keeping.

To write the book's final draft, I locked myself away in retreat. I'd like to thank Vera O'Hagan and Allan at the Old School House Creative Writing Centre, Haltwhistle, Northumberland, for the huge meals, moral support and fantastic setting, and also, for the last laps, Angela Wright, who readily made available to me her house in Duke Street, Whitley Bay, over a two-week period.

I must also thank my agent, Tina Betts, of Andrew Mann Ltd, for supporting the idea when it was just a mad gleam in the author's eye.

I'd like to thank Homer too. His epic *Odyssey* gave me support on my more humble version . . .

Preface

When preparing for my penniless odyssey, I came across an Indian custom of going on pilgrimage at the age of 50. How would Western society handle such a thing? I imagined the multinationals patting their employees on the head, come their half-century, with the words, 'Off you go, then, a pilgrimage on full salary, and we do hope you return spiritually enriched.' Maybe not.

Luckily I'm not the wage slave of a multinational, so when the idea first came to me in those small hours of the morning that cheat you of sleep, the main obstacle in my way was common sense. How would an individual fare, travelling through our country, denied the facilities we take for granted: food, shelter, money? Would he or she survive in a nation which often shows a soured face to the world? Unrestricted generosity and open-handed charity do not immediately spring to mind as attributes of modern Britain.

Other cultures accept the wanderer. Monks walk penniless with their wooden bowls in several Eastern societies. They do not starve. And the monks in turn offer sanctuary to the traveller. This seems a good arrangement, and one that doesn't depend on a huge gross national product. Yet, as Orwell pointed out in his essays, in our country 'tramps' are usually treated as scroungers, despite the fact that their way of life is infinitely harder than most, and one which many so-called honest and decent members of society would be unable to survive.

There is a certain degree of romanticism about life on the road. It's fed by countless US movies, Jack Kerouac books, that deep sense of unrooted freedom in all of us, a casting off of dull responsibility and duty. Is there any romance to its reality?

I'd done a fair share of travelling and written a good many travel articles. But never a travel book, and never without the security of a wallet. Despite poverty in Britain, shelter and food are – happily – something most of us don't have to battle for daily. Hunger is a temporary state, relieved if need be by a Twix or a Mars bar until the next meal comes along. Most of us need never wonder where we will sleep that particular night. What would be the effect of removing such 'luxuries', and at the same time having to travel long distances? The thought both fascinated and appalled me, and put me in mind of what a playwright friend, Rod Wooden, once said: 'Write about something you fear.'

Once the idea took root, it nagged at me like a toothache. What would the journey be? Land's End to John O'Groats? Too predictable. And too far. I decided 500 miles seemed a good distance. A check on the map showed Plymouth to Edinburgh would fit the bill. Many pilgrimages had started at Plymouth. And I would be journeying between the most southerly cities of both England and Scotland.

What next? I phoned a Buddhist friend, Yann Lovelock, who'd spent some time with a begging bowl on the streets of Birmingham. He advised me to visit my local Buddhist monastery, Harnham Vihara, only 30 miles from me in Northumberland.

Harnham is a small monastery (six monks, two novices) housed in former farm buildings perched on a hilltop. Some of the monks had experience of wandering penniless, and as I sat and ate a strange combination of Thai spicy food and arctic roll, the monks Punnjo and Suvaco talked to me. 'You will find it very hard,' said Suvaco, 'but eventually you will gain strength. It will be part of your journey through life, so you must.' There was practical advice, too: carry a torch and brolly; take some moleskins (padded foot protection).

The monks also lent me two important books. *No Destination* is the extraordinary autobiography of Satish Kumar, who, inspired by Bertrand Russell, undertook an 8,000-mile peace pilgrimage on foot from his native India to America. He walked through deserts and over mountains, crossed Russia in the winter, and was thrown into jail. He carried no money, but delivered packets of 'peace tea' to world leaders. Kumar also undertook a British pilgrimage, walking to this country's holy places such as Glastonbury, Lindisfarne and Canterbury. He now lives in Devon. The other book, *Peace Pilgrim*, is the story of the American woman (known only by the book title) who, over three decades, walked more than 25,000 miles, penniless, through the USA and Canada in the name of world peace, her name emblazoned across her T-shirt. She walked into her seventies, fired by her beliefs. She would walk until offered shelter, fast till she was offered food. Sometimes she walked through the night. Compared to these two remarkable people, my odyssey began to take on the dimensions of a Sunday stroll.

Kumar wrote, 'Walking in itself was an end, a form of meditation, a way of being. The outer journey became the inner journey.' There would be an important difference with my journey. They walked with a definite mission: high-profile peace pilgrimages. The writing came later. My own walk would have no definite 'mission', and I would be fired by the doubts most writers feel. My journey would be specifically as a writer. I would not expect people to throw open their doors for me. Who would know me?

I went back to other books: J.B. Priestley's *An English Journey*, a fascinating study of this country in the '30s, though Priestley travelled as a famous man on coaches and trains, and stayed in comfortable hotels. And Orwell's *Down and Out in Paris and London*, with its startling evocation of life on the bottom rung. Both books are important social as well as literary documents. I had less of an idea of my ambition for my own book, except that it must speak for itself.

A theatre director friend, Lesley Hanns, lent me Richard Mabey's book *Food for Free*, a guide to sustenance to be had from hedgerows, roadside verges, etc. – though most of the food needs cooking, and somehow I couldn't see myself foraging for fungi or goatsbeard. My friend Sarah Davidson offered her dog, a seven-year-old King Charles spaniel, Sam.

'He'll walk forever,' she said, 'and people will like you.' I'd thought of a dog and, though a bit minuscule, Sam looked cuddly. He might mean friendlier welcomes on doorsteps, as well as solace in those hours of loneliness and sagging spirits. I could snuggle him in the cold. Against which it was an extra mouth to feed. But I made the decision. Sam was on the team.

I decided the following rough daily plan: travel at least 15 miles, find food, find shelter, write 1,000 words. Simple, eh?

I was entering an unknown world. Not up some remote river in a far continent, not crossing a hostile desert, but in my own land. Yet I felt it might be as removed from my normality as any 20,000-foot mountain peak or impenetrable jungle. I would be seeing my own country through a distorting mirror. I would need to adapt in ways I still could not imagine. I knew there would be loneliness and despair, as in all expeditions. Few are glamorous or exciting at the time. Only in the achievement, in the telling and the retelling, does the kudos attach itself. And how would my physical and mental energies hold out? Would I be able to carry on walking? Or writing? Was the whole idea facile?

A few journalist friends asked if I wanted pre-publicity. I said no, dubious about the kind of high-profile travel writing that comes with celebrities, camera crews, teams of researchers. I believed the best writing was with notebook and pen, and any media circus distorts that which it attempts to record. Nor did I want gimmicks – travelling with a deep freeze or suchlike. Would I beg? I watched the Channel 4 series *Beg to Differ*, and decided that sitting on a street corner, hand outstretched, was not my style. I brushed up my mouth-organ techniques, mastered a few tunes, and opted to take one along as another possibility. I thought, as a poet, of penning the odd bespoke verse in return for grub or shelter. I decided to write a daily haiku, those gemlike three-line poems imported, along with Nissan cars and sushi, from Japan. Traditionally, these were always 17 syllables. The Western haiku, however, was less formal.

Making these little plans cheered me. For much of the

month before I set off for Plymouth I was incredibly appre-
hensive. I visited the toilet three times more than average.
The prospect of my journey to come haunted me, if you can
be haunted by the future.

I packed my bag. I needed to travel light. Spare under-
pants and socks, lightweight sleeping bag that folded as small
as a loaf of bread, two tops, jacket, small umbrella, cheap
camera, basic wash bag, two small notebooks, one large
cloth-bound notebook, one fountain pen, three ballpoint
pens, map, spare sandals (in case my Caterpillar walking
boots gave out), two bin liners, bottle of black ink, spare
trousers, Indian hat. Harmonica. How would I wash clothes
or body? I had no idea.

As departure grew near, I kept asking myself why I was
doing it. I hoped the journey would tell me. Sometimes a
writer needed to follow Kafka's advice: 'There is no need to
leave your room . . . the world will offer itself freely to you
unmasked. It has no choice. It will roll in ecstasy at your
feet.' But I also knew this wasn't enough. We had to go 'out
there' to discover what was 'in here'.

Being a fairly fit sort of chap, I did no special training. I
would set off mainly in blind ignorance of what awaited me.
Sam had a special trim, and I walked him along the clifftops.
Fine. And another 499½ miles?

At 54 I would be four years late for my pilgrimage.
Against which, being a fairly impoverished writer, I had a
freedom not given to better-off wage slaves. I needed
permission from no one. I just needed to get up and go.

The Eve

Thinking back on it now, I can recall that small knot of fear in the stomach. I carried that knot with me down on the train from Newcastle to Plymouth and into the Astor Hotel, where it woke before I did the next morning. The knot travelled up country with me, where it shrivelled only slowly. It was only in the latter stages I realised the knot had gone. The knot, I now realise, was an inevitable travelling companion.

I'd had some trouble booking bed and breakfast in Plymouth. More than 14,000 Jehovah's Witnesses were also booked into the city that Saturday night for their annual shindig. This was more spiritual support than a man could bear, and I kept my distance.

I had with me the clothes I stood up in, plus one spare set of everything. I had enough money to buy food on the train and two pints of beer in Plymouth and to pay for the B & B, with a bit left over for the moleskins I'd not had time to find before leaving. I had no credit cards, no reserve or emergency funds, no secret stash of food supplies. I had no wallet, no address book. I had no waterproof clothing, because it was too heavy. I had a small dog. As far as I knew, no one in Britain had done what I planned to do – a fact that was more disturbing than reassuring.

The train journey lasted eight hours. Throughout, Sam sat patiently. The train, which began at Newcastle, slowly filled with normal-looking folk excited about their West Country holidays to come. Small children were wide-eyed with anticipation and counted off the stations. The north fell away behind us, the Midlands, the West Midlands, on through Birmingham, down, further down, heading southwest, night falling as we journeyed on to Exeter, Torquay and

Paignton until, finally, a little after 11 p.m., we arrived in Plymouth.

Sam and I stepped off the train as the bustle of people made their way along the platform carting bulky suitcases. Into their taxis they went and off to their hotels. Probably all year they had looked forward to the coming weeks, saved, dreamed.

First impressions of Plymouth were reassuringly stereo-typical of the West Country. A ruddy-faced, smiling police-man with that distinctive soft West Country burr directed Sam and me towards the Hoe and the Astor Hotel, our last guaranteed night of comfort for – well, for however long it took.

The fear I felt was an exaggerated version of something I always experienced prior to travelling. I had been across the USA several times, various far-flung parts of the (then) USSR, to Iceland, Israel, East Africa, always driven by the instinct to travel. Yet whenever a departure date loomed, and people would say 'Bet you're excited', the truth was other-wise. At such times my inclination was always to stay at home, drink a pint in my local, stay in and read a book, do nothing challenging or unpredictable.

This was similar but different. A small but powerful voice inside me, the kind of voice that stops us doing anything much worth doing, was whispering that I was being idiotic, that a man of 54 should have more sense, that I was making a fool of myself, that if I had wanted to attempt anything as daft as this, I should have done it 20 years ago. I told the voice to shut up, but it went on and on.

The West Country stereotypes did not last long. As Sam and I walked from the station towards the centre, the Plymouth pubs were chucking out. Gangs of youths were spilling onto the pavements, indulging that strange impulse of the young English male to roar and bellow tunelessly, and, as they made their way towards the nightclubs, they banged their open palms against the corrugated shop-front shutters. They were dark, hunched shapes, often staggering in unison. Above them the black hovering insect of the police helicopter twirled its angry rotors. It felt like a battleground, which was perhaps what both sides wanted.

On towards the Hoe – quieter, more sedate – and the reassuringly solid-looking Astor Hotel, with its Greek pillars, its white façade, its thick carpets, its wooden floors with the occasional creak, its walls of panelled, stained wood. All these combined to envelop me in a false sense of security. Within minutes of us arriving, a bowl of fresh chicken arrived for Sam. Manager Roy Hardy, and the other staff, were polite, helpful, charming. They knew of my mission but, more importantly, I was a paying guest, which was a luxury and protection I would soon have to abandon. Also, my credentials were known – I had booked ahead.

A warm, comfortable room awaited, with crisp, clean sheets, *en suite* bathroom and toilet, a shower, a television. I knew a hot breakfast awaited the next day. I could still push away the reality which was growing closer. I could indulge a little longer in the normalities, or even luxuries, of everyday life.

In the Astor, a wedding party from Preston had been at it all day. As residents, they were entitled to drink beyond hours. In truth, they all secretly looked as if they'd had enough and would have preferred to have gone to bed, but there was a principle at stake (the principle of being able to drink late). Therefore they would continue. There was more fun to be had.

A string bean of a man approached the bar and summoned the barmaid, a student called April.

'Have a drink yourself, sweetheart!' he said.

'I'll just take for one,' said April. 'Thanks very much. That'll cost a pound.'

'It'll cost bloody 50 pence,' retorted the string bean. 'That's how much we give in Preston.'

April carried on, giving occasional looks at the clock. She treated me to a pint on the house and at midnight – a time of night I would not see again for a long time – Sam and I left the Preston revellers to their merriment and made our way up to the room. I was not used to the companionship of dogs. Part of me believed dogs were a totally unnatural companion to humans, forced to cramp themselves into houses, driven neurotic by long confinement and virtually total removal from their own kind, made insane by urban environments. Dogs, I often thought, belong with dogs.

Mind, Sam looked a canny pooch.

The late-night movie on television was *Easy Rider*, about two men in search of salvation 'on the road' but ultimately finding only oblivion. Just what I needed. Within minutes Sam was asleep, curled on the bed. I watched Peter Fonda and Dennis Hopper get blown away.

Day One — Sunday, 26 July

Miles travelled so far — 0

Far from home
My son's biroed name
Fades from my skin

The Road to Hell — A Plethora of Paperweights — The Reluctant Rector

As I lay in the soft white sheets of the Astor Hotel at 6.25 a.m., Sam barked his announcement that the odyssey was about to begin. I lay staring at the ceiling, enjoying for the final moments this protective womb. I rose, showered and wrapped myself in the fluffy polar bear of a towel. I shaved. I took everything from my backpack and laid it on the bed, partly as a stock check, partly to remind myself what I was about to undertake. The pack, which I had borrowed from my 14-year-old son Dylan, had one main zipped compartment, one inner one and two side ones. During these first days I would be constantly rearranging my meagre possessions, finding the best position for each.

I took up and fondled my sturdy Caterpillar boots. I felt an affinity with them and their task of conveying me 500 miles. I undertook the long, careful process of lacing them, a process I was to repeat more than 100 times.

In the downstairs dining-room, holidaymakers were planning their annual fun. The Preston string bean was already helping himself to the self-serve breakfast and, for some reason, shouting 'Alrightee!'. One man poked suspiciously at the prunes. Women on diets ate fruit and yoghurt and looked miserable. I tucked into a full English breakfast: egg, bacon, sausage, mushrooms, beans, tomatoes, fried bread, tea and toast. Plus seconds of toast. Plus more toast gathered up from other tables and stuffed into my pockets. And small containers of butter. I gathered them against my instincts; I was so full I was convinced I would never be hungry again. I

would simply walk up the country with this full tum. I knew
cold toast tasted like place mats. But took it anyway.

The hotel gave Sam a bowl of bacon and sausage. I watched
the wee fellow devour it. The holidaymakers were folding out
maps, poring over brochures, planning excursions, working
out ways of spending money. This was a problem I didn't have.
I wondered if any of them were Jehovah's Witnesses.

For the last time I returned to the bedroom, enjoying the
delicious transience of those final moments of luxury. The
fleeting quality itself imbued them with magic. Two minutes
lying on the bed. I closed my eyes, listened to my own
breathing. Then up, the lead put on Sam. He had an old-
fashioned lead, not a monstrous thing that came reeling out
of an ugly plastic box, tripping up passers-by. I did not wish
to play him like a fish. I'd written up the first pages of my
diary and emerged into the bright and breezy Plymouth
morning. It was 9.35 a.m.

Up on the Hoe, with its magnificent sweep of the bay,
they were preparing for a vintage bus rally. A posse of old
jalopies, plus 14,000 Jehovah's Witnesses, all on the same
weekend. I stood next to Sir Francis Drake. He looked as
pompous and remote as most statues, though the hand-on-
hip stance could have turned him into a gay icon.

Plymouth had been the launch pad for many great
odysseys: Drake, Captain Cook, Scott of the Antarctic. They
all headed south. My own journey that day was to be due
north. First mistake. From my position on this peninsula,
north-east would have been preferable. My paltry book of
maps – soon to be discarded as inadequate – suggested the
A386 to Tavistock as the best option. Other minor roads,
some not on my map, were far better.

Was I merely impatient? Ignorant? Stupid? Probably the
first. In Plymouth's spacious pedestrianised centre, where
every thoroughfare was Drake this, Armada that, Mayflower
the other, I learned that the chemist, where I hoped to buy
padded insoles for my feet, was closed for another 30
minutes. Half an hour in a month's odyssey is little enough
to wait. I didn't. Off I marched. Mistake number two.

I was also to learn an early lesson. Without money, cities and towns were alienating, depressing places. They were fuelled by consumption, by buying and selling. Anyone unable to carry out these basic activities was immediately ostracised.

Walking out of Plymouth involves a six-mile uphill gradient, an all-morning journey. We passed people washing cars, trimming hedges and lawns, carrying home the ridiculous bulk of Sunday newspapers. We passed shops, garages, hotels, signs to car boot sales. And even at this stage, my sense of alienation from the motor car was growing.

In midsummer, the A386, for one man and his dog, soon became a nightmare. As the city fell away, the road turned into a long, pitiless affair. Cars and other vehicles thundered past incessantly in each direction. We were buffeted by walls of wind; we were at times forced to take refuge in the narrow, pot-holed, often untended grass verges. With their padded comfort, their Van Morrison CDs, their air-conditioning, the motorists screamed past us in a relentless torrent, a blur of coloured metal. This was our first road. And I would have given all my money to get off it. Except I had no money. And, having decided on that day's route, I stubbornly stuck to it. Several times the fat, overgrown hedgerows pushed us alarmingly close to the whooshing traffic. Poor Sam. I needed to pick him up and carry him like some panting accessory.

We found temporary refuge down a hotel's country driveway, through landscaped open land on which Dartmoor ponies grazed peacefully. Suddenly the bedlam was shut out as if a door into the main party room had been closed. The Moorland Links Hotel faced out across spacious, well-tended grounds, seemingly a universe removed from the road to hell. We walked to the entrance. Sunday diners reclined in comfort, the smell of roast beef was in the air, I could hear the tinkle of the dining-room piano. In the foyer more people were relaxing, some drinking in the comfortable bar. This was an oasis. But of what use to us? As we stood there, the young female receptionist behind the desk asked, 'Can I help you, sir?'

It was the first real defining moment, the first time my totally impecunious state struck home.

'I'd, erm, like a bowl of water for my dog, if I could.'

She disappeared and came back with a bowl, which she put down on the thick pile carpet. Sam drank eagerly. I looked around, realising I was in this place but not of this place; it was the first of many places I could look at but not touch. I wanted to walk into that bar, order a pint and a round of sandwiches and sit down.

Sam had finished the water.

'Thank you,' I said, and we walked out.

By now the afternoon sun was fierce. I lay on the grass under the shade of a tree and watched the cars come and go over the hotel's cattle grid. I took out two small triangles of cold toast, used my finger to spread them with butter from the containers I punctured with my nail and shared them with Sam. Sunday lunch. And what would Sunday tea be?

We had walked nine miles. After eating our fill (*sic*), I secured Sam's lead to my arm, stretched out and went to sleep. As I drifted off, I saw the hotel as a metaphor. I imagined myself in the Third World, staring glumly at a satellite television gaudily presenting before my eyes the consumer excesses of the West. To see, but not to have. I realised what this meant.

After 15 minutes I woke. Drivers were still leaving the hotel. I thought of that road, wondered if I could get a lift for a few miles. I approached one middle-aged couple as they slowed for the grid. They looked at me with disdain, did not reply and accelerated away. Nothing dramatic, but enough to knock me back. I picked up the bag, summoned Sam and headed back towards the road to hell. I felt Sam's fear and confusion as once again we approached the rolling thunder. I have no idea why I simply ploughed on. Later, when I was in touch, I would have found another solution.

A few miles before Yelverton, having survived more of the same, we found another temporary haven, a large outcrop in a spacious area locals simply called 'the Rock', brilliant for kiddies to climb and a magnet for Sunday picnicking families. They sat alongside their cars in their striped fold-up chairs, with their gingham cloths, their hampers, their trannies, their footballs, their tennis racquets, their sandwiches, their giant bottles of Coke.

By now I was hungry. For several moments I walked around the grassy area, plucking up courage. Finally I approached one family.

'I wondered . . .' I said.

'Yes?'

'. . . if I could just – have some water for my dog?'

I envisaged one week hence we would be found: one human skeleton, one canine grotesquely inflated through excessive intake of water. I looked on the bright side. Which was the two remaining small triangles of toast. These I ate on the grassy bank, against a background of laughing, playing children. ('Did they care nothing for me?' I wrote in my diary.) The act of writing comforted me a little, though against this the reality of having no money whatsoever was like an ever-growing, ever-darkening shadow.

The first offered food was not totally expected. Sam and I walked on to Yelverton. I had talked to virtually no one all day, and my feet were sore. I found myself striking up an admittedly one-way conversation with Sam. His contribution was a large, brown-eyed stare. Passing Yelverton rectory, I saw the rector pushing a lawnmower across the grass. I decided to approach him and strode through the gates and up the path. Please do not laugh at my request.

'I wondered if I could have some water for my dog?' I asked.

I seemed incapable of speaking any other words on this journey. Sam did not need water. I needed food. What on earth was I doing? I had little idea.

'Is that all you want, water?' asked the rector, a dark-haired, middle-aged man.

'Well, erm, I . . .' I mumbled, '. . . anything else, naturally, would not go amiss, that is . . .'

The rector turned and walked towards his front door. I followed. Suddenly he swivelled on his heel, held up his open palm before me as if denying the anti-Christ, and said in a very loud voice, 'Do not enter the rectory!' He then led Sam and me back to the garden, motioned to us to sit on a garden seat and went inside. Some minutes later he emerged with an ornate tray on which was water for Sam, a large mug of tea for me and chocolate digestive biscuits. These he put down on the seat.

'Thank you very much,' I said. 'I wouldn't have come inside, actually. I . . .'

'If you knew what had happened here . . .' he said, and went back inside.

I would discover the facts later. Meantime, slightly confused by this mix of charity and guardedness, I drank the tea, ate the biscuits, listened to the soft drone of the bees, breathed in the fragrance of this classical English garden's many flowers and plants. I closed my eyes for a few moments and allowed it to enwrap me. Later I carried the tray to the rectory door and rang the bell. No reply. I wrote a small thank-you note and left it with the tray on the porch. My first – mixed – experience of Christian charity on my journey.

We should have turned right in Yelverton and struck out north-east across Dartmoor on the B3212. Instead of which we stayed on the A386. Inflexible. Unable to adapt. Blindly ploughing on. Of course, we would have missed the Yelverton Paperweight Centre. Paperweights were not an item that had crowded my thoughts over the years. Apart from a book on DIY, they may well have been bottom of any fictional shopping list of mine. So why was I suddenly asking proprietor David Hunter all manner of questions on the centre, like some keen *Down your Way* reporter? My feet were aching as he told me that a paperweight could fetch a quarter of a million dollars and informed me that the centre had been started by Bernard and Dorothy Broughton, who'd brought 800 paperweights to Yelverton. Hundreds of them lined the shelves in this attractive wee museum. Not one of them weighed down paper. I wriggled my toes. We left.

For what seemed an eternity, all signposts said 'Tavistock 5'.

The hedgerows were now more than ten feet high, and their generous girths pushed Sam and me further towards the traffic. At the Halfway House a sign proclaimed, 'This pub is football-free.'

The good weather had gone. A steady rain set in. My feet were more sore. I felt my spirits droop. Up went the small brolly. We arrived in Tavistock in the early evening to find the town wet, empty, uncheering. Both Sam and I had walked enough on this day. We now faced the prospect of finding food and shelter. I was tired and hungry and wanted such things merely to be put before me, to sit down in warmth and comfort.

All doors seemed excessively closed. To knock on them did not appear an option. What would be your reaction on a wet Sunday night, a total stranger on your doorstep? Would you gladly invite him in, show him the spare room? I had not yet galvanised myself for this task. Nor was I in the right environment. I stood on a wet street corner and realised that I would face this, day in, day out, for a month. Walk all day penniless. Then find shelter. And food. The rain thrummed onto the brolly and dripped off. Sam looked up at me as if to say, well, come on, what do we do now? A few youths, hunched in a corner doorway, eyed me. It was 7.30 p.m. I wanted to be home.

From a large church I heard the sound of strong, in-tune singing. This was the parish church of St Eustathius, Tavistock. It was packed, the main evensong event of the year, with a visiting choir, the Exon Singers. We walked through the churchyard, through the door and stood at the back, wet, bedraggled, sorry-looking. A packed congregation gave full vent to their lungs. The hymns sang out on the glory of God, of Christian charity, of mercy, of compassion. Men in well-tailored jackets and ladies in tasteful frocks leant back their heads and gave forth the church's music, spurred on by the choir.

The service over, they filed past me to the exit, mainly middle-aged, prosperous-looking, white-skinned – returning, I assumed, to warm, comfortable houses. I approached several of them and explained my situation, how I needed food and shelter. They were embarrassed. The couples looked quickly one to the other, as if for reassurance, as if for mutual strength when they gave their rejections. And strength they found, enough strength to push me away politely. A bothersome person. Rude. A stranger. All had a perfectly reasonable excuse. None was aggressive, impolite. None would help.

I approached the vicar, a friendly-faced, bearded man called John Rawlings. Again, that sense of some embarrassment. 'Normally we'd love to help,' he said. 'But we're all putting up members of the choir tonight. Worst possible time, yes, ah.' He looked beyond me. 'Yes, goodnight, thank you, yes.'

As he addressed me, others addressed him, thanked him, said goodbye to him. He was much in demand. I felt I was an irritation to these people, an unwanted presence. The significance of this was enormous. I was suddenly metamorphosed. I was no longer Peter Mortimer, writer. I was a down-and-out, a beggar, a person you crossed the road to avoid. I was in the house of God. And the house of God, it seemed, could offer me nothing. What hope did I have elsewhere? How could I possibly survive a month if the potentially most charitable institution was rejecting me?

The well-to-do parishioners were melting away, the church was emptying. As I stood in that church porch, it all seemed pious cant, the hymns, the ceremony, the prayer.

'He can sleep in my garage.'

These words came from a young, tall, bespectacled curate, a slightly studious-looking man called Geoffrey Boucher. He smiled at me. He offered me sanctuary.

Geoffrey Boucher drove me to his home. Not the traditional large stone house of the clergy, but a simple domicile on Greenland Council Estate. 'Actually,' he said, as I told him about my planned journey, 'you can have the spare room. I don't suppose you've eaten, have you?' As we got out of the car, he said, 'There's no culture in our society of people on journeys such as yours. You'll find it hard. It's sad, but true.'

Inside the house we drank hot tea. I told him of the Yelverton rector. 'Ah, yes. Last year, someone came just like you. The rector invited him in and was badly beaten and robbed. He's nervous.'

While Geoffrey made me pork chops, potatoes and vegetables, I removed my boots and examined my feet. I consoled Sam, who was also fed. The curate offered me Fruits of the Spirit, bananas, apples and oranges used in that day's sermon, each fruit marked with a virtue. I ate Patience (a banana) and Faithfulness (an orange). My shell-shock receded with the food, the warmth. I unpacked my bag. My harmonica was broken. My only means of busking was gone.

And I realised that on my journey people didn't know me from Adam. Or Satan. Why should anyone take a chance on me?

We sat and talked for two hours. My body felt drained. But I had shelter. And a man who seemed to know my great doubts, my insecurities about my journey. The day had traumatised me. Nothing truly dramatic. A shifting of my perceptions. Moving into a different universe. I had considered this journey in the abstract. Now came the reality.

When I went to bed, I lay in the dark, the silence, as huge doubts assailed me. Sam lay on the floor in a corner. He had symbolically turned away from me and was coughing and shivering. What was I inflicting on him? On myself? What foolhardy venture had I undertaken? How could I survive another 30 days? Even contemplating those 500 miles stretching away, a barren, alien, hostile, mammoth, penniless journey, filled me with dread.

Experiencing one of those dark, unrewarding moments when deep pessimism and nihilism most attack you, I resolved that come the next morning I would abandon this whole ridiculous affair. I would call a halt to this absurd venture. There was no shame, I argued, in recognising when something was wrong. And this was surely wrong. I had made a mistake. Everyone makes mistakes. A pity, but . . .

I drifted off into a fitful, uncomfortable sleep. My ridiculous foray was at an end.

Miles travelled so far — 15

Into the prison
Then out again
The innocent sparrows

Manna from Heaven — Loose on Dartmoor — Painting my Bedroom

A new day, a new perspective. I awoke at 7.30 a.m. in better spirits. Sam too was livelier. He was lying among my clothes on the floor. I took this as a good sign. He liked me again. I popped him his vitamin pill (I'd sworn faithfully to feed him one twice a day). He chewed it, swallowed it and looked up at me with those big brown eyes. 'Tell you what, Sam,' I said, 'maybe we'll not give up. Not just yet.'

As if to affirm the new optimism, I washed, then did my daily quota of press-ups. Breathless, I carried on talking to Sam. 'All we can do, Sam,' I said, 'is get through each day, and handle every situation as it comes up. I mean, giving up after one day. We'd be a laughing stock!'

In truth, I was still afraid of the journey. So be it.

I sat down and wrote my diary for an hour. Geoffrey had gone off on church business and returned at 9 a.m. I wondered, did any of his council-estate neighbours go to church, a middle-class pursuit in our country? 'No,' he said, 'so I come to them instead.'

Occasionally they smashed glass in his greenhouse; part of the price. He was a new-generation churchman. No cant or dogma, no clerical smugness. His sympathy to others was genuine, not condescending. Unlike many clerics, he seemed part of the world, not sealed off from it. I wondered if he'd survive long term. I felt he would. He was strong enough. I wasn't religious, but he was an inspiration for me. Spiritually, as opposed to religiously.

There were only four St Eustathius churches in the

country. St Eustathius, I learned, was a second-century Roman soldier martyred after a vision of a crucifix in a pair of stag's antlers converted him to Christianity.

Tavistock had been wet and miserable the previous night. As I had. In the gentle morning light it was a pleasant, open market town resisting the worst aspects of modernity. Abbots had owned it till the sixteenth century, and even into the twentieth the town was owned by the Duke of Bedford's family. End of history lesson.

Geoffrey Boucher had given me breakfast, but also hope. 'Look,' he said, 'it's going to be very stressful for you having to find food and accommodation every night after walking all day. I might be able to help early on. I vaguely know this man who runs a pub on Dartmoor, a day's walk from here. It's on your route. I've phoned him. You can sleep in his stable tonight.'

Into my mind came this wild, totally impractical idea. That each night my host would phone ahead, and thus I would leapfrog the 500 miles to Edinburgh, always booked up, as it were. Ridiculous, of course, but at that moment a psychological boost.

'In bed last night,' I confessed, 'I'd decided to give up.'

'You can't give up,' said Geoffrey. 'It's God's will that you go on.'

I skipped that one. He went on.

'This is your pilgrimage as a writer. Explain to people just what you are doing. You will act as a catalyst in their lives, wherever you go.' And suddenly my journey had a possible purpose I had never contemplated.

After breakfast, we went into town. My attempts to have the harmonica repaired were abortive. Deep down I knew it was not to be part of this odyssey. I walked into Boots with the small amount of money left for insoles and moleskins, the last commercial transaction I would undertake for a month.

I cut the insoles to shape and padded them down into the boots. The moleskins I attached to the sole and heel danger areas. All this I did in the church vestry, where souls of a

different sort were normally attended to. I stood up and
clomped around the church, feeling out the newly protected
appendages, the start of the long saga that was to be the
Mortimer Feet Story. I was comforted by cushioning. I was
ready for the open road.

Geoffrey offered to run me to the edge of Dartmoor, give
me a good start. On the inside of his windscreen, his licence
holder had an advertisement for Ecclesiastical Motor
Services. 'Vicars in distress,' he joked, and we both laughed.
He whizzed me round the side of Brent Tor, with the church
perched on its summit. How did they build it? It was, he
said, lit by gaslight. He pointed out other places of interest
before stopping the car.

I never got used to partings on the trip. They always jolted
me. As if, after a brief security, I was pushed out there again.
And my human contact was cut off. Geoffrey Boucher held
out something in his hand towards me.

'I want you to take this,' he said. 'It's for extreme
emergencies only.' In his hand was a ten pound note.

'Oh, no, I couldn't. I mean . . .'

'I know,' he said. 'You intend to carry no money. Fine. I
respect that. Only for an extreme case.'

Later, I would twice be offered money and twice refuse.
On this occasion I took it, knowing the importance of the
gesture. Yet even as I folded it, secured it at the bottom of an
inside pocket, even though I knew my fragility, I knew that
should I ever use it I would betray my trip.

We shook hands and embraced. I watched his small car
drive away. The previous day had almost flattened Sam and
me. Geoffrey Boucher had picked us up. It was part of a
pattern. Only later would I realise that.

We were now on the huge expanse that was Dartmoor,
one of the surviving wildernesses and, along with Bodmin
and Exmoor, one of the West Country's great trio of moors.
The day was bright and sunny, my feet were newly protected,
a roof for the night lay ahead. Last night's defeatism seemed
long distant.

We strode out under the huge Dartmoor sky. Sam was a

happy dog (he'd had a good breakfast too), my only irritation caused by his tendency to drift towards the centre of the road, a seemingly irresistible desire to be squashed like a grape by passing vehicles.

My bag was slung nonchalantly across my right shoulder. It weighed 16lbs and such nonchalance, as I was to learn, would slowly take its toll. The Tavistock experience had made me decide, where possible, to steer clear of both main roads and large towns. I hated the blur of traffic on the former, the alienation of the latter. Though an urbanite all my life, I decided on this journey to put my faith in the rural. The thought of arriving penniless, day after day, in large towns depressed me more than I could bear. I warmed to the thought of small settlements.

The road rose spectacularly, and to the south-east Dartmoor Prison came into view. It resembled a giant concrete factory, a grim building creating simultaneously a sense of the claustrophobic and the agoraphobic: the building itself alone in this vast landscape, yet its inmates locked inside small, cramped cells. I'd known the same sensation working as a fisherman on the North Sea.

We dropped down for our lunchtime stop at the crossroads village of Two Bridges. Why two bridges so close across the West Dart river? No one in the pub seemed to know. Nice spot, though. In a reversal of normal procedure, Sam bathed in the clear waters of the river, then rolled in the dusty soil. I sat in the grassy gardens leading down to the water. Again it felt strange to be among holidaymakers, flip-flopping in and out of the bar for beer, crisps and sandwiches. Several people patted Sam. I found myself wishing to be in the company of destitutes. The worst experience, when deprived, is to be amongst plenty. I had, from Geoffrey Boucher, two slices of bread and butter plus an orange.

Avoiding holidaymakers wouldn't be easy in the West Country mid-season. Locals were vastly outnumbered. A busload of Germans drove up. They spilled out, talking loudly, and spread themselves. I ate some bread, and gave some to Sam. Some people who walked past chatted. I felt my penniless state was a dreadful secret I was not prepared to reveal. I pretended to be normal.

We were the only two creatures to arrive at, and leave, Two Bridges on foot. We rested for 45 minutes, then climbed high again onto the moor. Dartmoor was a wilderness. But one with traffic.

We came across a strange sight high on the exposed moorland road. All manhole and drain covers had been covered over with strips of cardboard, then secured to the road with masking tape. We passed more and more of these. Was it installation art? Two-dimensional site sculptures? The explanation was more prosaic and arrived in the form of a hissing, steaming, piston-pumping, tar-laying machine slowly grinding its way along the road, leaving in its wake the black, sticky and gently smoking new surface from which would be peeled the protective covers.

I was working on my relationship with Sam. I attempted to keep him on the inside of me, away from the traffic. He strongly resisted this. Where possible, I also tried to keep him on grass, knowing how his pads could wear badly with long exposure to tarmac or metalled roads. He resisted this too. Sam wanted to be close to the traffic. He wanted to be on a hard, unrelenting surface. Why?

We walked for several more miles. Some blisters had developed on my feet. Despite the protection, they gave me some pain. Teething troubles only, I argued, as the high moor road eventually descended again towards the village of Postbridge and our night's destination, the distinctive white-painted East Dart Hotel.

These Dartmoor villages were like picture postcards. Too cute to be in a real wilderness. On the west side of Post-bridge spanning the river was the curious clapper bridge, the only complete one of its kind left on Dartmoor. Or any-where else in the world. It was built in 1380. Two giant granite slabs were supported by three stacks of smaller granite pieces piled up into bridge supports. It was basic, unsophisticated, strong, like it had been built by a three-year-old giant. It had carried people and vehicles for more than 600 years. How would Sydney Harbour Bridge rate against this record?

East Dart Hotel had been built by the great-great-grandfather of the present owner Alex Urwin, an erstwhile temperance house that had passed out of the family in 1936 but which he'd got back in 1996. 'Now they'll have to carry me out,' he said. He was a grey-bearded, slightly grizzled man. *En route* I'd decided I'd offer my limited services in any way possible. Sing for my supper and bed. 'How are you with a paintbrush?' asked Alex. For the next three hours I creosoted the outside of the very stables that would be my shelter. Even on a minimum wage I calculated that should cover a stable floor and a bit of grub.

Sleeping in stables sounded romantic. Not so. The stables were behind the hotel on a sloping path which led to the house of Alex and his wife Barbara. They looked like lock-up garages, featureless enclosures with bare concrete floors. Or not quite bare. As Alex put it in one of my trip's more memorable phrases, 'I'll just clear the horse shit out of your bedroom.' He shovelled up ample portions of it, leaving just a subtle hint of the bouquet.

Alex Urwin was a hunting man. I was not. His red jacket, which no longer fitted, hung on a wall. Wasn't hunting an anachronism? And a fairly male one at that? Were there any female huntsmasters?

'Heavens, yes!' he replied. 'There's even a Pakistani huntsmaster!'

What, on Dartmoor?

'Round here? No! We wouldn't want something like that round here!'

The village was on the border of four separate hunts for which the pub was a focal point. It was empty on my arrival, and remained quiet throughout.

After my creosoting, Alex offered me a bath. I changed into my formal evening wear: the striped top, sandals, light Indian patterned trousers. I cheekily asked Barbara if I could sling some other bits into the wash she was about to do. I then sat in the low, thick-beamed hotel bar, pleased that the quiet allowed me to write the diary undisturbed. Alex fed me with my first hot food of the day, a chicken casserole bar meal, plus two pints of cask bitter. I told him about the journey. I told him the three-hour creosoting had felt okay, using hands instead of feet. How I'd thought of begging, but had decided against it. 'I had one of those beggars come up to me in London once,' Alex said. 'I just told him to piss off.'

The odd person wandered into the bar. Alex gave me several publicity sheets and leaflets on the hotel. My own culture and his were far apart. Secretly I took off my sandals and socks and allowed the air to get to my feet under the table. I felt Alex might disapprove. The moleskins were still intact but I decided I'd remove them before going to sleep. Parts of my feet were turning a darkish red, as if brushed with rouge. But I was full of chicken casserole, had drunk two pints and would have a roof over my head.

I thought back to the claustrophobia and agoraphobia of Dartmoor Prison. For some reason I was feeling the former. Sam and I stayed in the bar till 9.30, then it was time to retire to our concrete floor. Alex offered me a thin tarpaulin sheet which would be my mattress. I made the mattress even more soft and bouncy with my black bin-liner. This was my first use of the magic sleeping bag. I pulled it from its tiny sack and it expanded miraculously, like some stage conjuring act. My main bag would act as a pillow.

Carefully I removed the moleskins from my feet and put them on the concrete, where they sat like curls of orange peel. I stretched out in the sleeping bag, while Sam's stomach rumbled like a malcontent volcano. He was generally restless, and I suspected he could sniff the hotel's two Labrador/Irish wolfhounds. They were big dogs and could have swallowed wee Sam with barely a burp. During the night, on the hour and every hour, Sam barked furiously, but gave no reason.

After the day's fine weather came the night rain. It thrummed its steady beat on the stable roof as I moved this way and that in a futile attempt to find lasting comfort. The stable was draughty, and halfway through the night I pulled

Sam into the sleeping bag with me for extra warmth. He liked this, but it didn't stop his barking.

I'd conjured up an image of the stable being warm with soft hay, and nearby the nuzzling bodies of warm cows. I looked on the bright side. I could barely smell the horse shit at all.

Day Three — Tuesday, 28 July

Miles travelled so far — 30

In the Dartmoor rain
The lonely hitchhiker
Sees cars brake for sheep

Everlasting Fire — A Life of Crime — The Moonshine Boy

Morning dawned to a grey sky, pouring rain and a draughty concrete floor which had failed to soften overnight. I drifted into consciousness around 7 a.m. and was aware of Sam in the bag, murgling and gurgling. I knew the hotel had eight bedrooms, and assumed people would be up and about preparing for breakfast. I had dire need of the loo. Come 7.30, the hotel was still in darkness.

I wriggled from the bag, pulled on my clothes and ran down the drive through the rain to try all doors. All were secured, no sign of life. I returned to the stable, walked about as the rain thrummed down, waited till I could wait no longer. I squatted down by the side of the stable and found relief, emerging to discover that Sam, as if in sympathy, had deposited four conical piles of steaming turd on the drive directly before the gate to the Urwin house. The two large dogs pressed against the gate were barking furiously. They were barking so much it was impossible for Alex not to wake, not to walk down to the gate, not to see the quartet of Sam's visiting cards in the middle of his driveway.

I tried to cover the offending foursome with the drive soil.

It was too meagre. I ran around in the pouring rain as the dogs barked on, located a large shovel, scooped up the evidence, hurled it in a projectile arc to some middle-distance long grass, and patted the drive surface flat.

There was still no movement from the house, nor the hotel. Nothing stirred until 8.30 a.m., by which time my fascination with the stable was spent. There were no guests in the hotel. The eight rooms were empty. Me in the cold stable, and no room at the inn. And it was a terrible day: mists, rain, a soaking-wet curtain drawn across the brooding moor. A day to stay indoors, with a warm fire, a good book, a hot drink. No day for a person to be heading across the exposed tops of Dartmoor.

My washing was dry. Not much else would be. Despite the weather, I was keen to be on my way. Alex had a bacon sandwich and tea for me, plus a large bone biscuit for Sam. I watched Sam chewing. Did he wonder where he was going? Who I was? If there was a superior dog somewhere?

We ate in the hotel kitchen. I packed up my belongings and prepared for the hostile road. I considered the mole-skins. They were sad looking. I decided my feet could do without them.

My only protection was the small brolly. Waterproofs were too bulky to carry. Besides, I was the kind of optimist who thought it would never rain, and who had had a lifelong aversion to dressing practically.

Off we went. The road rose and the mist thickened. Soon it wrapped itself around us, though not sufficiently to keep away the wild elements. The battle to stay dry was a losing one, and the higher we climbed, the more the odds were against us. This was not the day to be on high, exposed moorland. Who else was there? Absolutely no one. I would try for a lift, get off the Dartmoor heights as soon as possible. In this weather, only the hardest of hearts would hurtle past me barely bothering to look.

Every car hurtled past me barely bothering to look. Each one threw up curved sprays of water. Most had a single occupant. This was midsummer in the mild south-west of

England, but the weather smacked more of the Yorkshire moors in November. We had no food, no drink, nothing to nibble *en route*. We were heading off into the unknown, and the unknown was wet and miserable. We walked on for several miles, several dozen thumb-jerks. Sam turned into a wet dishcloth, and I considered wringing him out. Eventually, emerging from the mists, standing in total isolation, was the remote Warren House Inn, England's third highest pub, built by hardy souls on this Dartmoor peak in 1845.

I pushed open the heavy wooden door. The warmth of the fire came up and wrapped its limbs around me. There was no one else in the pub. I was probably the first customer of the day. Except I wasn't a customer at all. No money.

A word about the fire at Warren House. The fire had been lit on the day the pub opened. Since then it has never gone out. Naturally, as no one has lived 150 years, this must be partly hearsay, but the received wisdom is that the fire has blazed on all that time. Through two world wars, the invention of the motor car, the aeroplane, flickering while Victoria turned from a young woman to an old lady. The year the fire was lit, Alexandre Dumas wrote *The Black Tulip*, Robert Peel was Prime Minister, the pneumatic tyre was patented. I know – I looked them all up. The American Civil War still had to be fought, Gladstone hadn't even thought of his Reform Bill and it would be another 20 years before slavery was abolished in America. Each day the fire was built up; each night it was damped down and slumbered through the small hours. A century and a half of blazing and slumbering, and not a single match used. And the fire, all this time, waiting for this poor traveller.

I threw myself on the mercy of the young barmaid, Nicola Scaufe, confessing I was a penniless writer on a long journey, wet and cold. Nicola gave me hot coffee and told Sam and me to sit close to the everlasting fire, where I decided to bring the diary up to date.

I had a plan. I would wait in this pub, then hitch a lift from any customers travelling north-east, just far enough to reach the less-exposed lower terrain this side of Exeter. As with many plans on the journey, though, this one was stillborn. Over the next hour only three people came in, and all were travelling west.

The fire had still not gone out. Sam was asleep in front of it, and I was envious of him. I wanted simply to stay there. Not for 150 years. But a while longer. Nicola gave me another cup of coffee, and I finished the writing. The fire was drying out my combat trousers, my jacket. Steam rose gently. My body sucked in the warmth of the everlasting flame.

'There's a bus to Exeter at two o'clock,' said Nicola. I had another plan. It was 12.30. I would do some menial tasks around the pub, asking simply for the bus fare in payment. I thought it a splendid idea. Nicola too thought it a splendid idea. The only person who did not think it a splendid idea was the unseen landlord, who sent down his proverbial puff of black smoke via the slightly embarrassed Nicola. There was no alternative. Sam and I had to face the elements once more. This fire was not going out. But we had to.

Back on the heights of the moor, little had changed. The rain still rained. The mist still rolled and drifted. The elements had shown great patience in waiting for us. Dartmoor was keen its bleak delights should not be undervalued. Yet, in all this, I found some positive thought. My feet were painful but I took the decision they must, well, stand on their own two feet. I could not featherbed them for an entire month. The sooner they came to terms with the odyssey the better – starting now. Whatever pain or hurt they felt, I would simply walk off. It was merely a case of mind (or feet) over body (or blisters). The resolution sent a surge of energy through me, a spring in my step. I found myself shouting into the mist and rain, 'You can do it, feet! Just get on with it, feet!'

My brief celebratory mood was such that (remembering the book *Food for Free*) I picked a dandelion from a ditch and chewed it. It was unspeakably awful. I spat it out.

We finally began to descend. As the road dropped, the weather improved. The rain stopped, the mist went wherever mists go and in the sky was just a hint of blue. The wild moorland gave way to a gentle, tamed countryside, and we came into the small, quiet village of Moretonhampstead, where I embarked on a life of crime.

Sam and I were unburdened by any food supplies. Not a crumb, nor a penny to buy one. We passed the local green-grocer. No doubt he/she was a fine, upstanding individual, paying the council tax on time and giving donations to Oxfam and other worthy charities. None of which stopped me nicking a big apple. It was a Granny Smith's. I had nicked things before: rubber bands, envelopes. I'd made illicit phone calls from offices I'd worked in. As a schoolboy, I'd often dropped my cap over Woolies' display of Mars bars, then plonked it back on my head complete with one stolen bar. That said, I'd never really slid into the twilight world of the criminal.

I sat opposite the shop in the village centre and munched. I felt no guilt, only the sense of the tangy flesh putting much-needed sustenance into my tum. I half expected the hand on the collar, the firm, quiet voice of the police officer, 'All right, sunshine, you're nicked.' Forbidden fruit. I offered some to Sam. Possibly through conscience, possibly not, he declined.

By now, it was well into the afternoon. I had no idea where we might spend the night, where we might get a meal. But I still had half a Granny Smith's. Soon all evidence was in my stomach (I pushed the core well down into a rubbish bin) and we walked from the village, climbing steadily towards the hamlet of Doccombe, on a narrow, twisting road. Despite my foot optimism, the pain was growing.

Doccombe did me no good at all. On a corner was a fine thatched cottage. I peered through the window, spotted several painting frames and decided to investigate. I knocked at the door and a middle-aged man answered.

'I was just wondering,' I said in a cheery manner, 'is this a painter's house?'

'Yee-ees, sort of,' he replied, as if too much commitment would see him subjected to the tortures of the Inquisition.

'I'm a writer on a long journey,' I said. 'I spotted the frames. I like to stop and look at things.'

'Yes, I see.'

I felt he didn't see at all. The door was half open. His body blocked it. His eyes had narrowed slightly. I felt as welcome as the Jehovah's Witnesses. Who were all in Plymouth. Further conversation was not required.

'Well, thank you anyway,' I said.

He closed the door and I stared at it for several seconds.

'What I need, Sam,' I said as we walked on, 'is a happy, cheery face, a bit of comfort, as they say in the north-east.'

We walked another mile along the leafy road until we came across Red Valley Farm, an individual-looking settlement whose outer walls were adorned with a succession of small animal statues. 'Let's try here, Sam,' I said, and we did, walking down the path and knocking at the door, which was answered by a slim-looking woman in blue jeans. Her name was Jill Strange. She opened the door wide, and I felt nothing like a Jehovah's Witness. Nor a door-to-door salesman.

Sometimes I'd knock at a door and have no idea what I was going to say. Like here.

'I'm a writer on a long journey,' I said. 'I need somewhere to stay about five miles further on. Do you know anywhere? I have no money.'

'There's a cider-maker. He'd probably put you up,' she said.

We chatted on the doorstep.

'I suppose you could drink a cup of tea?' said Jill Strange as I turned to go.

Doccombe depressed me. Red Valley Farm cheered me up. As well as tea, there were biscuits – human for me, dog for Sam. And water for Sam. We sat on Jill's back step and stared at the gaggle of animals in the field by the river. Including a solitary turkey. I'd always thought a lone turkey was as rare as a lone Japanese holidaymaker. Didn't they live in great gaggling flocks, strutting their doomed way towards Christmas? Well, Jill had had two turkeys. One was called Bernard, the other, in a rush of predictability, was Matthews. Both were free from the normal expectation of Yuletide liquidation. Except they fought so much, and Matthews sulked so much, that . . .

'Yes?'

'We ate him.'

I ate another biscuit. I ate about nine biscuits. Two large mugs of tea. My problem was, when I got somewhere nice, I just wanted to stay. How about it, Jill Strange? Of course, I never asked. A few minutes later we were back on the road, pushing on through woodland, a steep climb, then through the Teign Gorge, which plunged down deep to the water from a narrow twisting road. We walked through Dunsford Wood, and took a small diversion to see Dunsford village, a place of such quaintness, olde worlde charm and thatched-roof gentility that some people might say 'aah!' while others might puke.

I looked one way up the street for Moll Flanders. The other direction for Tom Jones (not the 'Green Green Grass of Home' one). Neither. Nor a McDonald's.

My feet had deteriorated. I had discarded the moleskins but kept the insoles. There was no way my feet were going to give me long-term grief. I kept telling myself this, time and time over.

If thatched roofs are one English stereotype, West Country cider-makers are another, ooo-aar. We eventually reached our hoped-for destination, the bungalow of cider-maker Cliff Brimblecombe. Cliff was 67 and had a strong Devon accent and a glass eye. I had hardly explained my situation when he said, 'You'd best take the caravan. Just up the lane.'

His wife Evelyn appeared in the doorway behind him. 'I'm off to the WI meeting soon,' she said, half apologetically, 'but I'll make you a meal first,' and off she went. Possibly itinerants turned up here every day seeking food and shelter. Possibly there was a whole posse of them, just awaiting their cooked meal. Possibly feeding the wanderer was the natural Brimblecombe order.

A few moments later I was up the muddy lane, into the caravan and tucking into hot meat pie and potatoes while Sam crunched on some real dog food. I returned the crockery and cutlery to the house, where Cliff asked, 'Now then, what did you say you were doing again?'

He'd been a scrumpy-maker all his life, had now retired, but the business carried on and cider was still made on the premises, Farrants Farm. The cider house dated back to the eleventh century, and the fully operational press was 450 years old. 'Mind, there's a modern apple crusher,' he said. This was bought in 1933. Cliff led me round the corner, up more muddy lanes and into the cider house itself. The phrase that sprang to mind was medieval moonshine: low ancient beams, small dusty windows, strange cast-iron implements and the press. Three times as old as the Warren House fire.

Part of Cliff had retired. Part hadn't. As we walked round, he tut-tutted at small items he thought were misplaced, little jobs not done; he moved items, quietly fussed. He paused by one old beam and showed me the two dates carved into it, 1944 and 1946, done by himself in idle moments during his apprenticeship. He showed me everything: the press, the barrels, the channels down which the cider ran, the crusher. He took me through the entire process, omitting only the grand finale. A glass of cider.

After the tour, he said, 'I have to go out. You'm all right looking after yourself?' I'd taken off the boots and donned the open sandals. As we walked back to our humble caravan, I wondered why I was limping, and more on one foot than the other. I lay down on the caravan bed, removed the sandals and exposed my feet to the air. Sam showed an immediate concern for my welfare and began to lick the afflicted parts carefully. It was not better than sex, but it beat a jacuzzi or a steam room. I closed my eyes and thought of the length of England.

I examined the said areas. Blisters had formed and the dark red rouge was turning a strange plum colour. You might ask at this stage if I was a regular walker. If I had done the sensible foot preparations for the journey. The answer to the latter is no. As to the former, I was a non-car-owner and walked and biked most places within reasonable reach. I'd had the walking boots two years. Will that do?

We'd come about 18 miles that day, the longest trek so far. The 50-mile mark beckoned. Ten per cent. As I unpacked the bag and laid out my items, I realised my body was tired. I washed in cold water, laid out my purple socks for airing, cleaned my teeth and did some writing. What I really wanted was to be free of Plymouth's orbital gravity. I was sick of seeing the name 'Plymouth' on signposts, on the front of buses. We were still within the grasp of the city where we'd started. What kind of progress was that? We needed to leap past Exeter, put a second city behind us. I didn't feel like leaping anywhere.

I was learning to have early nights, early mornings. I was learning to do without normal distractions and entertainment. I'd not even thought of the telly. What was it? I looked at my feet. Perversity drove me to walk back up Brimblecombe Lane once again before retiring. I'd spotted and picked up a few snazzy leaflets around the cider house. They had such phrases as 'Step back in time with . . .'

Cliff's original cider-making sign, a primitive black-and-white affair, was still on the wall up the yard. But on the road outside was a flash-looking modern affair, a graphic design creation. My hunch was that since his retirement, the ancient cider house, the whole process, was being successfully turned into what the marketing men would call 'a vibrant, heritage-based product'.

For a short time I lay outside the sleeping bag. Sam gave me more tongue—foot medicine, the wee beauty. How silent it was up this muddy little lane. Just the slight rustle of wind in the trees.

As I drifted into sleep, I told myself that, lying like this, there was absolutely no foot pain at all.

Day Four — Wednesday, 29 July

Miles travelled so far — 48

The cider-maker's
Glass eye
Has seen it all

Village of the Dogs — The Motorway's Curse —
The Bells of Clyst Hydon

For the second consecutive morning I awoke to the steady beat of rain and a grey slab of concrete sky. I was immediately anxious about my feet, and from 5.30 to 6.30 I exposed them to the air. I wiggled my toes furiously. I had no idea what this would do, but it could do no harm. I was still determined they would heal themselves. Suddenly, this long-time believer in state intervention had become a free marketeer on foot care. Sam had slept at the end of the bunk, and he yawned himself awake during my toe wiggling.

There was, first thing in the morning, the small satisfaction of another day chalked up. I would study the map but cover up the route to come, like some schoolboy shielding his exam paper from cribbers. Much as I generally believed in looking forward, on this trip thus far I could only look back. To study the vast distances ahead would be unbearable.

Again Sam engaged in lick therapy. His preference was for the right foot. The reason was obvious but was only pointed out to me the following day. It had deteriorated more than the left because my bag was slung over my right shoulder in a vain attempt for me not to resemble some nerdy back-packer. The right foot offered more to lick.

As usual I had a plan. As often I abandoned it. I'd hoped to walk to the Devon Buddhist Vihara, which, my friends at the Harnham monastery in Northumberland had assured me, would offer sanctuary. I'd mentioned it to Cliff. He pulled a face and told me it would involve walking up the busy A30 full of roadworks, dual carriageway widenings, clogged traffic and, for all I knew, taxiing jumbo jets.

I also suspected I was 'running for cover', looking for the easy option. Being a stout sort of chap, I abandoned thoughts of the sanctuary. This was my first caravan of the odyssey. I still had some food from the previous night: bread and honey for me, dog food for Sam. I ate half the bread and wrapped the rest for the journey. A new eating regime was evolving. My three-square-meals-a-day philosophy was fading. What a few days ago I'd have seen as piddling was now a full breakfast. I'd hardly had to think about food, just shovelled it in. Now I was thinking.

My combat trousers had dried overnight, as had my green granddad shirt. My habit was to switch clothes at the day's end and dress for dinner. I had two pairs of thick tubed socks (purple) which I was wearing simultaneously for more foot cushioning. This made my feet hot during the day, and when I removed the socks in the evening they pulsed like over-active radiators. The policy probably added to rather than alleviated my foot problems.

I felt I was on my journey, but not yet part of it. I couldn't define it, but I still hadn't immersed myself. I was still an outsider. I was still knocking to get in. I was establishing some sort of routine. I woke early, wrote my diary, travelled all day, found shelter, wrote again, slept. Food came in somewhere when I could find it. Maybe I was still fighting against something. Instead of going with its rhythm. I mean, I was just a 54-year-old townie, after all.

I had the joy of a cold shave. One option was simply to let the beard grow, but while designer stubble could look attractive on a 21-year-old modelling the latest cologne, at my age it gave the look of an old wino, an appearance unlikely to advance the cause.

Despite the rain and the feet, my caravan ablutions that morning had a certain optimism, born of Cliff and Evelyn's open hospitality. As I shaved in the reflection of the caravan chrome, I babbled on to Sam. 'It'll be all right, Sam. You'll see. We just have to keep going.'

And the thought struck me. How come humans were the only animals who needed to shave?

I got too excited in my Sam monologue and cut myself.

At first sight, Cliff Brimblecombe had seemed a cosy, cuddly, traditional West Country cider-maker. I learned he was an independent councillor and chairman of Teignbridge Houses and Health Committee. His wife Evelyn was a sharp rabbit too. 'I'm a bit embarrassed just to happen on you like this,' I'd gushed the previous evening. 'You don't look embarrassed,' she'd said. She was right.

The official distance from Plymouth to Edinburgh is 500 miles. I realised this distance was the result of taking the quickest route, usually motorway. Staying away from big towns and main roads would add up to ten per cent to my route, or, if I really wanted to cheer myself up, on the original estimate of 500 miles, I hadn't yet started. It also meant at 15 miles a day I'd never make it in a month. I made another plan. I would try to walk the 15 miles every day but where possible cadge a lift every morning for five miles too. Why not just walk 20 miles a day? Because I was too knackered.

For once my plan, on its first morning, went according to, well, plan. Cliff offered to run me round the Exeter ring road. Sam and I jumped in the car. We drove through Devon country lanes whose 15-foot-high hedges arched towards one another like Denis Healey's eyebrows, a sense of being sealed off from the world being rudely shattered as we were suddenly sucked into Exeter's rush-hour traffic. Bit by bit I was beginning to realise that people who drove through the snarled congestion of rush hour twice daily, day in, day out, were plumb stupid. I could see thousands of them. Grim-faced, hunched over the wheel, arteries thickening with each passing mile.

We waved goodbye to Cliff and marched off. This was a long exposure to urbanisation, a 90-minute trudge round the ring road before we found the B3181 to take us north-east, and thereafter another long trudge to be free of the urban hinterland. What games could I play? Sniff the Four Star? Dodge the Nissan Micras?

The shops were full of goodies. I had a slice of bread and honey. Oh, and a small plastic bottle of water, acquired at Farrants Farm. I was getting worried. Too many possessions were bad for you.

I was longing to be free of traffic, but Sam and I were destined to have it dog (sorry) our footsteps all day. My plan now was to head to the village of Clyst Hydon. Thirty years previously my girlfriend Kitty had lived there as a student. I wanted to go to the farmhouse. Maybe they would put me up.

We were within easy reach of the (presumably) winding, sleepy Devon lanes. In theory our chosen route, the B3181, should have been quiet. It wasn't. I later learned it had previously been the A38 and had refused to accept the demotion quietly. It still harboured dreams of regaining A-road status and had persuaded every vehicle in Devon to zoom up and down it every day in the hope of reinstatement.

We passed a sign saying 'Dog Village'. What could it mean? A husky habitation? Dormitory town of Dobermans? Spaniel suburb? I owed it to Sam to find out.

We followed the sign from the main road. A motorist was sitting in her car at the junction. 'What is Dog Village?' I shouted through her closed window. 'This is,' she shouted back and drove off. A middle-aged man was in his garden tending his plants. 'Why is this called Dog Village?' I asked. He looked up startled, mumbled 'Dunno' and hurried indoors as if there'd been a warning of invading Daleks. I knocked at a door at random. An elderly lady peered at me through the kitchen window. She stretched up to the open part and yelled 'What?'. I stretched up too. I yelled too. 'I just wondered why this was called Dog Village.' I unstretched. It was her turn. 'Ask at the post office,' she said, and she unstretched too.

I walked to Broad Clyst post office, back on the main road. I stood in the queue as people handed over parcels, got disability benefits, filled in driving licence applications. 'I just wondered,' I said, as I reached the top, 'why Dog Village is so named?' (By now I was wanting to vary the question slightly.) The first assistant didn't know. She asked the second assistant, who mumbled something about the local history society being the people to ask. A third person piped up that the village had grown up around a pub called the Black Dog, by which time several people had joined the queue with proof-of-posting certificates, TV licence reminders, etc. It was time to move on.

Broad Clyst's fine church, St John the Baptist, stood behind a magnificent oak tree which fizzed like a giant green firework. The West Country happily still left its churches open without, presumably, the theft of too many altars. Sam and I had cause to thank Elsie Radford. She it was who provided the fine oak seat in the porch on which, after scoffing the bread and honey, Sam and I fell asleep, waking 15 minutes later.

Within a couple of miles, the B3181, with ideas above its station, went not only for A-road status but that of Brands Hatch too. The growth of thorn, shrubs and ferns made the narrow verges all but impassable and pushed us poor pedestrians closer to the speeding loonies. There was something else too. To the north-west I could hear a steady drone. It slowly grew louder. An airport runway? It was in fact the M5, converging on our own road to which it ran parallel for several miles, almost within kissing distance. Heard, but not seen, a malignant presence at our shoulder. We now had two sets of roaring traffic, or, if you counted both directions, four. At this stage I still relied on my pathetically small *Radio Times* book of maps. Absolutely faultless if driving between Birmingham and London. But for our purposes? For revealing those small, little-known roads?

We came across a strange oasis, isolated within a small stretch of land which had been surrounded by two mad roads, asked to surrender, but refused to do so. This was called Beare. Which followed Dog.

I knocked at the door of one of the cluster of fine old cottages. The man who answered fixed me with the wary look I was growing used to. His name was Robert Earle, and I asked him, or rather shouted to him, what it was like living between these two busy roads. 'It's okay,' he shouted back. 'I only notice when the noise stops.' I had assumed it never stopped.

What I really wanted from Robert Earle was a cup of tea, a jam tart, a ham sandwich, a soft settee. I was thirsty, hungry, tired. Robert stood between me and his open door. *No pasaran.* I played for time, asked him about his life, how he came to be here. He'd moved a few years back from Wiltshire.

'But this is as far west as I go,' he said, between juggernauts. 'Once you get trapped in that peninsula, you never get out.'

Sam and I moved on. 'Trapped in that peninsula'. What did he mean? I knew what he meant. It was beautiful. But I wanted to be free of it. This was our fourth day's trudging through it. I wanted to be in the lower belly of England. I wanted to be heading due north. I wanted a cup of tea. And I wanted to be free of the damned M5! All the way up this peninsula, nagging, nagging at your shoulder. Shoo! Shoo! It wouldn't go away.

Finally we turned on to a side road and walked up through the narrow, thickly hedged lanes. As these reached high ground, so the motorway drone came back. Another 40 minutes. Like Chinese water torture. We didn't want the noise. We had it. We did want the countryside. It was blocked off by the hedges. West Country claustrophobia. At Piper's Organic Meat Farm we stopped and asked for water, secretly wanting more. We got water from a man in a white coat and hat.

We had failed to pierce the skin at any of this day's locations. We were transients. Not connecting. Were we destined to wander in this unplugged way for a month? And what of my feet? They'd been whispering urgently to me: 'More protection!' I'd told them to shut up. They wouldn't. The pain was there only half the time. When the foot made contact with the ground.

I talked incessantly to Sam, there being no one else to listen. He occasionally cocked his head and looked at me, as if questioning some statement. I wanted to let him off the lead, but his kamikaze tendencies prevented it. His time would come. In more ways than one.

A few more miles of lofty hedgerows and we wandered into the secret village of Clyst Hydon. I say secret. Perhaps I should say shy. The village hid itself away from public gaze. It disappeared up lanes, it sidled off behind hedges. Its houses peeped out like diffident ladies behind fans. There was little sense of a village at all, but it was there all right. And it had a swimming pool. No shop. No post office. But a swimming pool. You could find one building in the village. Then you could find another. The problem was in seeing both at once.

I was looking for Town Tenement Farm, Kitty's erstwhile abode. Naturally it was hidden away. I approached the sixteenth-century farmhouse. A slim, bearded man with a full head of grey hair and legs as tanned as an oak sideboard eyed me silently. There'd been a suspicious man skulking around the village that day (probably looking for the shop). Unbeknown to me, Tom Coleman suspected me of being that man. Tom and his wife Jean still lived in this extraordinary building 30 years on. 'I am Kitty Fitzgerald's bloke,' I announced, which earned me an immediate cup of tea and removed all suspicion.

The big cottage had meandering corridors, wide oak beams, heavy slatted wooden doors, a spacious garden. I removed my boots and was immediately offered a bed for the night. Real beds were to prove a rarity, so much so that I would explore every inch of them. No sooner did I have a bed than I had a portion of fish and chips too. No sooner had I eaten these than Tom and Jean, keen campanologists, whisked me off to the village church (hidden away, now you mention it) for the bell-ringing session.

The sextet of ringers stood ready for action, each fingering the rope in the nervous way a gunslinger fingers the trigger. As I watched the ringers (Tom and Jean included) pull and jerk the bells into their beautiful peals, I was aware of two things. The English serenity of the scene. And the pain in my feet (I was now in my sandals). As I ascended the tower and saw the great cast-iron bells, the oldest dating back to 1616 and weighing 11 hundredweight, I was both aghast at the size and pissed off with my blisters. Meantime, at each peal, Tom and Jean's dog, Gyp, to the consternation of Sam, lay in the church porch and howled its canine accompaniment.

I had happened on a peaceful rural community. The kind into which Agatha Christie would immediately introduce a mutilated corpse. I had also happened upon people (Tom and Jean) who were able to give me good advice. Tom had done his own 200-mile walk on the Cotswold Way, and kept a word and photo diary.

He looked at me strangely. He looked at my feet even more strangely. He and Jean asked me questions. What preparations had I made? How were my feet prepared for the journey? What maps did I carry? With every question, I realised the paucity of my preparation. Tom, a much better organised person than myself, would mutter 'hmmm' at my replies. Never had 'hmmm' sounded so damning. My maps were no good. My method of carrying my bag was no good. My foot preparation was no good. Where was I heading? Edinburgh, I said, in a weak voice. Silence.

Something else unsettled me. This cottage had a link with my other life, with Kitty. I needed to leave this other world behind to complete my odyssey. Now it came and sat next to me. It unnerved me, confused me. I was all at sea. In Clyst Hydon. Tired. Sore feet. I looked at Tom and Jean. They were looking at me. What were they thinking? Had they recognised the foolhardy nature of my venture? Was I merely a buffoon about to get his comeuppance? The cottage warmly embraced me. I felt the gently pulsing heat of the Aga. But come morning I needed to rise, to go. I didn't want to think about it.

'This is a better book of maps,' said Jean, handing me the Michelin Motoring Atlas.

'It's too big, too heavy,' I said.

'Just rip out the pages you don't want,' she replied. 'It's ring bound.'

That night in bed I ripped out more than a pound in weight of superfluous map.

'You can leave your feet free at night,' said Tom. 'But in the day they need protection at the moment.'

'Wear your backpack properly,' said Jean. 'You must spread the load.'

Good advice, advice I needed, came thick and fast. I sat like a little boy and nodded. The session was painful and necessary. How concerned they both were.

In the big, beautiful farmhouse, in the big, beautiful bed, I spent a fitful night. Sam again provided the soothing balm of his tongue ('Saliva has many healing properties,' Jean had said). I lay awake and my mind drifted to those people who the next morning did not have to rise penniless, and with painful feet, to travel to unknown destinations. How privileged such people were. I wanted to be part of that great normal mass, that huge anonymous populace, who the next morning would rise and do ordinary things. I had been thrown into turmoil in this most peaceful and delightful spot. Yet come morning I would be up before the cockerel.

Day Five – Thursday, 30 July

Miles travelled so far – 66

Yanked towards heaven
The peaceful bellringers
Are dropped back to earth

Doom and Gloom – Farewell to Devon –
A Port in a Storm

Writing my daily haiku had become a necessary discipline. It was a different challenge to the diary entries, running at about 2,000 words a day. Fairly basic words, it has to be said – the distilling would come later. I tried for the haiku early. If I hadn't got one by midday I'd start to sulk. Getting the haiku gave me a boost. Boosts were what I needed. I woke up in Clyst Hydon, and there it was, hovering in front of me, the depressing fact. I still had nearly 500 miles to cover.

'Sam,' I said, feeling sorry for myself, 'let me be on Cullercoats beach, in the bar of the Queen's Head, in my own living-room, listening to Magic Sam.' (Magic Sam was a little-known Chicago blues singer. I'd bought his record at some sale or other. Sam – Magic Sam – that's probably why I made the connection.) Sam wasn't there. He'd slept in front of the Aga with Gyp. Once again I could have done with staying where I was.

I got up. Jean cooked me an appetising hot breakfast and also had sandwiches for my journey. Foodwise, I could have no complaints. It was just that I felt like shit. They'd been good to me, Tom and Jean. I'd needed bringing to my senses.

Tom gave me a lift to the village of Churchingford. On the way, he said, 'You know, if it really is purgatory, you don't have to carry on with it.' It was purgatory. I had to carry on with it. On the drive we travelled out of Devon and into Somerset – our first change of county. Only another 13 to go. Up and down the Black Hills we sped, and through the flat, empty expanses that had once been US air bases. The great yawning mouth of the south-west peninsula was growing wider. We were making progress.

The weather was nondescript. In the village, I shook hands and took my leave. What was that in Tom's eyes? Raging doubt. Was he thinking, how many miles this side of Edinburgh would he give up?

I think I was a little crazy that morning. My route went all over the place. At one stage I was even heading south. Could you believe it? I couldn't. I stood on the A303, checked the map and cursed myself. The traffic roared past and didn't give a damn. Where was I? Near the village of Buckland St Mary. A few miles north was some place called Staple Fitzpaine. I didn't have a clue what it was like, but a name like that had to have something going for it. We would head there. And do something.

The morning was a bit of a blur. I remember a small outpost called Newton, a derelict garage and a shop. It was sad and neglected the way I felt sad and neglected. I remember a kind lady called Violet Moss coming to the door; she had lived there 40 years and had watched the business wither and die when her husband became ill. She gave me a large glass of orange juice, Sam a bowl of water, and we all stood there, sad and neglected, because that was the way the world felt. And I saw the garage's peeling paint, and its uncleaned windows, and knew just what that garage had been through.

We left the main road and plunged into the quiet emptiness of the country lanes. Tom and Jean had given me new plasters for my feet. I now wore my backpack the right way. My new maps meant less chance of me falling into the sea. Lots of reasons to shout hurrah. Except I felt severely melancholic. And my self-healing-feet theory was in tatters. The buggers hurt.

'Sam!' I trilled, in a slightly pathetic attempt at self-jollification. 'Think of all those people in prison for years. Think of Terry Waite. Surely I can get over a few problems on the walk? It just means getting a grip, Sam, getting a grip!' Sam's small tail flicked back and forth like a fly whisk. He tugged at the lead. Maybe he knew something about Staple Fitzpaine.

The sun had climbed up from behind the trees and wobbled with heat in the sky. Staple Fitzpaine came into view, another leafy, secret, strung-out village, more large houses playing peek-a-boo behind tall hedges. I tethered Sam outside the Greyhound pub and walked into the bar with all the confidence a penniless man could muster. A few small groups sat and drank, munched crisps. In a bar at the back I could hear more voices, the clatter of knives and forks and plates. It felt like one of those large chain establishments with such names as the Beefeater or the Pop Inn, where overpaid interior designers created instant ersatz character.

The young male bar staff wore corporate white shirts and

ties. I asked them if they knew any farms further up for possible shelter. I may as well have asked them the local breed of sheep.

Once I had asked this question in a pub, most of my options had gone. Possibly I could sing, do impressions, produce bunnies from a hat. Or I could faint. Normally, I just left. Except the fates were kind. As I turned and thought of trudging away with Sam, an activity which on that day I relished as much as eating cold tea leaves, a young couple in a corner called me over. They'd been eavesdropping. What was all this marathon walk about?

She was Teresa Hurley, her partner was David Tackle, and peeping round the table was their twinkly three-year-old Levanna, whose second name was Oceanic. Sometimes a few words were gold-plated. You wanted to mount them in a glass case, bestow a knighthood on them. Thus when Teresa said, 'You can stay with us for the night, can't he, David?' relief swept over me like a tsunami. 'It's just a very basic council flat in Ilminster. But you're welcome. Have a drink.' The first wave was followed by a second.

I untethered Sam and brought him in. Dave plonked a beer in front of me. I laughed out loud in sheer relief. They laughed too. White shirt looked over. I needed them. They needed a distraction. Their 14-week-old daughter Shazia Starlight was detained in Ilminster Hospital, due to an inability to put on weight. No cuddling and holding their new baby. No putting baby to bed, washing and cleaning. Just travelling to the hospital, phoning the hospital and worrying, wanting the baby home.

We drove the few miles to Ilminster. Their small council flat was in a fairly featureless block up four flights of stairs. They lived a precarious existence. The flat had no phone, no television, not much space. David, who was 39, looked a bit like Sid Vicious. He worked when and where he could in the building trade. They didn't get out much. 'Often we can't pay the rent,' said Teresa, 'but we're madly in love.'

She'd led a chequered life. Dark-haired, 29, outspoken, spirited, several suicide attempts. Her body trembled slightly when she talked. 'If you were a businessman with a suit and mobile phone,' she said to me, 'you'd have no problems getting food and shelter. And they're probably the biggest crooks of all.'

Little Levanna was button bright. Here's a snatch of conversation between her and her mum.

Teresa: 'How many times have I told you not to do that?'

Levanna: 'Three many times.'

A truly responsible traveller would have spent what was left of the day taking in the sights of Ilminster and discovering its many fascinating features. As it was, I couldn't give a toss. I spread myself out on the settee and removed my boots and socks to expose my tomato-red feet to the air. The flat was dishevelled, untidy, chaotic. I felt at home. That evening we ate pizzas, drank beer and played Scrabble. Teresa was incredibly competitive, not just for herself but for Dave too, rearranging his letters for him. Laid-back Dave would shrug, toss the letters in, pick up seven more. The score meant little to him. It meant everything to Teresa.

The previous year Dave had been labouring on a building site. Teresa applied and got a labouring job there too. They worked side by side. How did the macho men react to her? 'I took no shit off any of them,' she said, peering over to get Dave a double word score.

Levanna gave me her necklace to wear and refused to go to bed unless Sam went with her. She had fallen in love with Sam. I was keeping a watch on his runny eye, cleaning it regularly. It seemed to give him no bother. The only universe I needed was the Scrabble board, the next can of Bass, the junk pizza. Sometimes Sam came and licked my feet. There was no edge to any of this. I would be sleeping on the settee. The room was totally wrecked by this time. Full ashtrays, discarded pizza trays, empty beer cans, the odd Scrabble letter. Nobody touched it. I stretched out and tried to sleep in my magic bag.

Some time later I woke to a rock station playing full volume in David and Teresa's bedroom. I waited to see if they'd turn it off. Meatloaf came on. Then Bob Seger. I wriggled out of the bag and made my way across the cluttered floor in the dark. I trod on an ashtray, slipped on a beer spillage. I slid about on an open pizza tray, kicked a few cans across the floor. I found my way to the living-room door, went to open it and found it hanging off (the next day Levanna would point at it and say, 'Daddy got angry!'). I knocked at Dave and Teresa's bedroom door as the music blasted through. No answer. I opened the door and could just make them out, entwined under the duvet. At the bedside, a ghetto blaster the size of a breeze block pounded 200 decibels of Deep Purple directly into their ears. They were both fast asleep.

I fiddled with the blaster for several minutes. Like all modern radios and CD players, it had a hundred buttons and I couldn't find how to switch it off. By the time I got the right one, it was ZZ Top. Maybe the silence would startle them awake? No. I made my way back to the room and over the obstacle course. I'd drunk several cans of beer, my feet were wet with Bass and my mouth belonged in the Sahara. Maybe, I thought, beer had foot-healing properties.

Day Six – Friday, 31 July

Miles travelled so far – 80

Wearing Levanna's necklace
Watching while
She bathes my dog

A Change of Plan – Spirited Feet – Party Time

I had come from two people (Tom and Jean) whose lives were much better organised than mine, to ones whose lives were infinitely less so. Chaos was a natural companion to Dave and Teresa's life. Orderliness and tidiness weren't matters of great importance. So what? I woke that morning in deep gloom. It was still only my sixth day. I seemed to have been walking through the millennium. I couldn't break free of this damned peninsula. I walked. I walked. I walked. I was still on it. I wanted to head north, yet day after day I was heading east, with just a nod towards my preference.

I heard Levanna's bright little voice. Even so, I wanted to pull the sleeping bag over my head and shut my eyes. Teresa brought me a cup of tea. I drank it like some condemned man. I had to get up. I had to go out on that road. I had to walk. David, Teresa and Levanna watched as I scrunched up my sleeping bag into its tiny container, as I packed my meagre possessions into my bag, as I pulled on and laced up my big boots, as I folded my maps, as I checked every item into place. Why were they looking at me that way?

'Pete,' said Teresa, 'Dave and I have been thinking. We both think you should take a break. We think you should rest up here for today. Tomorrow's Saturday, we could run you as far as you like, make up what you'll have lost yesterday and today. What do you say?'

I stared down at my purple laces. A day off? Was it in the rules? 'Let me think about it,' I said, and went into the bathroom, where I realised there were no rules. I came out of the bathroom. 'It's the most fantastic idea I ever heard in my life,' I said and collapsed on the settee. I burst out laughing again. They did too. To be free, for just one day, from the trials of walking, finding food, finding shelter. I'd blindly gone on. I'd as much thought of stopping as I had of walking nude. But why not? I needed it. Dave and Teresa had spotted that. I hadn't. Suddenly they were true friends. True friends can tell you when you're shagged out, mentally or physically.

One brilliant fact about the day to come shone and gleamed like a star. I had absolutely nothing I was obliged to do. 'Just rest up on the settee,' said Teresa. 'It'll do you and your feet good. You don't realise how good it will be for me, too, with Dave at work, Shazia in hospital. It can drive me up the wall.' The image of the condemned man returned. The governor had granted me a reprieve. Okay, a temporary one, but a reprieve. I stretched out on the settee. My feet, having girded themselves up for more torture, turned to ask me what was going on. I gave them the good news. My body, which had been using up its energy levels, took a short time getting the message. After which it chilled out.

Two hours later, with Sam, Teresa and Levanna, I walked into Ilminster, treading carefully in my sandals. In Boots, Teresa bought me a bottle of surgical spirit. She went into a phone booth looking hopeful and came out crestfallen. Shazia could not yet come home from hospital. I tried to cheer her. Back home we had bread and cheese and lots of tea. Levanna gave Sam a bath. I agreed to take her to the children's party at the local pub, where they all thought I was her grandad. On the way back she stopped and suddenly cuddled me close. 'You and Sam stay a long time,' she said.

My feet smelt like Ward Nine. I applied the surgical spirit at regular intervals. This task would have been useful if I'd started two weeks previously. Too late, as usual, but I kept doing it. All day I drifted in and out of sleep on the settee. I read several chapters of *The Hitchhiker's Guide to the Galaxy*. I woke to find either Levanna's smiling face or Sam's inquisitive tongue close by. Sometimes there was a cup of tea from Teresa.

And as I treated my feet, I wondered how Sam could walk for ever, no problem, and here was me with insoles, sticking plasters, moleskins, surgical spirit. Sam had the sense to spread the load across four legs, as did most mammals. Humans, as usual, had to be different. The result was inefficient feet and a global history of back problems.

A strange, surreal day, conscious, semi-conscious, unconscious, subconscious. I had hazy impressions of Orchard FM on the radio. The DJ played a game called 'What's in my hand?'. He offered as first prize in a competition the *Godzilla* soundtrack. The disorganised clutter was my haven. I had no money to offer these people who obviously had little themselves. They'd fed and housed me. I could give them nothing for that. Nor the petrol the next day. I shoved aside my guilt. They wouldn't want it.

After the excesses of the previous night, we were all in bed (or on the settee) early.

Miles travelled so far — 80

All day on the settee
Doing nothing
My journey advances

Foot Sense at Last — Mortimer the Cleric — The World of Colour

My sleeping habits were still bizarre. I woke on the settee at 5 a.m., began to take notes in my diary, drifted off again and was rewoken by Levanna pushing under my nose every book she owned, with the request I read them all to her that minute. It was 6 a.m. It was also 1 August, another month, another landmark on the journey. No more months to go.

Teresa had done oodles of washing for me here. I was a spankingly clean boy. And she'd made me cheese sandwiches for the journey. I looked at my feet, gave them a quick lecture and pulled on my two pairs of purple piped socks. I clomped around the house in my boots, getting to know them again. I packed my bag and made preparations for the road. I was nervous, stomping, like a racehorse waiting for the gate to spring. I had tea and toast. We all clambered into Dave's battered car. Two hundred yards later we were in an accident. As we waited for petrol at the local garage, an elderly man rammed into us with his car. The poor fellow got out and looked flustered. He'd dented our door.

'Oh dear,' he said, 'where do we stand now?'

'Where do we bloody well stand?' said Teresa, with dragon's breath. 'You give us the name of your insurance company, that's where we stand!'

The man looked terrified, as if Teresa might simply vaporise him.

A few minutes later we were back on the road. She was laughing her head off, we were heading towards Wiltshire, and I was to be treated to a big, big lift. The countryside passed in a blur, as the car pulled us further and further out of that peninsula. I sat on the back seat between Sam and Levanna. Sam's large brown eyes were turned towards me. Levanna's big blue eyes stared at me. She was silent. And sad. The nearer we got to dropping off, the heavier my heart became. I felt relief at finally moving to the belly of England. I felt melancholy at taking my leave of these people. I felt apprehension about how my body and feet would behave. The car stopped at a roundabout south of Melksham. We'd covered around 40 miles. Why not just keep going? To Edinburgh?

I stood at the roadside, watched the car speed away, saw Levanna's little face pressed against the back window, a small, white hand waving. For several seconds I stood stock still. I was feeling sorry for myself. I knew the antidote. Get going.

Sam and I were in a different culture. It felt like the south-east. We were close to the M4 corridor, with its business parks, its jets roaring in and out of Heathrow. The south-west peninsula had gone. In a blink, given way to the bustling, aggressive affluence. We were on the edge of the country's most well-to-do region. We would not be touched by it for long. Striking out north, traversing the M4, we'd find more expanses of tranquil countryside. I was unlikely to be corrupted.

Here was my dream: that the day's rest and the application of surgical spirit would see my feet reborn. There was to be no reincarnation. On the first steps, the pain returned. I had the insoles in the boots, and in my bag were more moleskins. For some reason I had not used them, but the time had come. A few miles north-west of Melksham, in the village of Shaw, I spotted the Shaw Clinic. My plan was simple, unambitious. Knock, ask for a pair of scissors, cut moleskins to shape, apply to afflicted areas, walk on, end of problem.

None of this happened. How fortunate. The clinic was a pleasant large stone building in its own grounds. The door was answered by a striking dark-haired woman in a white coat. White coats always fill me with confidence. I asked if she had scissors. She looked wary. What did I want them for? Because I was travelling more than 500 miles without money, because my feet were giving me constant grief, because I had some moleskins and wanted to cut them, because I had to get to Edinburgh. There was a pause. She looked me up and down, as if I was an object on the *Antiques Roadshow*.

'Just wait in the garden a moment, would you?' The last person to say this to me had been the reluctant rector of Yelverton. I sat down on the white metal chair by the white metal table. How pleasant the flowers, plants and shrubs were. I knew the names of none of them.

The woman's name was Sheila Carter, she was a fully trained chiropodist and this was her own complementary medicine clinic. A few moments later, her delicate hands were carefully examining all aspects of my feet. I closed my eyes, heard the soft drone of the bees, felt the warm southern sun on my face, experienced the sensuous touch on my feet.

'The feet are severely bruised,' she said. She turned their undersides for me to see, patterns of florid red resembling an old map of the British Empire. 'The problem is, you need them to heal, but you also need to carry on walking.' I nodded. Of course. But she would have the answer! 'What I'll try to do is take the pressure off the worst areas. I'm not sure how well it will work.'

Oh, but it will! She would see to it! I looked around at the garden, the large house. I said, 'I have no money whatsoever. I'm not able to pay you.'

'Keep your feet still while I do this,' said Sheila Carter. She applied two cushioned sections, rather like ring doughnuts, to the balls of my feet. Each was smeared with friar's balsam (an old-fashioned mix I wouldn't have associated with this clinic), given a strong adhesive and then skilfully bandaged so that the skin was still allowed to breathe. It was a work of art.

'I want you to keep these dressings on as long as they feel all right,' she said. She cut into shape two more 'doughnuts' as spares. The heels were also painful, but less so, and I hadn't the cheek to mention it. How paltry my moleskins seemed against these professional dressings. How on earth would I have continued without Sheila Carter?

'Thank you very much,' I said as I put my socks and boots back on. 'You've no idea what this means.'

'There are no guarantees,' she said.

Sam and I took our leave. I wanted to cuddle her, but didn't. We walked on, growing ever closer to the M4, through the village of Biddestone. The dressings had removed the pain from the front of my feet. It had transferred to the back. I stopped, sat by the roadside, removed shoes and socks, and stuck the two reserve doughnuts on my heels. My entire body would now be supported on cushioned doughnuts.

A large, posh car drew up alongside and an electronic window purred its way down. It was Sheila Carter. 'I'm worried about those feet of yours,' she said. This made two of us. 'It's such a long way to walk. I'm driving up to Lancashire with my husband tomorrow. We could give you a lift.' Two large dogs were in the back seat. They were especially interested in Sam.

I could think of nothing nicer than driving up to Lancashire with Sheila Carter. 'Thank you,' I said, 'but it would rather defeat the object. I have to journey mainly on foot.' She smiled. Another plan came to mind. 'Maybe you could drop me the other side of the M4?' I asked. 'I hate walking close to motorways, it drives me mad.'

She opened the door. I climbed in. How comfortable the big, soft seats were. As I closed the door with a soft click, the rain set in. On the back seat, Barnie, the Irish wolfhound/Border collie, and Lela, the labrador/terrier, leaned forward to sniff at Sam, who went for the world's tunnelling record inside my coat. The car drove noiselessly. The windscreen wipers glided over the glass like a pair of champion skaters. We crossed the motorway. Sheila Carter pulled up at the roadside. It was teeming down.

'No hurry,' she said. I took out one of my cheese sandwiches and munched it, more slowly than normal. The rain beat on. 'Take your time,' said Sheila Carter. I took out my second sandwich. I munched that too. We stared at the clouds. Like mucky cotton-wool.

'Well,' I said eventually, 'I suppose I'd better . . .'

'Yes,' she said. Rain hit the windscreen and exploded into petalled flowers.

'Thanks again, then.'

Moments later Sam and I were back on the road. The M4 was at our backs. For the second time that day I stood by the roadside, watched a car disappear and realised what I had to do was walk. We strode out, in the direction of Tetbury. The rain had set in hard. The brolly was up, Sam was taking on water. Trucks and cars threw up their sheets of spray. We battened down and carried on. After some miles, through the gloom the distinctive church spire of Tetbury's St Mary the Virgin was on the horizon. The spire seemed a beacon. It called to us. We responded.

Once into Tetbury, we made for the church and walked in. A peacefulness wrapped itself around me. I decided to write up the diary. It was a large Georgian Gothic church. It had eight bells, I discovered, the earliest dating back to 1722 (a Johnnie-come-lately compared to Clyst Hydon). Elsewhere in the country, churches were locked and barred. Not here. Locking churches, I told myself, solved nothing.

I sat at the table by the entrance, took off my wet coat and hat, and spread them out behind me. Sam lay next to them, and as the thunder rumbled its tummyache outside, I took up the pen. Only later did I realise that next to me on the table was the collection plate. To most of the visitors I appeared as some kind of clerical official. This made them all put money in the plate. There weren't many visitors, but the loot soon added up. No one had the nerve to pass without contributing. The few who had the nerve on the way in had lost it by the time they were on the way out.

The irony struck me. A penniless wanderer, writing about his penniless wanderings, and next to him a plate filling up with money. I wrote on. People approached, I indicated the plate. Some came clutching postcards. I indicated the wooden box. There was no sign of the clergy. Who was in charge of this entire large church? Me.

A small incident took place which linked two worlds. One

man, kneeling in a front pew, was forced to beat a hasty and embarrassed retreat when his mobile phone's trill shattered the godly peace.

I wrote for about an hour. I collected about six quid. Better than my normal hourly rate – except it wasn't mine for taking.

We had now passed into our fourth county, Gloucestershire. The accents were changing, but the one generally thought of as 'West Country' stretched, in various forms, across hundreds of miles, through Cornwall, Devon, Somerset, through Gloucestershire, Wiltshire, all tagged with the general 'ooo-aar' label. For some reason, we associated this accent more than any other with yokels in smocks. Country accent? They must mean West Country. Why not Yorkshire, Lancashire, Northumberland accents? Was it all down to cider advertisements?

What an agreeable little market town Tetbury was! Surely a natural resting place for tonight? Well, no. I called at the local tourist office. I called at several over the month. I thought they'd be interested in me, a writer travelling through their terrain. I thought they'd be flinging hospitality at me. They didn't. Not even a cup of tea or a jam tart in any of them. At the Tetbury office they suggested I tried the Ormond Arms for a night's shelter. In the small public bar, the locals leaned on the counter, narrowed their eyes and moved tongues around their mouths as I put my case. The landlord was not at home, and the barman slowly and surely moved his head from one side to the other as I talked. One regular tossed an apple in my direction. They all laughed. His name was Ian Woods and the apple was a red russet, which I hate.

'Try the Crown,' said one of them.

I did. Same speech. Same reaction. For some reason I returned to the Ormond.

'What's at Avening?' I asked. Avening was three miles distant.

'Nothing at Avening,' they replied.

'How about on the road to Avening?'

'Nothing on the road to Avening.'

I'd put the apple core in a waste bin. I knew Tetbury was not for us. My feet had been holding up well post-Sheila Carter. We set off. The rain had cleared, the evening was settling into a calm sky, the gentle sun stretched out the hedgerow shadows. I had no idea where we were going. I just felt good to be leaving.

The road to Avening offered huge swaying fields of corn each side, a sense of space, light. Ninety minutes later Avening appeared in front of us, clinging to the hillside. It was Saturday night, 7 p.m.

Saturday night wasn't like any other night. Saturday night had an anticipation of social and sexual excitement. Increasingly this had little to do with reality, but I would still feel it when in my Zimmer frame. It had been branded in from teenage years. It began with the reading of the football results just before five o'clock. It had to do with shaving, showering, gelling hair, slapping on aftershave, stepping out to see what the night held. Some Saturday nights I stayed in, watched *Match of the Day*. It didn't affect anything. It was still Saturday night. I might be ironing pillowcases. Still Saturday night. Or walking into Avening. Still Saturday night.

I pushed such things from my mind. My first stop was the post office/shop. As I walked in, a strident voice yelled, 'No dogs!' I tethered Sam outside. Inside, a slightly formidable-looking middle-aged woman stood in my way. As I spoke, her body began to revolve very slowly, like a watch in a jeweller's window. By the time she replied, she was almost at right angles to me, removing the need for any real contact.

'No money? How can you stay anywhere with no money?'

I began to explain. The woman shrugged and moved to the back of the shop. It was spitting with rain again. I walked through the village. I could see through windows into houses. The normal things people were doing – eating, watching television, lounging – seemed incredibly precious. Some were getting ready to go out. Spend money. They would think little of it. We took it all for granted. Except me, at this moment. Homeless, foodless, penniless.

Down the hill was The Bell pub. Again a small group of

locals looked hard as I walked in, Sam in tow. The barmaid seemed friendly, and her suggestion was unexpected.

'Try the College of Colour Therapy, back up the village, small road to the left. They'll probably help.'

The College of Colour Therapy? I was puce with anticipation. We found the road, a pair of gates, a drive, a second pair of gates, and there was Brook House, a large fourteenth-century stone structure, built at right angles.

I rang the bell. The door was opened by an extraordinary-looking man. He had a shock of white hair and a white beard, a cross between an Old Testament prophet and an eccentric scientific genius, the latter reinforced by the Germanic accent. He was 78-year-old Theolonius Gimble, a Bavarian who came to England in 1949. He was a genuine prince of Burgundy and since 1970 had run his College of Colour Therapy in this rambling stone building. It taught the therapeutic and harmonic benefits of light and colour.

Theo had published 14 books on the subject. Students came from throughout the world. At that very moment he was exhausted. Not because he'd recently got married to an Irishwoman a good 30 years his junior (surprises came thick and fast here), but because they'd both just completed running the final fortnight of a year's course with 17 students.

Not that I learnt all this on the doorstep. 'I need shelter for the night,' I'd said. Theo turned and went to look for his wife. The phone rang. I heard the answerphone: 'Please leave your message, preferably in colour.'

A highly coloured mobile swung gently inside the front door. An eight-foot grandfather clock was at one side. To the right a splendid banister ran upstairs in a wide arc. Corridors ran off in all directions. On the purple wall opposite, a large, brightly painted greeting read 'Bienvenu aux mariés' ('Welcome to the newlyweds').

His wife Carmel appeared, a slim, tall, elegant woman, almost birdlike in her delicacy. Like her husband, she looked tired. 'Of course you can stay,' she said. 'Excuse us being exhausted. We will make you as welcome as we can.' She led Sam and me down a corridor, into our small partitioned room. The door had a sign saying 'The Blue Room'; it was lit by a single blue light. There was another sign, saying 'May Peace Prevail on Earth'. I had a bed, a small table. I sat on the bed for a moment. 'Well, Sam,' I said, 'there's a turn-up.'

I changed into my evening wear: sandals, Indian trousers, striped top. Carmel had shown me the bathroom and I expected that to be it for the night. I would go hungry. I made my way along the corridor with wash bag. Carmel appeared. 'When you are ready, come and have a drink with us in the music room,' she said and swished away.

The spacious music room had a grand piano, a pianoforte, various musical instruments on the wall, large windows reaching to the ground. I reclined on a big, soft settee. I had a glass of chilled white wine in my hand. With Theo and Carmel were a young French couple, Laurence and Bona. Laurence was an aromatherapist, and a dab hand with animals, as Sam was to find to his benefit. Bona was a musician and composer. He had the same birthday as my son Dylan.

During the war Theo had been imprisoned for three and a half years, much of it in solitary confinement, much of that in darkness. The experience had inspired him to discover colour's true potential. Out of the darkness had come vibrant colour. I was on the wavelength straightaway. My own house was obsessively coloured throughout, a quarter of a century of organic process. British pastel and all it stood for was my sworn enemy.

I'd be okay here.

Carmel asked to look at my feet. She massaged them carefully and tenderly, avoiding Sheila Carter's dressings. She was an extraordinary woman, with an almost telepathic link to her husband. 'Your voice is very tight,' she said. 'What's that fear inside you?'

I told her. The fear of my journey, of not being up to it, physically or mentally. I lugged this fear with me like a small suitcase. She continued the massage. A few minutes later I started to cough. I hardly ever cough. Coughing is so rare for me, Lloyds have a large bell they ring if it happens. I coughed and coughed. For no reason. 'Don't worry,' said Carmel. 'That's just the fear being released, the tightness. Just cough away.' I did, for most of the evening. I used up two decades' worth of coughing.

I'd left Sam in the Blue Room, spread out on my other clothes, for his security. Contessa, a beautiful white Alsatian, had been rescued after a history of beatings which had left her nervous with other dogs. She was ten times the size of Sam, who, for once, would be better off alone.

While we talked, Laurence went off to see the wee fellow. She massaged his little legs, returned and gave me advice. 'Massage his legs every night from the feet up,' she said. 'It will help him. And here, this is to massage your own feet and calves, make them supple.' She gave me a small bottle of sweet-smelling oil. That night and every night I used it as prescribed. The mere act of rubbing the oil into my skin was therapy.

I had fallen into a wondrous house. Food appeared, a sizzling hot barbecue, chicken legs, sausages, ribs, burgers, chops. I tore at them like a wolf.

'In England,' said Laurence, 'people no longer go on a real journey. They simply travel.' She was right; people were shuttled off on package tours, herded on safaris, made surrogate journeys on telly's travel documentaries. I was beginning to discover real travel. I was beginning to appreciate the outer and inner journey.

Between coughs, of course.

Before we ate, Theo, whose general knowledge was encyclopaedic but who was a man of great modesty, produced two coloured candles. He lit the first. 'This is for peace in the world.' He lit the second. 'This is for Peter's journey.'

Up some rickety stairs from the kitchen (the second time I looked I couldn't find it, such was the meandering layout of the house) was the chapel, a non-denominational room, again liquid with colour. Stained glass was inset into the taffeta-covered door. In the centre of this secluded room was a golden cross, various candle holders, a Tibetan sounding bowl, small cymbals. We knelt on the floor. Theo lit another candle for my journey and rubbed a leather pestle around the rim of the copper bowl which eventually produced one beautifully sustained harmonic note. The cross, said Carmel, created a protective aura around an individual. It would help me on my journey. 'What would also help you,' she said, 'is a colour bath. Given your mental state at the moment, I think turquoise or blue would be best.'

She was not talking Radox. Into the bath water I shook two small drops from a small bottle of natural concentrated blue dye. Like some magician's trick, the water was immediately a vivid blue. In went two drops of green, and my bath was instantly transformed into a shimmering turquoise.

Bathing was not easy. I managed to lower myself into the water, propping my bandaged feet above the taps. The turquoise sea embraced me. I closed my eyes and gave myself over to the liquid which shimmied in curling patterns on the wall. I was in a colour bath, in the home of a Burgundian prince and princess. I was fed, wined, bathed, sheltered. All given freely, without fuss. As if charity was the most natural thing in the world. And as I let the waters take me, I grew for the moment sad that in our world Brook House was such a rarity.

After my bath (so powerful was the colour I half expected to emerge as the turquoise man), I pulled Theo's thick, white bathrobe around me and made my way back to the Blue Room. Sam had been fed, watered and massaged by Laurence. He had spread out on my combat trousers. I pulled out my small sleeping bag. Downstairs, one top and one pair of pants had been washed and were drying. Sam seemed pleased to see me again and snuggled up close as I wriggled down. As we drifted off to sleep, I heard the gentle gurgle of the trout stream as it flowed under the wooden bridge in the garden. Both Sam and I were almost away when he suddenly cocked his head and opened both big eyes in surprise at hearing me cough.

Miles travelled so far — 134

The two women
I just met
Stroking my naked feet

My Semi-Conversion — Classical Summer — Bring on the Hunters

A lot of people gave me a lot of good advice on my journey. In some ways I felt parts of my journey belonged to them. Tom and Jean at Clyst Hydon had instilled some sense into me. In Ilminster, Teresa and David had realised (when I hadn't) that I needed a break. At Avening, after I'd risen, washed, written up my diary and walked along for a breakfast of cereal and toast, Carmel said, 'When you feel the need to stop, don't resist it. Let it shape your journey. If you want to dwell somewhere a short time, just do so.'

I took her good advice sooner than she could have thought. That Sunday morning, she and Theo were going to the service at the Holy Cross of Avening church. I decided to go with them. A strange decision. I'd not thought of going to a Sunday church service in decades. My visits were limited to weddings and funerals. I usually enjoyed the latter more than the former. In the past I'd often overdosed on supercilious vicars spouting abstracted guff from ivory-tower pulpits. I felt the Christian religion had lost its way in Britain. How come churches were featuring prominently on my odyssey, I wondered? Why did I want to go? Maybe the ceremony would tell me.

The church dated back to 1080 and had a distinctive Norman tower. We walked up the gently sloping drive and Theo pointed to the rowan tree just inside the gate. 'My first wife's ashes are buried there,' he said.

Carmel was a newcomer to the village since the wedding. The villagers were still curious about her. The Sunday service was among the week's social focal points.

It was a beautiful service, free from cant or pontification. As we walked into the church, the organist played 'Smoke Gets in your Eyes'. There was no pulpit, no pews, just wooden chairs. The new female vicar, Celia Carter, was away, and the simple service was led by two young lay women preachers and included three children. Something about it just cut through. The hymns were not the usual dirges. For the first time I could remember, a normal church service made me tearful.

What was it? Something about a group of people gathered for a reason that was important to them. A belief in something. Our society tended to believe in nothing. Our dreams were fastened on such confidence tricks as a lottery ticket.

Nor was the sermon gobbledegook. It was of the real world, a vivid description of the Kurds' plight under Saddam Hussein. The main message was that the good people of Avening, compared to many in the world, did not know they were born. It was not put quite so blatantly. This struck a chord with me. This was why I had needed to come. My own journey was telling me many times over how in the comparatively affluent UK we took for granted things much of the world had never known. We were sheltered from most of the planet's miseries. We swallowed our anti-depressants, trudged off to the therapists, lost ourselves in drink or drugs. We were pathetic. We'd had the good fortune to be born in a moderate, affluent, temperate country and climate. For some reason this left us empty, unfulfilled.

Carmel leaned over to me, resplendent in her flowing colours of the rainbow, and whispered, 'Since Celia arrived as vicar, there's been none of that old-style sermon nonsense.' More female vicars, please! Away with the reactionaries!

The lesson was read by seven-year-old Camilla Delamare with an unflattering, uncomplicated innocence, after which the congregation emerged into Avening's soft morning light. I breathed the air deeply. Back to Brook House, its large, peaceful, secluded garden, its small wooden bridge, its 60-foot-high lime tree, its octagonal summer house. 'The octagon is a good shape to focus you before you leave,' said

Carmel. 'Why not sit in it a while? It will help your journey.'

I knew I could not stay overlong. Maybe few people could. Part of me longed for the peace and calm Brook House offered. Everyone in the world should visit Brook House. Another part knew a writer or a painter or any creative artist also needed a restlessness, a conflict. Too much calm could still the vessel. But it had been a revelation.

Carmel had made me sandwiches for the journey. I'd not yet passed a whole day in abject hunger, nor taken on the appearance of a down-and-out. I'd shaved every day. My clothes didn't hum.

This promised to be a hot day. I sat in the summer house and got focused. Despite the aggressive snapping of Contessa, Sam seemed relaxed and chilled out under Laurence's care. I'd given him his first leg massage that morning. (Ever massaged a dog's leg? It feels like something from a barbecue.) He'd had his vitamin pill. He sat at my feet in the summer house. I was okay. Brandy and coffee. It was already two o'clock, and Theo and Carmel had agreed to run me a few miles to keep up the daily average.

I wanted to visit the chapel one more time. I sat in silence and thought of all the people I had stayed with. From nowhere I arrived, was briefly a part of their lives. And was gone. I was totally reliant on them. What did I offer in return? Not much. Each stop made its impression on me. What impression did I make on them? I didn't have time to find out. After ten minutes in the chapel, I came out. Sam and I climbed into the car. I took one last look at Brook House. It believed in the power of colour. Power for most people was an altogether different, less beneficial thing. It showed us another world. Farewell.

After a few quiet miles of country lanes, Sam and I said goodbye to Theo and Carmel outside the small village of Winstone, south of the A417. I had lit a candle in the chapel, and thought of it still burning.

This was to be our hottest, quietest day so far, a day spent walking the tiny, narrow, silent Cotswold lanes, the beautifully sleepy countryside opening up into large rolling hills.

The sun was intense, the sky a cobalt blue; there was the occasional sound of a starling, the thrum of a combine harvester, the soft gurgle of an unseen stream. The feel was of a classical English summer's day in a classical English county. We were close to both Cheltenham and Gloucester; several main roads ran close, including the unceasing M5 (which had dogged our path for a week). Yet once these main roads were left, we were plunged into a soft, silent world.

North of Winstone, the map showed our road crossing the busy A417. I am in the process of issuing writs. 'Dear map-maker, our client wishes to inform you of the following: far from crossing the A417 as indicated, his road ran down parallel with it for three-quarters of a mile, through an underpass, then back up again another three-quarters of a mile, depositing him a few yards from where he had started. We wish to inform you that the main road was steeply banked and high-fenced, making any other crossing of it impossible. On behalf of our client we would also wish to inform you that while a mile and a half may seem to you a trivial distance, to our client, travelling on foot with a 16lb pack, a small dog, suspect feet and a journey of approximately 400 miles still to come, it is an intolerable and unnecessary addition to an already onerous odyssey. Further frustration was felt by our client arising from the fact that when he began this unnecessary diversion, he witnessed a signpost stating "Elkstone 1". When he completed the diversion, it was to see a second signpost. This also read "Elkstone 1". We await your offer of compensation . . .' etc, etc. I didn't go that much for Elkstone anyway. The other villages hereabouts looked natural. Elkstone seemed a bit ersatz rural chic.

With this day's heat, and the bag pressing down, my back was turning into a hotplate. I was, though, beginning to establish some pattern to the walking. Best progress came from disciplined spells of walking, then periods of rest and foot airing. Despite my protective doughnuts, the cushioned insoles and Sheila Carter's expertise, the constant pounding of the tarmac was taking its toll.

I tried walking on grass. Often there wasn't any. Other times Sam fought tooth and nail to be on the hard, man-made surface. Sam was a good pooch. He took everything in his stride. That stride wasn't very big, though. Part of me still felt a dog should come up to my calf, not my lower shin.

Bit by bit, we were chipping away at the monstrous mileage. We'd passed into Gloucestershire, and soon would be leaving the south behind. Already we were nudging the periphery of the Midlands.

Hot days brought water problems. I had my small plastic bottle from Clyst Hydon. In such heat, we rapidly glugged it empty and needed to knock on doors when no rivers appeared for refills. Hot days also meant sleepy stops. I could fall asleep at the drop of a hat, though I tended to keep it on. I'd prop against a shady tree and remove boots and socks. If there was food (as today, with the Brook House sandwiches) I'd share it with Sam, down some water and close my eyes. Sometimes Sam could be asleep quicker than me, but not often. Fifteen minutes later I'd be awakened, as if by a magic fairy.

Through the sleepy villages of Colesbourne and Withing-ton, on through this sleepy day till 7 p.m., by which time the golden sun was beginning to tire. We were late looking for shelter. The next village *en route* was Andoversford. That would be the one. My plan was normally this: enter the village, act on impulse.

For the first time I called upon the police. Literally. I had nothing to fear. The door of the police house/station was opened by a woman whose most prominent feature was the dramatically peeling sunburn on her nose. I tried not to look at this too much as I spoke. Suddenly there were more noses. What seemed like a pack of ferocious dogs was try-ing to push past her. It looked like they wanted to eat Sam, who shrank behind me and made himself as small as a toy dog in a car's back window. Above the clamour, I asked about possible shelter for the night. Police custody. The lady with the peeling nose, whilst keeping the pack at bay, suggested I tried other dogs, the Cotswold Kennels, half a mile distant. I never got to meet the police officer, her husband.

Back up the main road and up a lane, we came across the small settlement. Several humans lived there, along with 100 hounds, 14 horses and three ponies. And, tonight, one peripatetic guest. I was about to enter the world of foxhunting. Who'd have thought it? Townies rarely get close to this world. Unless it is to lay aniseed trails or wave placards. I'd never met a foxhunter in my life. For the next few days I'd hardly be able to move for them.

There was a small terrace of three houses. I knocked at one, the home of huntsmaster Julian Barnfield and his wife Julia. He was a foxhunter. She was a vet. For some reason I found that funny. Julia listened to my tale. 'You can have a mattress in the back room,' she said. 'The spare room's being decorated.' Sometimes it was as simple as that. In I went. In came Julian, a fit, healthy-looking man, close-cropped hair, that soft-collar checked shirt beloved of ruralites. A hundred hounds – did he know them all by name?

'Yes, of course I do.'

And every morning he took them for a two-and-a-half-hour walk on the small country lanes.

The children, Gemma (eight) and Laura (five), were fascinated by Sam, who was far removed from a foxhound. Gemma tried to draw him. Not appreciating the discipline of the artist's model, Sam declined to stay still. 'Take a photo,' I said. 'Draw him from that. Send it to me for the book.' She took the photo. I never saw the drawing.

In the back room, I took off my pack, my boots and my socks. I changed my clothes. I laid out and checked all my possessions. Gemma and Laura knocked and came in and watched me. They gawped at me as if I were from Planet Zog. What was I doing? Walking every day for a month. And I had no money? That was right. How did I live? I depended on generous people like their mum and dad. They examined my bandaged feet. They looked at the massage oil. They unscrewed Sam's little bottle of pills and sniffed them. They fed him one. I told them his feet needed massaging and showed them how. They did it.

In the front room was a hugely welcome fry-up. I sat on the settee, barefoot, tucked in. Julian sat in his armchair. Draped around his neck was his 'shadow', the foxhound Jesse. He hung there, looking – ironically – like an old-fashioned fox fur. The weather came on the screen.

'See that?' said Julian. 'A terrible forecast. You'll get soaked tomorrow. Got anywhere to stay?'

No, I didn't have.

'I might be able to help,' he said. 'Not much fun being drenched, then having to look for somewhere to stay.'

Jesse swivelled an eye towards me. Forward booking? I'd not had it since Dartmoor. I tucked into my sausage and bacon with relish. Or was it ketchup? At such moments the world seemed perfect, anxiety drained away, the next day's uncertainties were forgotten. I had shelter. I had a beautiful inlaid desk on which to do my writing. I was fed. Sam too. I had possible shelter the next day. Day eight. So far no sleeping in hedgerows. I'd not been beaten up, nor starved to death.

Julian went to the phone, then came back. 'No reply,' he said, 'but it'll be okay. It's too far for you to walk in a single day, though. We'll give you a lift for the first part.'

We'd talked little of foxhunting. I'd mentioned I was anti, Julian had shrugged his shoulders as if, on such brief contact, he wasn't over-concerned in opening up a fierce debate, and, as I speared the last sausage, I felt the creeping tiredness in my limbs and thought of that sleeping bag. I guess I felt the same.

Miles travelled so far — 150

Fed with his wife's ashes
The rowan tree
Will flower brilliant red

Exposed in Ledbury — A Journey Too Far — The Smithy as Saviour

The symphony of awakening comprised the baying of foxhounds and the patter of rain on the dining-room window. I listened to the first movement, opened my eyes and found Sam on my chest staring back at me. Since I'd started massaging his legs, he seemed especially affectionate. I just hoped he wasn't getting any ideas. Time for his vitamin pill. Laura and Gemma would do the honours. For many dogs, such a pill needed to be ground up in half a ton of Pedigree Chum, then force-fed through a plastic funnel. In Sam's case, I said 'Pill!', he opened his mouth, I popped it in, he chewed, swallowed, blinked, and that was it.

Where did I live, asked Laura. Near a big town, I said. 'I hate big towns,' she replied and pulled a face. I thought of her in ten years, all disco glitter.

I was changing my survival technique. At first I'd been tentative: knock on doors, possibly ask for water, a bit of chat, slowly edge towards requests for food or shelter. Now I was more head-on. I was a penniless writer. How about it?

The sky was an unwashed grey, and the wind was shoulder-charging the windows. A pig of a day. I washed, dressed and sat at the kitchen table. Julian did his best to cheer me up. 'You'll get a real soaking today. The forecast is for a lot of rain, and winds up to 50 miles an hour. This is no day to be on the road with a small dog.'

I waited for the bad news. After the toast, I opened the kitchen door to let Sam out for ablutions. He stood at the open door and for the first time demonstrated the efficiency of reverse gear as great squalls of rain lashed down. He reversed right back into the centre of the kitchen. 'Sam,' I said, 'if I have to go out there, you have to go out there.'

Julian gave me the address and phone number of the kennels ahead. 'Just get there,' he said. 'I'm sure they'll put you up.'

I'd had little time to look around his own place. It covered 130 acres and had its own point-to-point course. Its few families lived in each other's pockets. I wondered how they got on. Why had there been no soap opera, no fly-on-the-wall documentary?

I shared a final cup of tea with Julian and, almost from some sense of duty, broached the thorny topic. 'Isn't foxhunting out of date, cruel and unnecessary?' (No sugar, thanks.)

'There's a lot of ignorance,' he replied, and was as calm as you like. 'The fox is dead within seconds of being caught. What people don't realise is that the countryside today is laid out the way it is mainly because of field sports. In theory the best method of killing a fox is at night, a gun and a torch, but it's too indiscriminate, and you're never sure if the fox is dead. But the fox is a pest, believe me, and sheep farmers round here would agree.'

I made some sort of muffled acknowledgement to this. He seemed quite a gentle man. But then I'd met lifelong pacifists who were a pain in the arse. Oh, for easy answers.

Both Laura and Gemma had fallen in love with Sam. 'Whenever we have a new dog now,' said Laura, 'we'll call him Sam.'

I was to journey beyond Tewkesbury in a strange vehicle. I named it the Knacker Truck, the Flesh Wagon. My driver I named as a dealer in death, a body-snatcher, a Dr Corpse. He was actually quite normal-looking, kennel man Gary Irwin; his somewhat battered wagon had the task of picking up carcasses from neighbouring farms to feed the hounds. There was a strange putrescent smell. Another landmark on this waterlogged morning – Gary would run me across the M5 and we would finally be free of that seemingly endless tentacle which wriggled its insidious way from far down in the south-west peninsula up into the West Midlands. The M50 also ran up north-east. Within a short space of time, my journey involved crossing not one, but two motorways. Gary seemed to read my mind.

'I'll drop you just past the M50,' he said. 'How's that?'

Brill.

'What's Tewkesbury like?' I asked him.

'Never been,' he replied.

Our planned destination, Clifton Kennels at Tedstone Delamere, was far distant. We needed all the lift we could get. I'd got sandwiches from Julia, and my feet were tapping on the van floor. At one moment I convinced myself they were improving. Ten seconds later I was convinced of their terminal decline. I needed a definite sign. I'd get one.

On such a pig of a morning, sitting in a warm, dry (if slightly unsavoury) cab, witnessing the intemperate weather outside, there was a yearning not to open that door, not to go out into the wild elements. As someone once said, though, a man's got to do . . . Sam and I climbed down from the cab on the A438, eight miles south of Ledbury. The first few miles of walking didn't seem rhythmic enough, as if the body needed to lubricate itself, establish its pattern.

It was a valley road set in rolling wooded countryside and, behind, both Elgar's Malvern Hills and the Black Hills were prominent. I'd mentally prepared myself for a day of rain, my valiant wee brolly was pitted against the elements, my body was hunched up to protect itself, angled for best resistance against the wet. There was, then, almost a slight sense of being cheated when, a little more than an hour later, the rain stopped. And there was the brolly hassle, the need to pull it free from where it was tightly wedged in the corner of the bag, open it up, redo the bag. This was necessary every time it rained. I got so fed up that sometimes I'd walk stubbornly through the rain unbrollied. 'You can damn well just stay in the bag!' I'd shout. What did the brolly care? I got wet.

At Hollybush, we came across a strange sight. All Saints, a

small, isolated church, stood at the roadside. It was surrounded by unfenced grass on which grazed a flock of sheep. I resisted all puns, even though the flock included a black one. I realised I would probably never again see a church surrounded by sheep.

Sheep, as someone might have said, are nature's lawnmower, and the grass was perfectly trimmed. The graveyard was some sight too. Death may as well be colourful. Every gravestone here was a brilliant floral explosion. It looked a good place to die. In the porch was a certificate – the church was in the 'Excellent' category in the Best-Kept Churchyard competition. Those sheep had every right to look smug.

There was more surprise and brilliant colour after we'd walked a few more miles along the valley to Eastnor. Eastnor had what I realised was not that common – an aesthetically pleasing post office, a low-slung, thatched-roof building, half-timbered. On its front hung a variety of wire baskets dripping with brilliantly bright flowers. You walked to the post office up a gently sloping garden path, a short journey which itself meandered (I said I'd never use that word!) past shrubs and plants ablaze with colour. This was some way to get your Giro.

Inside was Lilian Earle, who'd been behind that counter since 1972. I had my *Down your Way* hat on again. 'How long has it been a post office exactly, Lilian?' I asked. She wasn't sure. She ferreted around and produced some notes scribbled on the torn-off side of a Jaffa Cakes packet. These notes suggested the first postmaster had been a Mr Sam Manwaring in 1902. The price on the Jaffa Cakes packet was one old penny; it was a time when you knew where you were with a Jaffa Cake.

By the time we reached Ledbury, my water bottle was again empty. I had talked to Sam about the possibility of travelling through Wales, which, had it any thoughts on the matter, may have felt left out of this odyssey. But it meant trekking through the Bristol conurbation to cross the Severn Bridge, heading directly west for a longish spell. Either of these activities was likely to bring me out in spots.

This Elizabethan border town would have to do. I realised my feet were now subject to more treatment than a seasoned hypochondriac. I applied the surgical spirit from Boots. From the College of Colour Therapy came the massage oil. From the Shaw Clinic they had their dressings. My feet had no excuses for below-par performance.

Ledbury meant Herefordshire – another county. In the town centre, opposite the distinctive Tudor buildings, I sat on a wooden bench. The town was busy with lunching office workers and shoppers. This is what I did. I removed my socks and boots and placed them on the pavement, where I also placed the surgical spirit and the massage oil. I applied each in turn to my feet, which I propped up on the seat. No one sat next to me. My feet enjoyed the Ledbury air, and asked for more of it. I left them propped up unrobed (except for bandages), took out Julia's cheese sandwiches and munched away. I looked up to see two small children standing staring at me, wide-eyed. Their mother pulled them away. Maybe she didn't like cheese.

I needed water. I also needed to check out my potential night's stay. Opposite was the tourist information office. I made myself as respectable as possible (i.e. put my boots back on) and walked in. There was one woman at the counter and she was rushed off her feet. Ledbury was a popular place. I asked if she'd try the phone number for me, and told her I was penniless. Slightly abashed, she did so. There was no reply. I told her I had no one else but her to rely on, what could she do? She was brilliant. She knew the local master-of-the-hunt-cum-blacksmith, name of Michael Roberts, and she would phone him. He answered.

I told him I was a penniless writer. I hoped to stay at Clifton Kennels, Tedstone Delamere. I'd spent the previous night at Andoversford. Michael Roberts, without so much as a blow-your-horn, had promised he would fix everything up at the kennels. I just had to arrive.

A queue was forming in the office. I pushed my luck. Could my dog possibly have a bowl of water? Could she possibly show me the kennels on her map? Oh, that was a good map! Could I possibly have a photocopy of that page? And the water? I failed to get this good lady's name. It obviously begins with Saint. A tupperware bowl of water arrived for Sam. A photocopy of the map arrived for me. The queue grew.

Sam lapped at the water greedily. I watched him. I licked my dried, parched lips. Sam lapped on. Lap, lap. The queue was still long. The lady was busy. There was a limit to my cheek. Still Sam was lapping. My lips grew drier, more parched. I was in that film. *Ice Cold in Alex.*

Sam stopped drinking and gave a watery snuffle. There was still an inch of liquid in the tupperware bowl. I looked around me. People were busy studying maps, making enquiries. What did they care? I dropped on all fours, out of sight of the counter lady (but not most of the customers), picked up the bowl and thirstily drank out of it.

I had to bother the lady again. Sam was fixing me with a strange eye. What was wrong with him? Ah, yes. How far exactly was it from this place to Tedstone Delamere? About 14 miles. I sat down for a moment in the office and took the statistic on board. We'd already come about nine. Outside, a watery sunlight was pushing its way through the cloud. We faced our biggest day's walking yet. 'Let's go, Sam,' I said, and we took our leave. The sun, tentative at first but now seemingly reinforced by assertiveness training, was growing hotter. I'd feared being washed away on this day. Now we might be cooked.

Several miles from Ledbury we walked through the small village of Bosbury. A small, defining incident took place. A gaggle of young children spilled out of the village shop. Each had an ice cream or ice lolly. I watched the laughing, playing children skip away up the street, sucking or licking their cold delicacies. I was seized by an almost overwhelming desire for such a treat. I realised it was impossible to satisfy this desire. I could feel that ice cream slipping down my throat, that frozen fruit water filling and cooling my mouth. The shop window advertised all manner of ice creams. Inside, the gently humming fridge would house enough to satisfy a child army. I needed just one. A raspberry ripple, a chocolate chip flake, an orange lolly . . . such a small pleasure. So impossible for me.

I knocked at a door in the village. A kindly, elderly lady called Pansy Watkins answered, spotted my face, which was like a red balloon, and offered a whole pint of orange juice for me (plus bottle refill) and a bowl of water for Sam. Did I like orange juice? Yes, any chance of another pint?

And why was no one else in the world called Pansy?

As if to add insult to my thirst that afternoon, we were walking through a terrain of vineyards and hopyards. We had been walking for more than three hours since Ledbury. The sun took pity on me. It went somewhere else. The catch was, the rain came in its place. For the first time I had the sneakiest of suspicions we would not make that night's destination. A check on my photocopied map brought a flutter of panic. Tedstone Delamere was still two or maybe three hours' walk away. My feet were getting serious about hurting. My body felt it had gone ten rounds with Naseem Hamed. We walked on, Sam plodding faithfully at my side.

And, on the ninth day, Mortimer did pause by the roadside and did announce to the world, 'Sod this!' Without the poor feet, maybe the tiredness would have been okay. And vice versa. It was the deadly cocktail of the two that did it.

We crossed the A4103, coming into a village called Ridgeway Cross. I was fazed again, and for a short time headed off the wrong way. This was no help at all. I knocked at a door by the crossroads. A middle-aged man answered. He looked a bit suspicious, but I was beyond all that. 'I need to make a reverse-charge phone call,' I said, 'and I'm whacked.' The man disappeared and came back with his mobile phone. I sat on the wall and phoned Michael Roberts. He was the kind of guy who'd happily accept a reverse-charge call from someone he'd never met. He was also the kind of guy who'd respond to the out-and-out cheek of the following request.

'I'm all done in. I'm in a bad way. I'm still some distance from the kennels. How about dropping whatever you're doing, no matter how important, and coming to pick me up?'

'Just keep walking towards Acton Green,' said Michael Roberts. 'I'll find you.'

Herefordshire was full of saints.

My temporary host by this time seemed satisfied I wasn't a mugger or a burglar. His name was Keith Johnstone. He sat me down in his kitchen, where I slumped like a bag of coal. He gave me a cup of hot tea.

'Ha! Ha!' That was the sound of me laughing. A kind of deranged, flood-of-relief laugh, a laugh only understood by those in similar circumstances. Somehow I was able to hold a moderately interesting conversation with Keith Johnstone before thanking him and heading off. I was some yards up the road when he shouted, 'Don't you want this with you?' My backpack.

The road to Acton Green was – predictably – up a steep hill. Sam and I walked it for about three weeks before a ramshackle van passed, stopped, turned and came back. Michael Roberts was a big, friendly bear of a man with a wild ginger beard, a rural Brian Blessed. His personality occupied a good deal of space in his immediate vicinity, but I couldn't imagine anyone objecting. You might just have taken him for a third-generation blacksmith, which was exactly what he was. His grandad had moved here to be the smith in 1904, and Michael had been banging in horseshoes and other things for 42 years. I couldn't imagine him as master of the hounds, but he was. He laughed a lot. His was a big, excited voice, and as we drove off, he pointed to his toolbox, which he had made on his very first day as a blacksmith.

He was both blacksmith and wheelwright, and based at Blingsty. He tossed a horseshoe across the cab. 'You'm best carry him for luck!' he said, and roared like a friendly bull. We drove past Brockhampton School, the only one he had ever attended, aged five to 15. He referred to most objects as 'him'. When talking of his toolbox he said, 'Oi made him on moi first day.' Of his rickety van, 'Oi'll clean him at the weekend,' he said. 'You'm gotta take a chance on people!' he remarked and roared again, as if he rescued penniless wandering strangers as a matter of course.

I was shagged out and Michael Roberts was showing enough energy to light a medium-sized city overnight. He took me to see his forge, his smithy, then he ran me to Clifton Kennels at Tedstone Delamere and dropped me off.

How did I know this was to be probably the defining place of the journey? My initial impressions were hazy, as though I was looking through a lens smeared with Vaseline. There was a modern bungalow, some white-painted farm buildings, a sloping lawn, what looked like kennels at the top. There was the tough-looking terrier man Peter Harper, the shy young kennel man James Cook. I remember Peter describing how he let loose ferrets to disgorge the fox once it had gone to ground. When it came up, he shot it. 'Don't like doing it, though, see?' he said in a distinctive Welsh accent. 'I'm frightened of guns, me. Someone has to do it, though.'

I remember sitting down in the bungalow kitchen, Peter cooking a pan of chips. They looked like the wings on the Angel of the North, and came with cold meat. I remember him telling me chief huntsman Roy Tatlaw (whose bungalow this was) was on holiday in the Lakes, but not to worry. I was welcome. Next day I would get some real sense of this place. My first night I was exhausted. Sam too. And incredibly mucky. I stood him up in the bath and sponged him down. He came up fluffy as a new towel. In the cupboard the dog food was stacked twice as high as him. Sam was okay.

I remember the ping-hiss as Peter Harper opened the beer cans as we sat around in the bungalow living-room. At about which time I began to come alive again. And anyway, I could tell he wanted to sound me out about foxhunting, this townie who'd happened on the scene, this scribbler. What was he about? I was eating their food, drinking their beer, sitting on their settee. What did I think of their lifestyle?

The dusk slowly settled on the land. I stretched out on the settee by the picture window which looked out on to the lawn sloping up to the white-painted kennels. It was a quiet, well-furnished bungalow. The kennels and buildings lay up a sleepy road. Hardly a sound of traffic interrupted us. Nobody seemed surprised to see me. James spoke hardly at all, looking up shyly, a sheepish smile, that Princess Di style.

I'd decided hunting people weren't like others. They felt under siege, felt a traditional way of life was under threat from those who didn't understand it. Maybe bear baiters and cockfighters had once felt this. Foxhunters said it wasn't a sport but an essential way of life. Peter kept nudging me towards a statement. 'I suppose,' I said, 'I don't know that much, except it never quite seems fair. A hundred baying hounds in pursuit of a solitary fox.'

Foxhunting was a conduit for a way of life. Hunters put forward logical reasons for its continuation, but it was more the social cohesion, the bonding. If some miracle drug, food or method of controlling foxes had been discovered, thereby eliminating the need for hunts, I didn't think the hunters would be that chuffed. Did I say all this or just think it while popping open another can? And did I begin wondering that, while I wasn't religious, wasn't pro-hunting, both seemed to give certain people a sense of purpose when so many of us were lonely, isolated, living lives that seemed to have no meaning? Or was I just falling asleep on the settee?

That's where I would fall asleep. It was my bed. I'd stashed my bag and possessions one end of it, made a little base camp. Up the sloping lawn, 120 hounds were snoozing, no doubt dreaming of a bushy red tail.

Peter talked on in that Welsh lilt. I joined in, drifted off, joined in again. Outside, the kennels darkened. Both Peter and James were staying at the bungalow. At 10 p.m. both went to bed. James had spoken about a dozen words, most of one syllable. He was of that rare breed in the countryside, a teenager working on the land.

I laid out my sleeping bag and wriggled into it. Sam was to get two companions. First in walked Pickles, a tiny Jack Russell, so called (I presume) because he'd fit inside an onion jar. He was followed by the slow and elegant entrance of Bruce the lurcher, whose walking speed was reduced to that of Black Rod through an injured hip.

Sam got to sleep with two other dogs. As usual, I was sleeping alone. It had been a long, long day on the road. I stretched out, pulled the plug on my body and willed the fatigue to drain away. When I closed my eyes it was with the confident, but false, expectation that I would have a long and untroubled sleep.

Day Ten — Tuesday, 4 August

Miles travelled so far — 181

Walking all day
At evening I drink
From the same river

Feet of Flame — Staying Put — Enter the Hounds

A terrible night. A night to end all nights. I lay awake in the early hours. My feet had swallowed the sun, Mount Vesuvius, Dante's Inferno, one dozen electric arc furnaces, a dragon's breath — and the annual output of a Colman's mustard factory as an afterthought.

Beneath the chiropodist dressings my feet burned as only a tormented soul in hell could burn. Purgatory, thou art my feet. So hot were my feet that when their 1,000-degree alarm system woke me, I yanked myself instantly from the sleeping bag to lessen the fear of spontaneous combustion. The journey had caught up with my feet. Was that a mixed metaphor? At that moment I didn't care. The feet felt bad. The body felt little better.

I remembered Ledbury, remembered thinking, '14 miles? We can do it, Sam, let's go.' We couldn't. Put my feet in water and they would have sizzled. Touch my body anywhere and it hurt. These were the dark hours, the lonely hours of the night, when something crept up alongside me, whispered in my ear, 'Why not give up?' then crept off again.

Sam was awake too, uneasy too. He'd been overwhelmed

by pooches. As well as Bruce and Pickles, a flinty grey mongrel called Fly had wandered in, and in the shadows I'm sure I could make out other vague canine shapes. I lay on my settee, I drifted in and out of a feverish sleep, I tumbled into vivid haunting dreams, all of which involved failure. All this, and I was still to hear the Greatest Hits from the Canine Massed Choir of Clifton Kennels. It began just after dawn. First there was one long descending howl like a falling mortar shell. Other dogs joined in, possibly a dozen, then more. They joined in and broke off, joined in and broke off. Always enough to make the howl continuous but disjointed, a bizarre Greek chorus of dogs. Not even in the most lurid werewolf films, where creatures had faces like unmown lawns, had I heard anything to rival the howling hounds of Clifton. Nor were they ten-minute howlers. These pooches could keep at it. And they did.

I rose at 7 a.m. I dragged myself off the settee like a slack bag of sawdust. When Peter and James rose, I was slumped over the kitchen table. They offered me tea and toast. I needed another chiropodist. Perhaps Sheila Carter, with her gentle hands, would drive up in her big car and make everything all right. Perhaps I would just wake up in my own Cullercoats bed, no bad feet, no nightmare journey, no sweat. All a dream. Perhaps I'd better shake myself and look through the Yellow Pages.

I found a chiropodist, Helen Chapman, in the nearby town of Bromyard. 'My feet are terrible. I have nearly 300 more miles. I have no money. I'm a writer,' I said over the phone. Or maybe I said something else.

'I can't see you until tomorrow at 4.30 p.m.,' said Helen Chapman. 'It sounds to me like you shouldn't be doing any walking today anyway. Remove the dressings, soak your feet regularly in warm salt water. Walk as little as possible.'

Did you hear that, dear reader? She said, 'Walk as little as possible.' I had been ordered not to walk. Helen Chapman, obviously a much-respected figure in her field, had commanded it. Much as I would have liked to, how could I disobey?

'Look,' I said to Peter, 'she can't see me till tomorrow, so . . .'

'Stay here as long as you like,' he said. 'It's no problem.' He spread the marmalade on his toast.

Sometimes there is a delicious sense in having matters decided for you. Helen Chapman had told me what to do, or what not to do; Peter Harper had treated me as if I was as much a part of the place as the main gate. I had time to sit back, to look.

Firstly I removed the dressings from my feet. Sheila Carter had fixed them well. They were more secure than Elton John's wig. I peeled them off slowly, having little desire to remove four layers of skin at the same time. What a strange act it was, like the opening up of a mummy's tomb. The feet were badly damaged, the colour of ripe plums. I didn't look too closely. Uncovering them made me feel good. I bathed them in warm salt water, and this made me feel good too. They sighed to be in the open air. How bad were they? Could Helen Chapman fix them? Could I still walk more than 300 miles?

And what about Clifton Kennels? As my feet snoozed away in the salt water, I looked around me. I had landed in a small, tight-knit, isolated group of hunting folk who were holding the fort while their master was away. They lived in his house, ate his food, drank his beer, looked after his hounds. The hunting season began in September, when the hounds would hunt up to three times a week. For the moment they were looked after by three vastly different males.

Peter Harper was stocky and powerfully built, with do-it-yourself tattoos; he was one of the few 42-year-olds able to celebrate a silver wedding. His wife lived in Caerphilly, and he spent his working time between the two places. He had a quick Welsh accent, and his eyes were quick and mobile like a fox's. He seemed laid back and tough at the same time. James Cook was incredibly slim (how come his trousers didn't slide off his hips?), 17 years old, tall and so shy you expected a blush each time he spoke, yet behind it you felt a reserved intelligence. And I met the third member, the wild card, Johnnie James, who lived seven miles away. He was in his early fifties, tall, stooped with a slightly stiff awkward walk, a shock of black curly hair and features from a Goya cartoon, that inbred rural intensity. I would find him staring long and hard at me. Did he have any idea who I was, what I was doing there?

'That's my dog, Sam,' I told him. He looked at Sam.

'Sambo,' he said.

'No, just Sam,' I replied.

'Sambo,' he repeated and walked off, like a slack-stringed puppet. He was the only man in England of his age I'd ever met who had never seen the sea.

I would see Johnnie James's job in all its gruesome reality the next day. He skinned the carcasses and prepared them for the hounds. His own small universe was in the yard up alongside the kennels. There was the incinerator, whose acrid fumes often drifted down the sloping lawn. There was his shed of death, a grim, windowless affair where his deeds were done. Sometimes the fumes from the carcass remains would drift over the hounds' open-topped compounds, causing them to pad and pace their territory restlessly.

That morning, after the foot soak, I washed some clothes and walked up the lawn to hang them out to dry. The hounds caught my scent. They hurled themselves against the bars, large, muscular creatures, barking, howling, yelling. I imagined the feelings of the solitary fox, 100 of these in pursuit.

I would not be walking that day. Nor possibly even the next. How much did this matter? Not as much as before. The journey created a shape. I had to mould myself to it. And something told me that Clifton had been waiting to show me things. For the second time, my stay at one place would be more than one night. But Clifton Kennels were very different from the Ilminster flat. Come to that, which resting place had been like any other? None.

For the first time, I had a little territory I saw as my own. At the end of the long settee where I slept, I arranged all my belongings in small, neat piles. Sam recognised it as home territory and promptly sat on them. But I spent more time in this area than anywhere else on my trip. Here I would sit, several times a day, my feet in the warm salt water slowly shedding all the sticky bits and turning, where not bruised, as pink as freshly boiled lobster. From here I could stare through the large picture window up at the kennels. During the day, Sam slowly grew less uneasy at the massive canine presence. I felt the hounds were growing used to his scent and my own, little by little, plus Pickles was being less of a bad-tempered little buzzer with Sam (or was it the other way round?). Maybe Sam thought it was all over, end of walking. Maybe it was.

The weather was changing, the forecast for a long hot spell. From my grandstand seat I occasionally saw a group of hens strutting on the patio outside, and when Peter gave me two spankingly fresh poached eggs for my dinner, I offered the hens thanks.

I didn't do much at all that day. I didn't know at that stage what the men were doing either. My day was philosophical. Which meant, as I said, I did bugger all. I had time to reflect on having no money. It left you sealed in a bubble. You could see the rest of the world but couldn't really touch it. Sitting here, it was like there was no bubble. But I knew it was waiting for me. Towns and cities were mainly about making and spending money. This was their lifeblood, and to be in the middle of them without any was like being in a nightmare. You had no importance. No terms of reference. The countryside seemed less obsessed with buying and selling, more involved with being. Was this just a townie's rose-tinted specs? Maybe. Except I'd never bought into the rural idyll. Far too quiet for me. I'd feel I was missing out. But on this journey it was my natural home. The city wasn't. The city was too neurotic about housing a penniless wanderer. For one month at least, the city could get stuffed.

Miles travelled so far — 181

Fresh eggs on toast
In the cottage doorway
The watching hens

The Day of the Dead — Shaven Feet — The Skin Game

I woke at 5 a.m. twice the man I'd been the previous morning. I was like those people in the breakfast cereal advertisements. I was Mr Sunshine. The morning light was still a smudge outside the large picture window. By 5.15 I'd washed some clothes and hung them out to dry in the gentle morning air which felt as though it had just been born.

My feet got their first salty bowl of the day. These soaks, the rest, the exposure to the air had done them good. As I sat soaking them, I noticed Peter standing in the doorway. What was it? 'The feet,' he said. His 24-year-old son Jason back in Newport had suffered third-degree burns when a vat of boiling water spilt over his feet. He was out of work for seven months. 'Just seeing your feet like that . . .' said Peter, and walked away.

By the time most people had stirred, had worked up the conviction to drag their tired bodies reluctantly from bed, I'd washed my clothes, bathed my feet, eaten breakfast and was busy scribbling in my diary. You might say the day's rest had done me good.

I was keeping close tabs on Sam. I doubt he'd been this close before to 120 powerful hounds. In addition to which there was the small posse of dogs which padded around him in the house. Sam had seemed bewildered at first. He was now adapting, and I suspected him of having some fun with the pack. The first time he'd ventured from the bungalow back door and walked up the lawn towards the kennels, the hounds had set to with a monstrously loud caterwauling (dogerwauling?), baying and barking with such ferocity that

Sam had retreated faster than Dracula from the sunrise. But he was soon to learn that the noise was just that – noise. The audio bombardment wasn't dangerous. Plus he could play around with it. Bit by bit he ventured further up the lawn, until I spotted him strutting his full width like a model on a catwalk (dogwalk?) while scores of baying beasts hurled themselves against the bars.

The foxhounds were kept in five separate enclosures, one for dogs, a second for bitches, a third for dog pups, a fourth for bitch pups, and a rear enclosure for bitches on heat. In each enclosure were about 30 hounds. The enclosure was the size of a very large living-room, open to the sky, with a smaller enclosed sleeping area at the rear. Each day the kennels were hosed out thoroughly by Peter. The whole place was kept spotless and had a faintly Mediterranean feel with its white paint, its hanging baskets of flowers, its creeping ivy and its climbing roses.

What about so many big, powerful hounds in a relatively small enclosure? 'If hounds aren't happy they fight amongst themselves,' said Peter. 'You won't see them fight. And twice a day they get taken out for long runs on the roads.'

I was fascinated by the hounds. Time and again I'd return to look at them, be close to them. They were so fierce, so muscular, so aggressive when baying at the bars. I walked up to them and they rushed forward, pushing noses and paws through the steel, big softies climbing on top of one another to lick my hand, nuzzle me. I felt like some rock star at an airport, stopping at the crash barriers to acknowledge the adoring fans who'd waited all night. I felt like the monarch at the palace gates giving a brief glimpse to his ultra-loyal subjects. The hounds seemed desperate for affection. Soon I'd see how desperate they were for something else.

My appointment was at 4.30. It seemed unlikely I'd be leaving Clifton that day. I was secretly glad. Three nights in one location – a record for my trip. I decided to reorganise my bag, empty it totally for the first time. This is what I found. One piece of rancid cheese. Three hard-boiled eggs I'd carried from Clyst Hydon, which were decomposing.

One three-day-old meat sandwich mysteriously turning itself into something else. I threw the fetid lot away. I'd thrown nothing away previously. Food was scarce, precious. At Clifton I could eat what I liked, when I liked. I knew the luxury would be fleeting. It was all the more precious for that.

The phone rang. Farmer John Winterton, from Half Ridge Farm, seven miles away, had a dead cow for collection. I decided to go along with Peter in his battered open wagon. It was to be part one of my morning of death. This sheltered urbanite was about to witness sights not previously seen.

We drove under the warm sun along the quiet country lanes. The farmer guided our wagon up through the fields. Lying on its side on the sloping grass in the middle of a large field was an eight-year-old Friesian cow. We'd all seen dead cow meat hanging from butchers' hooks. Most of us had eaten beef at some time. Seeing a dead cow in a field was different. Other herd members stood around, chewed the cud and stared. I noted the cow's swollen udder, milk that would never be drunk.

Peter backed the wagon up close to the corpse and slung the steel hawser around the cow's neck ready for winching. There was a slow whirring sound, and the neck stretched grotesquely from the pull of the hawser. I found myself stupidly wondering if it was painful. Finally the beast was dragged forwards, up the ramp and into the open back of the wagon. The cow was too long. Peter needed to yank it so the head was pushed up against the back of the cab. For a moment it seemed this rearing head was alive, seemed its large brown eye, like an open tin of golden syrup, was staring directly at me. Then the head slumped, the illusion was gone. Peter wedged in the feet and bolted up the end of the wagon. We drove off. 'What did the cow die of?' I asked. He shrugged his shoulders. By the time we arrived back, there was already an answerphone enquiry from the vet. Dead cows were a sensitive issue.

The cow would be skinned by John James. We dumped the body at the top of the yard on the concrete. It lay by the incinerator and the carcass room (the room of death), that awful, windowless enclosure where entire skinned carcasses hung from the ceiling.

It was the room of death on two counts. Locked inside at this moment was a sheep a farmer had brought in to be shot. Peter opened the door, a loaded pistol in his hand. The sheep, sensing what was to come, scampered frantically among the hanging cadavers. Again, we'd all seen parts of sheep and cow carcasses hanging in a butcher's shop. An entire skinned cow was different. Enormous, misshapen alien beings, florid red. Clouds of flies buzzed furiously around these unrefrigerated bodies in this hot room that smelt terribly of death.

The frantic sheep ran round and round, bumping into the cadavers, causing them to swing slightly, which in turn caused the flies to chorus more loudly, more angrily. After a few moments of this desperate dodging, the sheep was caught. Peter took it firmly by the neck and dragged it towards him. And now it seemed the sheep knew its fate. It grew calm and, in an act of either resignation or supplication, lowered itself in front of him and was perfectly still.

The stink of the rotting flesh, the heat, the buzzing of the flies, the lowered head of the sheep . . . I noticed Peter's gun hand was shaking. He put the gun to the sheep's head and pulled the trigger. The gun jammed. I could hear my own breathing. And Peter's. Again he pulled the trigger. Again it jammed. I was thinking of the sheep. Of the heart, pumping blood; of its organs, going about their business, doing what they were meant to do. Keeping the sheep alive. For the third time, in this room of death, Peter put the gun to the sheep's temple and pulled the trigger. There was a sharp crack, the animal shuddered as if from an electric shock and slumped to the ground. For a few seconds its limbs twitched. Then it was still. Not once did its expression change.

The carcasses were still gently swinging, the buzz of the flies was growing less excited. The sheep was dead on the floor.

'See?' said Peter, his voice trembling. 'I'm shaking, see? I bloody hate guns, I do.' He stared down at the ground. I saw his exposed, vulnerable side. I knew what it cost him to do these things. He talked on, rapidly.

'My son, see? Got shot by a gun in an accident, didn't he? The bullet lodged in his temple, didn't it? Blinded in one eye, he was. I bloody hate guns.'

We both stood in that room of death, the sheep at our feet.

'You need a cup of tea, Peter,' I said finally. 'I bloody well do as well.'

We sat in the kitchen, drank hot tea, ate biscuits. The experience receded, like a dying wave, became bearable.

Then it was feeding time for the hounds. They were fed every other day. They were never fed the day before a hunt. The hunger I would see would be the same they'd have when chasing the fox. In one feed the hounds would devour two cows, or up to a dozen sheep. This was not like feeding town doggies. This was not Pedigree Chum spooned out into Fido's bowl. John James cleared the centre pen of hounds. In each adjacent pen the hounds sensed what was to come. They pressed frantically against the bars, their teeth bared, their growls deep and menacing. They did not seem desperate for affection.

Using a large iron hook, John dragged in four enormous sections of cow carcass. At the sight and smell the hounds became frantic. The first feeding group were the males. Once the four sections were gathered in the compound centre, the hounds were let in. They poured through the open gate and set upon the carcasses. Such was the power and ferocity of the attack that the carcasses moved this way and that, tilting and sliding. The hounds tore off long strips of flesh, the way you'd pull mozzarella cheese from a pizza or stretch out chewing gum. They snarled at one another, raising their bloodied snouts from the carnage, bearing their own portion. The cage was a frantic moving mass of sharp-toothed hounds. John James rapped one hard with his stick and pulled it away. At the bottom of the slightly sloping pen, a dark reservoir of blood gathered. The hounds piled on top of one another, climbed across each other's backs, pushed and jostled and snarled. I imagined them at a small fox.

Before long the carcasses were picked clean. A giant ribcage rolled over onto one side, as if animate. These cuddly hounds were startlingly bare-toothed, their faces smeared red. John moved among them, an eye for those getting too fat, which he pulled away and shoved into the next enclosure. One hound escaped onto the lawn. He dragged it back and beat it with his stick. I sensed he was playing up to me, wanting to show his power over these beasts. The need to be cruel undermined that sense of power.

It would take almost two hours to feed the whole pack, after which John James would skin the dead cow and the dead sheep. He would hang them in his windowless room, with its putrid stench, its maniacally buzzing flies, close to the bitter, drifting smoke of the incinerator where the surplus body parts were burning.

A little later, the four of us sat in the big kitchen, drank tea, ate bread and butter. Peter said, 'My wife in Caerphilly don't like it here. Says it's too quiet. She don't stay long.' He paused and added, 'I like the quiet, me, it suits me.' Despite the death and carnage of that day, the blood-red rawness of the kennels' existence, Tedstone Delamere *was* quiet.

The days turned dreamily in this tranquil part of Herefordshire. The rolling countryside, the sleepy villages, the quiet, mainly unvisited lanes – there was little feel of dormitory country, the ersatz rural refuge for city dwellers. It was as if those who lived here worked here.

I was sucked into the slow tempo, where there was little expectation of the quick, the unexpected. The life fascinated me. At times it horrified me. I told Peter, told him I was still no fan of foxhunting. He laughed. 'You're half Irish,' he said. 'It should be in your blood.'

On my odyssey I moved rapidly from one resting place to another. Little time to make my own mark, or establish that of others. These kennels were different. I felt I knew something of Peter's complexities. On the first day, John James had treated me warily, padding around me like an animal. He seemed more approachable this day, asked me about my work. I told him of the journey, the writing. Those strange Goya features distorted themselves. He laughed out loud. 'Walkin' all bloomin' day wavin' a pen about in yer 'and! Some of us've got real work to do!' He paused a moment, then said, 'Think I'll come with you to Edinburgh.'

'You wouldn't get past the end of the lane,' said Peter.

John lived with his twin sister. There was also a battered old caravan at the kennels, where he'd go to watch television. He and Peter exchanged regular insults. James Cook looked on. The insults were swiped away by both sides as easily as you'd swipe away a fly. The banter was neither the friendly one of mates nor the hostile one of adversaries.

The trio had been thrown together by their master's absence. Normally they'd only drift in and out of each other's lives, Peter going back and forth to Wales, John working casually. The enforced closeness produced tensions, John half furtive, body curling over as you spoke to him, like some rodent resisting attack from a canine. He was a product of the deep removed countryside. The countryside had created him, and in the countryside he would survive. I couldn't think of him in a city. And James Cook. Shy, sensitive. He stared hard at a poultice he was to apply to a horse's leg. What did he do when not at the kennels? Not much. Girlfriends? Possibly. Drinking with mates? Now and again.

Between seeing death and carnage, I was still soaking my feet. My chiropodist awaited. I was 11 days out from Plymouth. I'd stayed in stables, caravans, on settees and had slept in two beds. People I'd never met before had fed and sheltered me. When I woke up each day I had no idea where I'd be the next night. This could be exciting. It could be horrible. I remembered what a music critic once wrote, about the two worst kinds of music: totally predictable, and totally unpredictable. In life too. If you're reading this, it meant I got through. The comfort of hindsight. I didn't have that perspective at the time. Lots of things could have toppled me. Feet, for one (or two). They'd been spending a lot of time under water. Why did it make me think of child-hood, feet in a bowl of warm water?

I got a close look at the bungalow. It was defined almost entirely by hunting. On the walls were loads of hunting photos and paintings. On the tables and sideboards there were cups for hunting. The bookshelves had bound copies of the *Foxhound Kennel Stud* book dating back to 1800. If you wanted to know a certain hound, certain pack, certain year, this was your place – every hound born to a registered pack over two centuries. There were huge leather-bound tomes entitled *British Hunts* and *Hunting* that would break your toe if they fell on it. Pick up any of the magazines scattered around. Not a sign of *Loaded, Computer Weekly* or *What Car*. They were called *Hunting* or *Hounds*. On the back of the toilet door was Roy Tatlaw's red master huntsman's coat. It would set you back more than £200. There were statues of horses, statues of foxes, statues of huntsmen with hounds. For the first time in my life I read the magazine *Hunting*. You always learn something. No one knows why a fox has a large bushy tail (or brush). Did you know that?

Back up the yard in the simmering heat, John James was about to skin another cow, the billowing bitter smoke of the incinerator curling patterns around him. The dun brown cow lay on its back, each leg in a stirrup, yanked up tight on steel hawsers. The cow's red glistening innards were pushing against her open vagina. The effect, reinforced by the splayed and stirruped legs, was like the moment of birth. The effect soon vanished when John set to with a large, sharp knife. He spliced and peeled off the cow's skin as if it were a satsuma. With its protective hide removed, the cow glistened like wet red paint. The hide was spread out on the ground like a carpet in some Eastern bazaar. The cow would be hung. I'd seen enough for one day.

I walked down the drive towards the white border fence. The kennels sat on a small hill in green and gentle country-side. The cluster of sheltering trees, the gentle slope, the white-painted buildings, the farmyard, the stables – at a quick glance, few would have suspected the presence of 120 foxhounds. A quiet country lane drifted past the front before wandering off into leafy oblivion.

I borrowed one of the push-bikes and cycled this lane for a few miles. It sucked me deeper and deeper into its tranquil sense of another world. My own life seemed galaxies away. I realised I had not seen a female in three days. My company was all male. Only Peter had even mentioned the existence of women.

James Cook drove me into Bromyard in the Land Rover. Not only would my feet be gently fondled once more, it would be another woman. I'd left Sam behind. As I sat in the waiting-room, I realised my intense irritation with my feet. People felt irritated when Saddam Hussein's name came on the news again. Like he was still at it. So were my feet.

After the blood and carnage of Clifton Kennels came the bright white clinic of Helen Chapman, the soft skin and smiling face of Helen Chapman. She popped me into her special chair and placed my feet into two elongated stirrup holders, which she then cranked up. I thought of the dun cow.

Once again I told her I had no money. Her calm smile made me feel silly for mentioning it. It was the most comfortable chair I'd ever been in. I melted into it. I retreated into the comfort and security of Helen Chapman's clinic.

'What you have to realise,' she said, turning my foot this way and that for examination like an item on the *Antiques Roadshow*, 'is that you're pounding tarmac every day with a pack on your back. Human feet were not built for it. It takes its toll.'

I was a naughty boy. I was being chided. More.

'You have to be careful with these feet,' she said. 'There's a condition called march fracture. If you got that, your feet would collapse, end of journey – to say the least.'

It sounded like a calendar reference – the splintered month. I was confident. Helen Chapman would know what to do. She was a female chiropodist.

'When your feet start hurting, you have to stop walking,' she said. 'Otherwise you're asking for trouble. It's simple. That way, at least they'll have a chance to recover for the next day.'

My Samuel Smiles self-help foot theory lay in ruins.

What happened next was that Helen Chapman shaved my feet. 'I have to remove the layers of dead skin,' she said. 'One reason they're hurting so much is that there's still liquid trapped under the skin and it can't get out.'

How many shaves do you have in your life? How many are done by a woman? To your feet?

As she carefully shaved off layers, I thought of the skinned cow again, and how I was much luckier. Helen then cut into shaped sections the support rubber to fix to my insoles for extra cushioned effect. More strong adhesive. The feet were then rebandaged like an ancient Chinese lady, but bigger. Would they get me to Edinburgh? Would I need a succession of chiropodists?

Crazy ideas went through my head. I would roller-blade to Scotland. Borrow a push-bike. Put Sam in the front basket. Or I could stay here, in this chair. Just close my eyes.

Helen Chapman had changed figures for feet. She'd been an accountant. Feet were more interesting. She liked the job, liked this part of the world. 'The natural hedgerows, the rolling countryside, all the different types of building, brick, stone, half-timbered. How could you not like it?'

We've always undervalued the English countryside. American film-makers had hijacked the romance of the open road. The truth was, travelling through the USA was often boring, hundreds of miles of unchanged terrain. In England the landscape could change dramatically in 20 miles. Why should Wichita sound more exciting than Wakefield? Films and songs, that was all.

I climbed down from the chair. My feet were jacked up on supports. I felt bouncy. I bounced around Bromyard for a bit, waiting for my lift home. It was like a small, sleepy Irish town. They even sold tickets for the Irish lottery. I wandered into a second-hand bookshop and sifted through the books. 'Can I help you, sir?' And, I suddenly realised, no, he couldn't. I'd quite forgotten my penniless state.

My final Tedstone Delamere evening. We sat at the kitchen table. Sam and the other dogs were spread out on the floor like mats. The evening was warm, calm. The sun sent long fingers through the open door to spread across the floor tiles and touch the fur of the sleeping dogs.

Much of the time there was silence. The occasional hen clucked and jerked its way past the door. A dog would open an eye, cast it lazily around, then close it. I had been in this place three nights. Not one of us four males had even mentioned the pub. Where was it?

Normally we were all in bed by 10 p.m. A good night's sleep, then up early the next morning. That was the way of life. Topics of conversation were different. Peter and James talked about the recent Moonlight Steeplechase event. They'd organised a ferret run, betting on which pipe the ferret would scamper up. As with all other events, proceeds went to the hunt. The hunt informed their whole lives.

After John had been run home and Peter and James had gone to bed, I sat for an hour in the kitchen with Sam as the light expired on its death bed. I felt melancholic to be leaving this place. It was three days since I'd been on the road. I was still a good way short of half the distance. How effective would Helen Chapman's dressings be? How many miles could I walk? Where would be the next destination?

A small incident ended the day. I let Sam on the lawn for his final wee. He walked boldly up several yards of grass towards the penned hounds. He kept walking further towards the compound than he had ever walked. He stopped and lifted his head. He barked at the pens. Not a single bark, but several strong, defiant barks, an I-am-not-to-be-intimidated series of barks. The barks brought down on his head the full canine chorus. Sam stood his ground, cocked his leg, peed, turned and walked back to the house. The chorus was still in evidence by the time he was sorting his bed among my clothes on the lounge floor.

Day Twelve — Thursday, 6 August

Miles travelled so far — 181

Heatwave at last
Carefully John
Removes the cow's skin

The Final Death — My Roadside Loss —
Life with the Belchers

For three days my walking boots had been in unmoving contemplation. Even boots had to gather their thoughts. I got out of the sleeping bag and spent a longish time looking at them. How often do we look hard at our boots? It was part of my mental preparation to leave Clifton Kennels. As usual I was up early. I was leaving the kennel men, the terrier men, the hounds, the carcasses, the world which was not my world. But all worlds had a heartbeat, and were better understood once this heartbeat was felt.

I considered lightening my load. What could I jettison? My head torch? I clung on to it for no logical reason. I pulled some loose strands from my hairbrush. A quarter of a gram gone. I tore three more pages from my map book. Later I regretted this. I would be unable to bounce future grand-children on my lap and boast, 'These were my maps!'

There was an atmosphere as we ate breakfast. Perhaps I'd overstayed my welcome. I was a stranger. I came into their world. It fed and sheltered me; I criticised it. Who could blame them? Or perhaps it was themselves. Ten more days before Roy Tatlaw returned. Ten days in each other's pockets. Peter had a strong, underplayed domestic instinct. Several times he cleaned up small things behind me: a crumb on the draining board, a spot of water on the table. Perhaps this irritated him.

My clothes had been given a good airing, washed, dried and neatly folded in the bag, which was free of putrid foodstuffs. The boots went on my feet like strangers. I clomped around the room like a freshly shod horse. My feet felt bulky but trouble-free. But only the open road would tell me the truth.

James and Peter took the pack of hounds for their morning exercise, more than 100 powerful beasts spilling out into the quiet country lane. Bringing up the rear on his dayglo mountain bike, cracking his whip like some misplaced circus master, was John. The great yelping, tail-wagging army moved off. I was left alone at the kennels with Sam. I was mentally prepared to leave, but would have to await their return. James had agreed to give me a mega lift – about 40 miles towards Shrewsbury – to make up my lost time.

I paced the patio outside the picture window. I felt the nervousness bubble up like a geyser. Part of me longed for a trouble-free, incident-free journey. Part didn't. I remembered what Martin Amis had once written: 'Happiness writes white on the page.' I gave Sam his vitamin pill. I gave him his leg massage. I cleaned up the slight discharge which was a feature of his eye. He was well fed and watered, had rested well, had passed through his ordeal by foxhound. Was he ready? I was unable to stay still. I paced like a zoo tiger.

A van drew up at the top of the lane close to the shed of death. Peter had told me that farmers sometimes dumped dead livestock without paying the fee. As temporary custodian of the kennels, I did my duty. The farmer was legitimate. He had brought a young calf with the correct forms, which I signed, feeling important. The calf lay on the concrete, a milky white liquid dribbling from its mouth. But there was something else. There, by the shed of death, with its fly-infested grotesque corpses, its sheep and cattle carcasses splayed out, there, still and inert, as if only sleeping on the concrete, was a beautiful, fully grown, deep russet and stone dead horse.

The exercising dogs returned later than expected. There was dissent among the ranks. Peter was shouting at John for taking them on a wrong turn. John was distorting his features and snarling back. How would these irritations resolve themselves over the next few days? It would be no concern of mine. We said our farewells to Clifton Kennels. I clasped Peter in an embrace he may not have been ready for. Into the Land Rover, a last look, and we were off.

Once on the A49 we headed virtually due north. This Land Rover was a country bumpkin, couldn't normally be doing with them big, slick, main-road motors. It usually poddled around country lanes. Didn't have fancy things like seat belts, for one thing. What was that tailing police car doing? Luckily it turned off. James was anxious. Seventeen, just passed his test. Anxiety produced speech. 'I hate bloody roundabouts,' he said, the only unprompted sentence I'd heard from him. This was my last chance to draw the shy lad out. I fired off a few enquiries. Each was fielded by a brief, noncommittal response.

We drove to the Shrewsbury ring road, then east towards Wellington. James dropped me off. I waved as he turned, set off and negotiated his first roundabout. The Land Rover disappeared. A fleeting moment of sadness by the roadside. Sam tugged at the lead. Sam was right.

I had ham sandwiches and water. Sam had crunchy food. My feet had been prepared. For the first hour our landscape was urban. Even a small town could take two hours, shops, pubs, cafés, everything reinforcing my penniless state. My last purchase had been cushioned insoles in Tavistock. Shopping was the modern religion. I was an atheist.

One irony about suburbs was they were often more foot-sympathetic. Most had grass verges; in the countryside the choice was often tarmac or treacherous ditches. I walked every available inch of grass. Sam had to toe the line. Were my feet to fail me this day, the end would be nigh. Or even nearer than nigh. They felt bulky, but each step without pain was a bonus.

Day 12 brought a momentous decision. In the history of global expeditions it may not rank with Magellan, Raleigh, Scott or Cook. For me it was momentous. My plan had been for us to journey up the west of England, through Lancashire and Cumbria into Scotland, moving diagonally across to

Edinburgh. I'd looked at the map and realised how inter-linked were the great tentacles of Manchester and Merseyside. The thought of penetrating that great urban mass filled me with more gloom than a Smiths album track. There was virtually no open countryside, and the landscape had motorways like the back of the hand had blood vessels. Instead, then, I would pull hard to starboard, head north-east across Staffordshire, into Derbyshire, the Peak District, up through Yorkshire, County Durham, Northumberland, enter Scotland by Carter Bar, and on to Edinburgh. Easy, wasn't it?

The decision lifted me. Captain Mortimer had charted the journey. Through the outskirts of Wellington, we turned and headed due north on the busy A442. Three days non-walking had left me rusty. After a short spell, we should have turned off on a minor road at Sleapford. Instead, we trudged on. The A442 was as flat and straight as a length of ribbon, bordered each side by a featureless landscape of fields the size of small towns, and not an undulating crease between them. The rolling hills and quiet hedgerows of Herefordshire seemed far distant. Shropshire, too, had its reputation. Gained, I suspected, in other bits. The road was busy too.

After five miles we stopped at the Buck's Head, a large roadside pub which I shall remember for two reasons. First, it had the worst painted sign I had ever seen. The buck's head in question was anatomically impossible. I gave the artist the benefit of the doubt. He/she'd been on acid or some such drug. Secondly, I suffered my only real loss of the journey (so far).

The pub had open gardens stretching down to the main road, with wooden tables and benches. We stretched out under the unspeakable sign, I removed my boots and socks, ate sandwiches, took a swig of water, fed Sam. I propped the bag up against the same unspeakable sign, stretched out and went to sleep, while the pub's alfresco customers were afforded an unrestricted view of the flat road, the flat fields, the endless traffic.

I woke 15 minutes later. Something was missing. My precious, unique, handmade, solid silver, 15-year-old iron press earring, crafted by Newcastle silversmith Jadwiga Billewicz. How alone my ear felt. Witness the following (as the pub's customers did). A fully grown man, without shoes or socks, with bandaged feet, a yapping small dog in attendance, scampering on all fours at the base of an unspeakable pub sign, nose sniffing the grass. (This last one was due to my myopia, and was in fact an illusion.) There was no sign of the earring. Somewhere near Wellington it lies neglected, or swings from the ear of a lucky Larry (or Laura).

Feeling more sorry for myself than is healthy, we moved on. We turned east along the B5062 towards Newport, a rural road that felt tamed by the neatly clipped verges. We were close to many population centres: Manchester and Liverpool to the north, Stoke and the Potteries to the north-east, and the looming shadow of Birmingham wasn't too far distant either. The day had become hot. The frigid summer of '98 had found some passion. Our small water bottle rapidly emptied.

By the village of Waters Upton, I knocked at the door of a small cottage. It was answered by an elderly man, Frank Williams. The elderly usually had more trust. Could I have water? He invited us into the kitchen, disappeared, and returned with orange juice and shandy for me, water for Sam. He asked about my journey. I told him. 'Wait here,' said Frank. He came back and pushed something into my hand. 'That might help you.' It was a one pound coin. What made some people slam their doors, others offer cash? I was touched, but declined, explaining how I wouldn't take money from people. I was speaking out loud what I'd known instinctively for days. I felt good, strengthened. I didn't want the money. But meeting the Franks on the journey was a tonic. And his accent. The sing-song of the south and west was giving way to a Midlands monotone. The accents changed like slow-moving clouds. No perceptible movement second to second. Then, hey presto – different.

Sam and I supped up, chatted on, said our farewells. A look at the map and I decided Edgmond would be our limit that night. I was out of practice at finding shelter, needed to crank myself up for the effort. Clifton Kennels had softened me up. Across a vast wheatfield, a complex of tall, brick buildings rose up suddenly. The complex was both impressive and lonely in its isolation, like a child's drawing of a single house on the horizon. We walked towards it down the side lane, then through a large white gate where the county's spider population was having a web convention. From the impressive frontage, double bay windows looked out across spacious lawns-cum-grassland. Up this stretch of grass appeared a flock of sheep. They rumbled towards us in that totally unterrifying way sheep have, and it took the raising of my right hand to bring them to a halt.

I rang the bell. Eventually a rather well-to-do, middle-aged woman appeared at one of the bays, which was slightly open at the bottom. She beckoned me over and leaned down to speak through the gap at the bottom. I did the same. We both looked as if we were kissing the Blarney Stone. The woman motioned to me to go round the back. I walked into the enclosed yard and she appeared at another window, this one head height, looking into a large, open-plan room, part kitchen, part living area. Sitting in the room, but with as much movement as to suggest an audition for Madame Tussaud, was a man reading a broadsheet newspaper. I assumed (rightly) he was the woman's husband. A certain patrician air attached itself to both of them.

As I explained my journey, my need for shelter, I had an almost overwhelming desire to touch my forelock. One reason I resisted was I don't have one. The house was Tibberton Manor, the couple were Peter and Ruth Belcher. After I spoke there was a short silence.

'I suppose,' said Peter Belcher, 'we could let him have the holiday cottage.'

'I suppose we could,' said his wife. It felt as if this conversation was taking place in my absence. There was a slight movement from the man. 'You say you have a sleeping bag?' asked Mrs Belcher. I resisted the temptation to say, 'Yes ma'am. I do, ma'am.'

'Yes,' I said.

She held up a key on a ring. 'The cottage is another quarter of a mile towards the village,' she said, and then, 'I suppose you haven't eaten?'

I blurted out something. Within a nanosecond a plate had appeared. On this plate Mrs Belcher had spirited up salad, quiche and bread rolls. She had secured it with cling film. I hadn't seen her hands move. She put the plate into a plastic bag. Into the bag in a blur of speed went one banana, two Weetabix, three tea bags, half a pint of milk.

'Return the key in the morning,' said Mrs Belcher. 'Simply leave it on this windowsill.' There was a rustle of newspaper. Mr Belcher was turning the page. When I looked back, Mrs Belcher was moving back into the room.

'Oh, thank you very much, yes, ah,' I stammered. 'I really am grateful. Perhaps when I'm settled in, I should call round and, erm . . .' The sentence, realising how idiotic it sounded, committed suicide. Mrs Belcher stared at me.

'Just return the key as requested,' she said.

The audience was at an end. I walked out a different gate from the one I'd entered through and went up the small road towards the whitewashed cottage. It had original slatted doors. Inside there had been some renovation. It was an attractive building, but with the impersonality of a holiday let. There was no bedding or towels. The electricity was off. I found the mains switch after a hunt. The rock posters and pin-ups suggested young clients. Sam and I shared the bread and quiche. I made myself a cup of tea, and we explored the building. Sam was unsure and blu-tacked himself to my ankle. I discovered a small upstairs room facing west over a huge field of corn, melting in the evening sun, which also spilled onto the floor.

'The writing room, Sam!' I exclaimed. I laid out my materials: notebooks, fountain pen, ink. I dug out a tea towel in the kitchen to dry myself and I changed my gear, by which time Sam was already stretched on the writing-room bed, his fur flecked with the evening sunlight.

There were signs of youthful exuberance everywhere. The toilet door had pinned to it a notice saying 'Poo Zone –

Radiation Risk'. A scribbled sign on a bedroom door read 'The Dirty Rat's Little Lair – All Fair Maidens Beware'. Pinned to the wall were glamour pics from *Loaded* and *FHM*.

That increasingly rare animal, a Series One Land Rover (discontinued in 1958), stood outside the front door. The spacious gardens looked east. At the bottom were two small brick buildings I thought would house bees. There was also a neat line of conifers.

What unsettled me? The lack of real roots, the furniture which had absorbed not one family's history, the pots and pans neatly arranged without clues. You looked at the arrangement of chairs and tables. They looked back at you blankly. They had no personal history. The open-plan stairs were a late addition. I suspect Sam had never seen such stairs. He climbed them, peering at the gap between each one. Dog logic suggested they were unable to support themselves. It took Sam three or four ascents before he succumbed to human building science.

My plan was this: walk into Tibberton village, seek the local pub, get myself a lift for the next day, ease my feet back in.

From the south, Tibberton was spacious and affluent, large houses with wide drives, usually two expensive cars, none of which bore CND stickers. This was BUPA land, lawns shaved with Gillette precision, hedges and bushes neatly sculpted. I imagined the local newsagent being well stacked with copies of the *Daily Mail* every morning. The village's north side, on the other hand, went what estate agents call down-market, ending up in a council estate. In the village centre, keeping the peace, was the Sutherland Arms, a traditional-looking English pub, oak beams, external hanging baskets and coloured lights. I walked into the pub.

Imagine being in a barber's chair and saying, 'Nothing, thanks.' Imagine getting onto a bus and showing the conductor your empty pockets. Not on. This didn't feel on. I had no loot. I asked the barmaid for the manager. She gave me a sidelong look and went away. The second barmaid waited for my order. Behind me I could feel the eyes of a small group of locals. Sam was tethered outside.

The landlord arrived. He carried in front of him an invisible force capable of resisting everything. I remembered a story by Stacey D'Aumonier called 'The Great Unimpressionable'. I explained my long, penniless journey, my suspect feet, my need for a short lift the next morning. The landlord's glazed look was followed by the short statement, 'Don't know anyone who goes that way.' He looked over at the locals. Their turn. They didn't know anyone else who went that way either. The unspoken question hung in the air: would there be anything else?

Hell, why should they help me? Who was I anyway? I walked out, closed the door, turned and made the crucifix sign. Childish, of course. I was a person who wanted to be cherished and loved. I couldn't understand it. How on earth could anyone reject me?

Back at the holiday cottage, I found an old black and white television in a corner. I plugged it in, moved the indoor aerial through an interesting series of geometric formations, banged the top of the set and produced some sort of picture. The horizontal hold had gone. The image passed in front of me like I was seeing it from an open lift. The picture was bad, but the Western was worse. I switched it off.

The quiche and bread had already worn off. Was it possible to get full of quiche? Who invented the daft stuff? It wasn't even spelt right. Hunger drove me to minor crime. I'd found a tin of baked beans on a shelf and, having scourged myself with scorpion claws, put them aside for breakfast. I decided Sam could have the Weetabix soaked in water. I also found a large pack of pasta, already opened. I decided I would eat some of that, and for punishment this time I scoured myself with a Brillo pad. I boiled the pasta in a pan, mixed in some Lee and Perrins sauce, shook on some black pepper and downed the spicy dish. Feel free to use the recipe.

It was 10.30 p.m. This was quite late for us. I stretched the sleeping bag out on a bare mattress in an eastern-facing bedroom. If there was morning sun, I wanted it. I snuggled in with Sam beside me. I lay there staring at the glamour pics on the walls. Female bodies. I could remember them.

Day Thirteen — Friday, 7 August

Miles travelled so far — 230

On the neatly trimmed lawn
The neatly curled
Dog turd

Running on Empty — From West to East — Camping It Up

My gamble paid off. The sun rose in the east, and came in the window. It woke me at 5 a.m. and I woke Sam. The cottage had felt lonely the previous night. In the morning it felt good. I felt good. I liked being alone in it. I walked about starkers.

I stood in front of a full-length mirror and realised I was losing weight. I rarely weighed myself and considered dieting a fraud visited on the neurotic. But the daily travel and reduced food intake was making an impression, albeit a minus one.

I was normally a big eater. Three square meals a day, and at times a round one. At home I kept fairly fit, but this journey was seeing my body going through something very different. There could be no doubt about it. There was less of Mortimer. As I stood there, I indulged in some small self-congratulation. Had I not managed to keep myself fairly presentable? Wash my meagre clothes regularly? Shave almost every day, do exercises most days? Write about 2,000 words daily in the diary, plus the haiku? Walk? At that moment, in front of that mirror, I felt fit and well. Sam and I would soon be at the halfway point of our journey. It had been much harder than I had imagined, but then, if you'll excuse the illogicality, I knew it would be.

My life had been thrown into a totally different perspective. Should I begin to analyse it, I'd end up in all sorts of scrapes. Best to act instinctively, stand back and distil it later. T.S. Eliot wrote, 'Old men should be explorers.' I wasn't an old man, but I knew what he meant. Time passed, we clung evermore to the familiar. Sometimes we had to cast it off. That's what I must have done. Felt dissatisfied. Pushed myself to something extreme. Just to see. And here I was.

I couldn't imagine handling money. I could fancy it, but not imagine it. Like I'd given up cigarettes. I still got a whiff, felt the tug, but knew I wouldn't do it. Money? I was destined to have none on the entire trip. As I thought this I looked down. On the wooden floor was a ten pence piece and a two pence piece. I picked them up and put them in my pocket. We'd see.

Other things were changing. I flicked back through my diary. The fountain-pen writing had altered. On the first days the writing had been scruffy, ragged, even lollopy. The change was almost imperceptible day by day, but within a fortnight you could notice it. I was still never going to win the calligraphy gold award, but the strokes were less scrawly, there was more order. These were the good things. Against that, I'd struck up no real contact, and my shelter was an empty cottage. I preferred people to furniture. Sam was good, but didn't get my jokes.

I opened the tin of baked beans I'd stolen. I gave Sam the Weetabix. I'd planned pouring water over these, but relented on this Scrooge act and let him have the milk. It meant I had black tea. There's always a reward for self-sacrifice. I discovered two small variety packs of cereal in a cupboard and stashed them in my bag. I packed. I'd brought a certain discipline to this, mainly because to leave anything behind would be a mini disaster. There was no going back. I'd line up everything I used. I'm not sure how many items there were, but I checked them all out, and I checked them all back in.

I cleaned up my rubbish. I switched off the electricity. I gave thanks to the place that had sheltered me, wrote a small note of gratitude and left it on the kitchen table. Leaving places was always strange, even depersonalised places. I would probably never see most of them again.

It was only 7.30 a.m., a beautiful morning, the blue sky tinged with a salmon pink. My lost earring still bugged me. But slowly I was coming to realise it was only a possession.

I had a plan. Return the key, crockery and so on to Tibberton Manor. Thank them for their trust and generosity. Enlist their help in finding a lift for the first few miles. I strode the quarter of a mile to the big house. The same window was ajar. Mr Belcher was sitting in the same seat. He was reading a newspaper. Presumably not the same one. There was no sign of Mrs Belcher.

'I have brought back the key. And the spoon and plate,' I said.

'Thank you,' said Mr Belcher, reading on.

'I did appreciate your hospitality. I have left the cottage just as I found it.'

'Yes,' said Mr Belcher.

I placed the key on the windowsill, the rest inside.

'I was just wondering,' I said, 'because of the state of my feet I'm not supposed to walk all day just yet. I try to get a lift first thing. I asked in the pub last night, but no one could help. I wondered . . . if you knew anyone who might help.' Once again my voice expired, like a totally clapped-out horse.

'I'm sorry, I don't,' said Mr Belcher. I found myself wondering what article he was reading. Possibly the crossword?

'Ah,' I said. 'I see. Well, thanks anyway. Goodbye.'

'Goodbye,' said Mr Belcher.

No lift. No food. I decided I would try hitchhiking. I swung my thumb for a few miles. I seemed invisible to the hundreds of cars which passed, whizzing their wage slaves to work. Most had a single occupant. Many travelled at 80 miles an hour. Boy, they must have loved their jobs!

We walked through Edgmond and I noticed a young

mother with two boys getting her car out of the garage. I decided to act crafty and hang around her gate, making a big show of poring over the map. A lift? Oh, well, how nice! Her name was Ann Lock, her sons Jack (six) and Jamie (four). The lift was only two miles, leaving me at Forton, just north-east of Newport. But, like a present, it was the thought that counted, and it bucked me up.

'Look out for the hedges and bends around Sutton,' yelled Ann as she drove away. The hedges around Sutton are pot-bellied. Anyone daft enough to walk the road is pushed out towards the centre. The bends around Sutton are blind. The result is that traffic cannot pass anyone foolhardy enough to walk (and I suspect Sam and I were probably the first in a generation or so).

For a short spell, I had in my wake a whole procession of vehicles. People behind a car wheel are not known for their patience; the frustrated fumings vibrated through the air. Secretly I enjoyed this rare instance of pedestrian power over motorist. We crossed over the Shropshire Canal and looked over the bridge to see a longboat dreamily passing under. They always looked like giant domino containers. I toyed with the romantic idea of hitching a ride. The canal (or rather the boat) was unfortunately heading north-west. Not to be.

By this time I had evolved a new method of walking. Sam and I would walk for 90 minutes, then rest for about 30, when I would remove my boots and socks and have a kip. I decided we needed a regular routine to enhance the chances of foot preservation. This was our second post-Helen Chapman day, and the feet were holding up. Plus we had moved into a new county, Staffordshire. The countryside was flat and not over-interesting. Which was just as well, as you couldn't see much of it; the high, forbidding hedges gave a view only of the sky.

It was still a bendy, dangerous road. Sam and I were forced to cross and recross to find the safest verge. I felt like a shoelace being threaded. I had not given up all hope of a lift, though I was soon to learn the lengths to which people would go to avoid a simple act of charity. At a Snax lay-by, I approached a middle-aged man and woman munching a sandwich in one of those four-wheel-drive Tonka toys. 'We're full up,' said the man. 'Got the dog in the back.' On the vast rear seat, barely visible, and no bigger than a packet of crisps, was a tiny terrier.

A mile further up the road, a large lorry was parked up in a lay-by. How about it, driver? 'I've only just stopped,' he replied in a broad Black Country accent. 'Be here a long time yet.' Two minutes later, his wagon hurtled past me without a second look.

Not everyone was negative. We stopped at Holly Farm, Wootton, attracted by the display of flowers. I knew good folk would live there, and Renee Slack offered both Sam and me water and biscuits. We had food!

Although this was not an attractive road, although there were no lifts, although we were not over-burdened with food supplies, my body was feeling looser, more relaxed. It felt oiled, felt like walking was natural to it, like it moved easily through the air, through the countryside. Maybe it had taken me two weeks of walking to learn how to walk. Maybe we urbanites had lost the ability to walk the real way. Maybe what we thought of as walking wasn't walking at all, more an unrhythmic shuffling down to the corner shop or pub. Only by walking long distances could we learn the secret rhythm of walking. I felt I could walk like most people couldn't walk, like I couldn't walk before. I didn't know what it was, I couldn't exactly define it, I just felt it. I was walking. And other people I saw up on their two feet weren't.

But I still had to take care of my feet. This was my latest plan. Sam and I would walk as far as Eccleshall, which would mean 12½ miles so far that day. We'd stand and hitch, whizz on a few miles, then walk some more.

We took up position outside Eccleshall Pet Clinic. For some daft reason I felt this was a good hitching location for a man and his dog. One million cars whizzed past, then a few more. I hated every one of them. I hated their occupants, who averted their eyes. I hated the tin cans they were driving.

I hated standing there. I even hated my thumb. I hated being so submissive. After 45 minutes of hating everything, I decided we should walk on.

Was it my appearance? Was it Sam? Was every motorist simply a selfish bastard? I didn't much like walking and hitching. It interrupted my flow, my rhythm. I had to keep turning, jerking that thumb, and it did nothing for the harmony of movement. From now on I decided I'd either arrange a lift at my night stop or do without. I jerked the thumb one final time. A Land Rover pulled up. It was a farmer, Nick Brandon, from Sandon Stafford Farm, and he offered to whizz us the few miles up to Stone, north-east of Eccleshall. This meant crossing over the M6 – crossing the Rubicon. We had always been in the west. We were to move into the east! From one galaxy to another. As Nick's Land Rover crossed the bridge, I let out a highly significant whoop of joy. 'What's all that about, then?' he asked.

The plan was to walk through Stone – not a bad little town – and find a night's shelter somewhere the other side. The day was still sunny and hot, and it would soon be time for our 30-minute break. We took it on the north side of town, on the grass verge of a sloping drive up to Coppice Farm. No sign of activity from the farm, a cluster of white-painted buildings. I lay down in the shade of a small bush, removed my boots and socks, thought about something to eat, realised there was nothing, took a swig of water and fell asleep. Sam too. I would be woken (I fantasised) by a friendly farmer offering bags of healthy food and a big bouncy bed for the night. I awoke to nothing at all. The farm was still silent. I examined the Bromyard dressings, replaced my socks and boots and walked up towards the buildings.

I knocked at a door. No reply. I stood in the yard and shouted. Nothing. I climbed an outside set of steps to another door. No reply. I walked round the back, looked in a caravan window and the startled face of a woman looked back at me.

Three generations of the Harnforth family from Matlock were on holiday at the farm. Several of them suddenly appeared, as if from nowhere, and were friendly with it. There was a jam sandwich and pop for me. Water for Sam. Luckily I had a link with Matlock. A friend had once run the Boathouse pub there. I'd travelled to visit him and had been so keen I'd run across the road and under the wheels of a lorry. They'd carried me into the pub on a stretcher.

I'm not sure how much this story helped me with the Harnforths. Chris Harnforth knew the pub well. His daughters Rachel and Catherine were open-mouthed about my long saga. Something told me I'd be all right for a night's shelter. Instincts weren't always correct, though. Chris looked a bit sheepish. 'Well, you see, there are rather a lot of us, and the decision would be my mother's anyway, and she's taking a nap, and . . .'

I felt my chances gurgling away like washing-up water. Not to worry. There would be other places. And what right did I have just to walk in and expect a bed? This was England in 1998.

Sam and I walked on and tried the next large detached house up the road. The door was answered by a man stripped to the waist with a very brown chest that had spent all its life under a sunbed or on a beach in Lanzarote, both of which were alien territories for me. The man smiled as he opened the door, smiled as I stated my case, and smiled when he said no can do. Why not try the scout camp a little further on?

Two rejections. I began to feel weary. That's the way it was. You got yourself ready for the day's walking, and at the end you got yourself ready for stopping. Except you couldn't stop when and where you wanted. The decision wasn't yours.

Half a mile up the road was the leafy entrance to Kibbleston Camp Site. I'd had little to do with the scout movement for decades. I remembered sitting around a fire while a large man with incredibly hairy legs made strange signs, made us say strange words such as 'dib-dib-dib' and 'dob-dob-dob' and checked our woggles. I'd never been sure of Baden-Powell, and wondered if scouts were an anachronism. None of the teenage lads I knew gave it a second thought.

Kibbleston was 55 acres of secluded woodland. Sam and I walked through the leafy, shaded paths. Rabbits leapt out in front of us, the trees opened up into peaceful glades. We could hear hammers knocking in pegs, see the flash of a few tents. Deep in the woodland we came to the wooden reception buildings. Inside was a youngish man with a fresh face and ponytail – the warden, Paul Westwood. I threw myself on his mercy. 'Well,' he said, 'officially we're not allowed guests, but you've got an honest face and you've come a long way, so we'll put you up.' Scouts? Won't hear a word said against them.

A man called Harry appeared. Every organisation had a Harry. Harrys kept the world going. If chairmen or managing directors were off sick for a day, it made little difference. With Harry absent, things collapsed. Harry did a bit of everything at Kibbleston. He led Sam and me through the wooded paths to Kibbleston Hall. This was a site of former glories, the erstwhile seat of the Spode family. You'll have drunk from their cups and saucers. It was built of brick, like every building in Staffordshire, and had seen better days. It was in a state of disrepair. It reminded me of an aristocrat who'd lost his fortune gambling and was out in the street. Shabby, but obviously with breeding.

For our very own use Sam and I were given a fairly spartan but comfortable eight-bunk room. Toilet and washing facilities, also spartan, were across the way. It was a bed, a roof. But what of food? The hunger pains had begun to gnaw.

'All the scout groups will be cooking up soon,' said Harry. 'I'm sure they'd share.' And he took his leave. I laid my gear out on a top bunk, washed away the hot dust of the day, changed the clobber.

This was a huge forest area. Paths led off in all directions: into the trees, into glades, out into open pasture areas. Small armies of scout troops were encamped here and there. I walked through the forest and drifted from group to group, plucking up courage to ask for some grub. Why was I nervous? Paul had been generous, Harry had been friendly. But I felt like a wandering outsider. Get on with it.

I approached a Devon group. An obvious group leader was ladling out hot grub. I put my case. Could I have some? She looked me up and down like a suspect in an identity parade. 'Food supplies are on a strict budget here,' she said. 'So much a head and none to spare.' She returned to the ladle. Sam and I wandered onto other parts of the site. A second group gave the same response.

I stood and hovered near a third group. Waves came off them. The waves said the following: 'We are a special group of people who have come away for a special holiday. We have come to this forest to do our own thing. The last thing we want is strange men approaching us begging. Please go away.' And suddenly I saw myself in a new light. A suspicious character. A strange man wandering among groups of young boys. These leaders were moral guardians too. They had to watch out for people like me. I'd be lucky not to get arrested. I wandered about the forest. I had no idea what to do. Neither did Sam.

I came back to the reception area and went into the office. Paul was busy with new arrivals for the weekend. I hung about, shifted my weight. He was still busy. I butted in, explaining my failure at finding food.

'Oh, yes,' said Paul. He was checking lists, turning pages, giving out site locations. There was a queue of scout leaders. 'I suppose that's understandable. They do have tight budgets, yes.' He was talking to me, but his attention was elsewhere. The man, understandably, had things to do.

'I wonder,' I blurted out, 'if I could just have a cup of tea?' Paul waved a hand, didn't look up.

'Sure. Machine's just there.' He carried on.

'Ah. Yes. But you see, ahem, as I explained, I have no money at all.' The sentence seemed to hang in the air. Everyone in the office looked at me. There was a pause.

'Of course,' said Paul, and smiled. He took out some money, went to the machine and pressed some buttons. 'Sugar?' I shook my head. It was lemon tea. The heat surged through me, the first hot sustenance of the day. I felt like a beggar. It was mid-evening. All over the site people were tucking into bangers, burgers, beans. I walked out of the reception office and wandered back into the forest like a member of some lost tribe. One thing I had learned. When you felt really low, do something. So I did.

One tent was pitched on its own, with a man, a woman and two boys. I sensed they weren't in a group. They had a barbecue. They were cooking. I walked up and came straight out with it.

'I'm pretty hungry. I wonder if you could share a bit of your food with me?'

'Sure.' The man had a strong Black Country accent. 'There's not that much, but you're welcome to it.'

He was Dean Coffield, a paint sprayer from Dudley, a former scout leader who'd broken loose. He was here with his wife Sharon, their 12-year-old son Jon, and Jon's mate Jamie Sutton. Sharon had one of those open, sympathetic faces. She looked like she'd give anyone in the world a second chance. She'd planned to go and work with Romanian orphans, but the onset of rheumatoid arthritis had prevented it.

We sat around the beating heart of their fire. There were sausages, beans, garlic bread and what we Midlanders call pikelets and the rest of the world calls crumpets. The sun sank, the fire's presence grew. How come they were there, on their own?

Dean had been asked to run a group in Dudley, had built it up for a year, but then left. 'Scouting's finished,' he said, spearing a marshmallow, which he swung into the fire. 'It's seen as a middle-class thing these days. Loads of kids wouldn't even think of joining. There are loads of other things for them to do.'

Here he was. An outsider. Feeding another outsider. I had to do nothing except sit and eat and talk. I ate large amounts, drank mugs of tea. I tossed bits of burger to Sam. He stretched out, toasted his tum. The boys ran in and out of the trees, returned with wood for the fire.

I was on a scout camp. I had been given shelter by three arms of the Establishment. The church had sheltered me.

The foxhunters had taken me in and given me shelter. The scouts had given me a bed. What could it all mean? I felt conflicting feelings. Scouts seemed removed from modern Britain. Yet all around me in this forest, young people were busy. They had things they were doing, getting on with. I knew how many young men in inner cities led drifting, bored, meaningless lives, a kind of tedious futility that saw them drifting into crime. I'd seen them at close quarters on the desolate housing estates, been shocked by the brutality of their existence. What was the answer?

The night had drawn in. I'd eaten well. As I rose to go, Sharon shoved a plastic bag in my hand. 'For breakfast,' she said. 'Come and say tara in the morning.' An hour previously I'd faced a hungry night followed by a hungry morning. Now look.

Our path was through the ever-darkening woods from which we could hear voices. As we approached the dark shape of Kibbleston Manor, a scoutmaster appeared.

'Not going to bed so soon?' he said cheerily. 'This is when all the fun starts!'

But my day's fun had finished. I liked to rise early, to write my diary when the morning was fresh, while the world snored. The more simple I made my routine, the happier I became.

This night virtually marked our halfway stage. Edinburgh was still far distant. But how far away too Plymouth now seemed. I chose a top bunk, pulled Sam up with me and wriggled down into the sleeping bag. I pulled Sam up tight, and we began to drift off straightaway. I could hear the shouts and laughter in the wood as both boys and men went about their night-time games.

Day Fourteen — Saturday, 8 August

Miles travelled so far — 250

Too hot to dance
Except for the cows
Caught in the heat haze

The Big Spender — Fool's Paradise — Walking Backwards

Could it possibly be, I mean, not to make too big a thing of
it, but was there just the teeniest chance – nothing more than
that, mind! – but just a slight hint maybe, perhaps, you
know, the possibility . . . that my feet were improving?

It was my first thought on waking. In city terms it was
again ridiculously early, 5.30 a.m. There were words to write.
Exercises to do. Preparations to make. And Sam was barking
for a pee.

I threw open the bunk-room door. The sun filtered
through the trees and a slight mist ghosted its way round the
wood. In this, the most atrocious of recent summers, the
weather's bad temper was finally sweetening.

Washed, dressed, exercised and scribbled, Sam and I
packed the bag and made our way back to Dean and Sharon's
campsite. The coffee pot was already on the open fire.
Sharon's bag had contained milk, cereal, cake and doughnuts. I gobbled some down. Kept some for later.

I'd leant on this family enough. Now I leant on them
some more. Was there any chance of a short lift? 'I'll take you
about four miles,' said Dean. Dean was brill. They both
were.

I wondered why people associated certain attributes with
certain accents? Cuddly and rural for the West Country.
Sharp practice for Cockneys. Slow and ploddy for Black
Country. Racism. Ageism. If accentism had been easier to
say, people would have recognised it.

The four miles saw off the A520 and left us near Blythe
Bridge. But where were we? East or west? North or south? In

the Midlands? We were everywhere and nowhere. Journey-wise, we were in No Man's Land. Officially we were in Staffordshire. The terrain was flatter than a London pint, but was beginning to change. Ahead lay Derbyshire and the Peak District. I felt the landscape unfolding itself like a blanket, opening up before us.

A word about Sam's olfactory habits. Items of little interest to humans offered a whole universe to him. A tuft of grass, a piece of fence post, a small patch of waste ground would arouse his intense nasal curiosity. At the journey's start I'd tugged him away impatiently. Now I realised this was a vital part of his journey, the universe of smell. We reached an understanding. Sniff breaks were allowed. But not over-indulged.

It was a brilliantly hot, sunny day. Before Cheadle we made our first stop, under a shady tree, dappled in sunlight. From where I lay, rolling hills now heaved their way to the horizon. Bootless and sockless, I stretched out, my bag for a pillow, and watched the sun's mottled progress through the branches. I then fell asleep.

My stops routine was now well organised, and was important to Sam and me, for both physical and psycho-logical reasons. Walk 90, rest 30. Repeat as required. Do not deviate. Resist early temptations to increase former. Pacing vital. Look forward to small delights during stops: a nibble of cheese, a small apple, a biscuit. Always air feet. Always sleep. Always face forward. Face forward. I never looked back. Not even when I knew the view was breathtaking. On the map I never traced forward. On my route I never looked back.

We could see for 20 miles. Two minutes from the road, all noise of traffic blotted out. Only the slight breeze, the valley spread out before us, the giant tree dropping its protective arms, my wiggling feet.

I examined the Bromyard dressings. The rear ones were beginning to disintegrate. The discovery resulted in a short stab of panic, that feeling when you snap off part of a tooth, or realise you've lost your wallet. How would my feet cope? I would find out.

I had dog biscuits for Sam from Sharon. He showed them total indifference, so I boxed clever. I'd noticed that whatever I ate, Sam would eat. I popped a biscuit into my mouth. I chewed on it, making exaggerated, semi-orgasmic noises of pleasure. 'Mmmmm, that's nice. Mmmmm, lovely, yes, mmmmm.'

I chewed the thing for a full minute, then offered him a biscuit, which he ate. While he was busy doing that, I spat the foul thing out.

We walked on, past the sign to Alton Towers. Imagine the fun I could have had there, penniless. Except I wasn't penniless. By Cheadle, the day was oven hot. We passed an open market selling fruit and veg. I thought of the 12 pence from Tibberton. It had arrived by chance. I'd spend it.

'How much for one of those Granny Smith's?' I asked a stallholder.

'Twenty pence.'

'All I have in the world is this twelve pence.'

'Take an apple.'

For a full mile I rolled the apple in my hand, stroked it, tossed it in the air, anticipated its juicy, bittersweet explosion in my mouth. I think I overdid all this. Sam and I missed our turn.

At my speed, missing traffic signs was difficult. Between seeing a sign and acting upon it, I had time to write a short story.

I'd also been distracted by thoughts of my Indian hat. On hot days I wore it to keep the sun off my tonsorially challenged bonce. On wet days, to keep it dry. As a result, the hat was continually damp. It grew wet from the rain or it grew wet from the sweat of my brow. It was never dry. The hat seemed to be made of a unique, non-drying material. Such material could have commercial possibilities. Line buildings with it and render them more fire resistant. Or maybe . . .

You can possibly see how we missed the turn. Instead of heading on the A521 towards Kingsley, we were on the B5417 heading towards Oakamoor. This was not disastrous.

Few things were. And had we gone the 'correct' way, we'd have missed two delights. First, climbing the steep hill out of Cheadle, we passed a large campsite on the left. I jumped a fence at the sight of a tap and filled the bottle. Then, looking up, I saw on the opposite side a large and very strange building, around which thronged whole hosts of people. The building comprised two large brick edifices at right angles. Superficially they had the imposing aspect of a Victorian mill. On the roof, picked out in giant tile letters, were the words LES & MAVE.

The façade covered the history of architecture from classical Greek to the modern day. The windows, doors and appendages were part Gothic, part rococo, part classical, part Regency, part Victorian. There were more large letters, picking out in relief YOU ARE NOW ENTERING FOOL'S PARADISE. A carpark in front of the building was full. People were teeming everywhere. This huge place had a name. It was called Les's Horse and Cart, and was a perfect example of English eccentricity.

Sam and I walked up. Outside was a great sprawling mass of items on sale. I saw no actual horse and cart, but did see just about everything else. A quick walk round a small part of the exterior revealed stocks of the following: petrol pumps (garage forecourt variety, old style), mangles, milk churns, lamp-posts, village water pumps, road signs, telephone boxes, horse-drawn caravans, shop-window dummies, wrought-iron gates. The place was packed, mainly with couples who'd woken up that morning, turned to each other and said, 'I have an irresistible desire to buy a milk churn.' This was just the outside. For all I knew (no dogs allowed), inside they had surplus atomic submarines, bulk supplies of false ceramic legs and economy-size telegraph poles.

The place was run by Les and Mave Oaks. I realised that to meet them would be anti-climactic. Imagine if Les had worn a shapeless cardy. We moved on, leaving behind this impressive cathedral of the useless and the glorious.

A few miles on and our second stop, another shady tree, another view across the shimmering green lands of middle

England. I glugged at the bottle, removed boots and socks. The rear foot dressings were now well and truly in a state of disintegration. I had no choice. I had to remove them. 'This is the moment of truth, Sam,' I said.

Imagine removing them, walking and finding feet full of pain. What then? I replaced socks and boots and took a cautious step forward, as important to me as Neil Armstrong's had been to him. Under those woolly socks, the heels of my feet were completely naked. Without help or support. Alone. The sensation was strange, being accustomed to the dressings. But the pressure did not make me yelp. We walked on; each step lifted my spirits.

The small village of Oakamoor appeared like some Brigadoon. The road, steeply wooded countryside on each side, plunged down into the River Chunet valley. Oakamoor = more oaks – more of lots of trees, in fact. They'd pulled a thick curtain round the village, removed it from all the nastiness of the world. They'd dropped it here, with its small bridge, its waterfall, deep and hidden away. Its inhabitants had turned their backs on the Euro, Noel Edmonds, the Premier League and the Abbey National mortgage rate to live happily, secreted away in their wooded magic valley.

Or so I could fantasise, as we walked through and up the steep hill the other side, rising slowly like a diver to the surface, the familiar world. The slope saw Sam puffing like a train and me puffing like a much bigger train, the heat under my backpack enough to grill a T-bone steak. Up we climbed, finally emerging from the valley and the leafy shade.

We went through the tiny village of Cotton and back to the reality of the day. Which, let's face it, wasn't bad. Once out the valley, the countryside spread its great wide wings before us, and we turned briefly north-west to pick up our original route. How philosophical I was. There is no wrong turn, I thought, only an alternative one.

We were on a ridge top and the panoramic vistas shimmered in the heat haze. The slight breeze was no more than a baby's breath. The day belonged to the sun.

We were making good progress. Stop number three, a wall just below a large farmhouse at a remote crossroads up high. I ate one of Sharon's small doughnuts, half a sandwich, two swallows of water. Biscuits for Sam, boot and sock removal, and sleep.

Voices from the farmhouse woke me 15 minutes later. I decided I'd refill the water bottle. I was at Brockyard Farm, Cauldon, and facing me through the top of the stable-style slatted door to the kitchen was Freda Chadwick, a gutsy, lively woman who, mercifully, had never heard of small talk. She lived here with her husband, John, a commercial wagon trader. I leant on the lower part of the door, asked for water and told her a bit about my journey.

'Are you totally mad?' asked Freda. 'No, I mean it, are you? A writer? What have you written?'

I boasted of my small collection of worst-sellers.

'How old are you?' she asked.

'Fifty-four.'

'Fifty-four!' She leant backwards and shouted, 'John, come here!'

John appeared, a middle-aged man looking slightly uncomfortable. He had a prominent pot-belly.

'He's fifty-four, he is,' said Freda, and pointed at me. 'He's older than you, do you realise that?'

John nodded weakly as if to signify yes, he did know that. He shot me a look.

'Older than you!' repeated Freda.

John looked down at his pot-belly. One thing I did not have to worry about on this odyssey was a pot-belly. John did not appear over-enamoured with having been dragged out to be the subject of an unfavourable comparison.

'He's travelling from Plymouth to Edinburgh with no money!' exclaimed Freda.

John's response, another nod, the hint of a murmur, suggested this was information he could take or leave.

'And he's writing a book about it!'

Nod.

This slightly strained triangle was interrupted by a sudden

canine confrontation. Freda had assured me their collie was the world's most peaceable dog. I had made a claim for Sam as the planet's leading serene pooch. The two dogs were suddenly stark staring mad, snarling, biting, clawing, a life-and-death, bared-teeth struggle in the farmyard. Serenity met peace and calm – and the result was mayhem.

We parted them and put one each side of the door. John had made his silent departure during the struggle.

'You shouldn't wear that hat,' said Freda. 'People will think you're a weirdo. Where are you going now?'

There was a village about another six miles up called Onecote, which we were heading for.

'Try Adrian Plant,' she said. 'He might just put you up. Here, have some of this.'

There was a cup of tea, fruit, biscuits and dog biscuits for Sam (my pack was rapidly filling with Sam's supplies). We'd been 40 minutes chatting at this high crossroads settlement. Off again. 'So what was all that about, then, Sam?' I asked him as we began the great descent towards the A52. He gave me a look. Surely it happened with humans too? Someone who just got right up your nose?

After a short spell on the A52, we turned on to another minor road and headed up towards Onecote. On the brow of a hill stood a giant mounted stone wheel, the southern border of the Peak District. The Peaks are considered Derbyshire, but we were still in Staffs. It was a mightily impressive border point. You walked past the wheel, over the hill and there! The Peaks' display manager had arranged them, laid them out specially. Peak after peak, a wide, sweeping panorama of them. All shimmering away in the heat. Talking of heat, my feet were like microwaved buns. Not hurting, just steaming.

As Sam and I dropped down to the village, how could we have known we'd be coming back again soon? Adrian Plant lived in a big house and wore a Panama hat which flapped a little when he nodded. He nodded a lot as I told him Freda had sent us, we needed shelter, and the rest. The only time he didn't nod was when I put it to him, how about it? That

Ready for the off: Sam and me at Newcastle Central station

BELOW: Day 1 – Best foot forward: Sam and I prepare to leave the Astor Hotel, Plymouth

Days 1–2 – Early salvation: the Tavistock curate Geoffrey Boucher

Days 3–4 – Old-style cider from Cliff Brimblecombe

Days 4–5 – 'If it's purgatory, you can always give up' – Tom Coleman of Town Tenement Farm

Days 5–7 –
Ilminster saviours:
Teresa Hurley,
David Taddy and
the irrepressible
Levanna

Days 7–8 – The world of colour:
Theo and Carmel and the College
of Colour Therapy

Days 9–10 –
Third-generation
blacksmith
Michael Roberts

LEFT: Day 10 –
The death of a
cow: Peter Harper
collects the dog
food

Days 10–11 –
Peter Harper and
the hounds

Days 13–14 – Sam gets close to the grub at Kibblestone Scout Camp,
with Sharon and Dean Coffield (front row), Jon and Jamie (rear)

ABOVE: Day 15 – A sign to drive a hungry man insane . . . Sam is unimpressed

LEFT: Day 15 – A well-dressed well: Muriel Mason in Bradwell

BELOW: Day 16 – Books on the move: the welcoming mobile library of Sue Chambers and Allan Calvert. Sam is in a hurry to press on

Days 20–21 – The good, the bad and the farm: Hughie Bird on the combine

Days 21–22 – Pigeons at the Ritz with Joyce and Ron Crozier

Days 22–23 – The Italian Geordie, Ernie Auriemma

Day 24 – Getting on with the neighbours: the remoteness of Northumberland

Days 24–25 –
The huskies of
Fellside with Bernard
and Joy Whiting

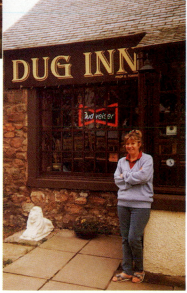

Days 26–27 –
Final resting
place: Pearl
Cunningham
outside the
Dug Inn

Day 27 – Journey's end: I've made it to my publishers'
(the bike is not mine!)

time he shook his head, but look, why not try the local farmer, Andie Andrews?

Okay. He sounded like a ventriloquist's dummy (Andie Andrews, that is). He was in a battered old shed on his farm, an elderly man who looked at me closely while I talked. Maybe it was the hat. From nowhere he produced a can of lager and handed it over. He then produced an open tin of dog food. He scooped out a spoonful and dolloped it onto the dirty concrete floor, where it landed like a cow pat. Sam sniffed it, but nothing else.

No grub for Sam. No shelter for us. Like decibels, rejections were logarithmic. So the second was more significant than the first, and so on. Andie farmed in Onecote, lived in Leek. 'You couldn't put us up in your home in Leek?' I said. See, I was getting desperate. He looked uncomfortable, and why not? I might have been a mass murderer, anything. 'Thanks anyway,' I said, and we left. I wondered how long he'd leave the dog food on the floor. The lager was warm. I didn't like lager, and I didn't like lager in cans. It wasn't Andie's fault. I pushed the can down into a litter bin.

A third attempt at a night's shelter was no better. 'Sam,' I said, as we stood on the village's main street, 'I'm getting pissed off. No one wants us.' Not so much pissed off as rejected. I'd been amazed how vulnerable I was, how knocked back by rejections. Especially three of them.

Onecote was a small, stone village, quiet. I soon realised that at one time they'd passed a by-law commanding every citizen on Saturday night to dine at the Jervis Arms, my next target. Through a small porch, the pub had doors to left and right. To the left was the main lounge. It heaved and churned like a full sea, people packed in at the bar, standing around, sitting at tables. To the right was a small, undistinguished bar-cum-store, with not a soul. Bar staff hurried through here from the kitchens, bearing steaming plates of appetising food into the main room. 'Excuse me, I just wondered if . . .' The waitress was past me, turning to say, 'No dogs, sorry.'

I tethered Sam in the porch and went back into the small

bar. The same waitress returned. Jollity wafted through, the smell of roast chicken, steak pies, gammon and pineapple. I stopped her and told her I needed shelter and had no loot (what an attractive proposition this must have sounded!). 'Ask the landlord,' she said and was gone again. The next moment she appeared with a steaming mug of tea. 'Drink this,' she said, and was gone again. I had no idea what she might do next. There was no sign of the landlord. It was getting on.

'Right,' I said. I sat down in the small, empty bar and began to write my diary. Night-time brought two pressures: finding shelter and writing the diary. I'd get rid of one of them.

The landlord was Peter Hill, a fit-looking, shaven-headed man in his thirties. He emerged as I was scribbling. Would he throw me out? 'Would you like something to eat?' he asked. The pub needed renaming – the Unpredictable Arms. A few moments later plonked down in front of me was a plate of burgers, chips and salad, plus a golden-brown pint of cask ale. Sam peered through the door from the porch. I threw him bits. I ate. I scribbled. Until the eating and the scribbling was finished. And all we needed was the shelter. Peter Hill emerged from the lounge again. 'I don't do bed and breakfast,' he said. 'There's these people up the road, they'd probably put you up for nothing. Check them out – here's their brochure.'

I looked at the B & B leaflet. How far?

'Oh, about a quarter of a mile that way,' he said, pointing the way we'd come, and disappeared into the hungry throng next door. The building didn't ring a bell. No matter. We set off.

This felt doubly strange. Retracing our steps seemed out of synch. It was history, and we were going back to it. Plus my body and feet adjusted themselves at the end of each day's journey. Break time. Now they had to get up again.

The place was called Townfoot Cottage. Me, Sam and the backpack walked the quarter mile, then another quarter mile. We walked a full mile. We passed a crossroads where we'd taken a break. We passed the giant stone wheel. Something perverse kept me going, pushed me on to find the elusive Townfoot Cottage.

We walked one and a half miles. There it was. Locked up. Empty. In darkness. No reply at the door. I sat down on the step. The odyssey had taught me to be fairly stoical. I took deep breaths. I almost managed to obliterate the burning desire to nuke the Jervis Arms. Sam panted at my side. What was I piddling about at?

'It's not my fault, Sam, come on.' And we set off back for the return mile and a half. The sun was beginning to dip behind the hills, the day's heat was sliding back. We had walked three totally useless, irrelevant, extra miles. We had been in or around Onecote for three hours. We had no shelter.

The village itself was dark on our return. And quiet. Except for the Jervis Arms. All the noise, activity and energy of the village was wrapped tightly in the lounge bar. The other bar was still empty. In the village centre was a stone bus shelter. I lay on the seat, measured it. It was short, and not the most enticing prospect. But what was the alternative?

I went back to the pub and tethered Sam in the porch. Through the serving hatch I could occasionally see Peter's head, like a buoy in a swelling sea. I trusted my instincts. This sometimes got me into bother but elsewhere proved advantageous. My instincts told me Peter Hill was a good bloke. He was my man.

My head was stuck through the serving hatch, jerking about. I was waving my arms, trying to catch Peter's attention. Behind me the unstoppable wave of food continued, more steaming plates carried by the waitresses. I was half blocking their path. I imagined them back in the kitchen, pulling pained faces at one another: 'It's that bloke back again!' Everyone in the crowded lounge seemed to notice me except Pete, who had now disappeared again into the throng.

I sat down once more in the small, empty and somewhat glum side bar. Pete popped his head round the door and came over. What I wanted to say was at the end of a hard day's walking, with your feet still in a parlous state, an extra three miles of fruitless trudging was not a barrel of fun, and now I was stranded, with no options at all, because at ten o'clock on a Saturday night, who would put up a wandering stranger?

'There was no one at the Townfoot, Pete,' I said. 'It was a mile and a half each way.'

'Catch you later,' he said, and was gone. Catch you later? Did that mean I have provided accommodation for you? Did it mean no need to worry? Or did it mean I might just possibly, at some future time in your life, accidentally bump into you; now clear off?

My feet had not liked the extra walking. They argued, quite rightly, that at this time of night they were off duty.

Back and forth went the plates. Full and steaming one way, empty the other. Everyone in Onecote was eating. Plus all members of their extended family. Plus people they'd all met on package holidays over the last ten years. Plus ex-college friends. And there was probably a Jervis Food Chat Line too.

I took off my boots and socks, the least I could do for the feet. I was a useless nuisance. I didn't know what to do. Two young couples with babies came into the small bar, bought drinks, sat down. They looked over at me. Why so strange? A solitary man, sitting barefoot without a drink on a Saturday night? So?

'Would you pass me that newspaper?' I asked one of them.

The man picked up the paper on the table next to him and glanced at it.

'It's a week old,' he said.

'Oh, that's all right,' I said, and laughed nervously. The man passed it over, slightly warily. I thought maybe I'd just walk on. I'd need to replace boots and socks first. This might draw attention to myself. I smiled over at the young families. Weakly, they smiled back. Perhaps if I just closed my eyes, went to sleep, what then? Peter flashed by.

'Peter,' I said, 'I'll just go to the bus shelter and . . .'

He gave me a cheerful wave and was gone.

And then the Unpredictable Arms lived up to its name. Another few minutes, and me having glumly decided the bus shelter was the best option, Peter reappeared, a foaming pint in his hand. He plonked it down in front of me, said, 'I'll sort something out. Drink this,' and was gone.

Whole scenarios change in a second. The world is dark, then light. The touch of a wand – transformation.

'Cheers!' I shouted across at the two families, and took a long and welcome draught. The newspaper? Totally unread. Twenty minutes later, Peter appeared again, said, 'Follow me,' and led me out the back of the pub, across the yard, up some stairs and into a holiday cottage. 'It's let from tomorrow,' he said, 'so you must leave it exactly as you find it. You can sleep on the bed but not in it. Okay?' And he was gone.

Peter Hill for Prime Minister. For World President. For Inter-Galactic Chief.

There was a large bedroom with double and single beds, a lounge, a kitchen and a posh bathroom – with hot water. I found teabags but no milk. I lay in the hot bath, drinking black tea, my bandaged feet propped up on the taps. It was 11 p.m. – almost the middle of the night for me. My face was an electric hotplate from the long, hot day. I stared at my feet. The front dressings were now also disintegrating.

'Be bold, Sam,' I said, and after the bath set to. The inner part of the dressings was still securely fastened and resisted so much my pulling and tugging that I almost sensed the feet protesting, 'No, Pete! That's stupid, Pete!'

One last tug and the dressings were off. The feet which for more than a week had been swathed in bandages were naked, two large pink things. I did not have the nerve to look underneath. The Unpredictable Arms, Onecote – a watershed. The unfettering of the feet. They were now well into the second half of their long and painful cycle, though only later did I see the pattern. The feet had struggled on.

I walked round the flat, on the soft carpets, on the hard covering in the bathroom. Sam followed me. I took out my sleeping bag and laid it across the posh-looking cover on the double bed with its plumped-up pillows that made me feel the world was all right.

I snuggled in, and Sam snuggled close to me. I felt a great affection for him on this night, and stroked the orange and white fur on his head as we both drifted off.

The recurring image as I went to sleep was that of the giant stone wheel marking the start of the Peaks. It appeared in front of us, time and time again, and we kept walking past it.

Day Fifteen — Sunday, 9 August

Miles travelled so far — 272

After walking twenty miles
I enjoy the fly's journey
On my cooling feet

On to Gluttony — Day of the Birds — Undressing in Public

I tried not to think of how far lay ahead. The maximum onwards projection I normally allowed myself on the maps was the day's journey to come. Sometimes I traced our journey back to Plymouth and, in the absence of anyone else to comment, said, 'Well done!'

We were more than halfway. Why wasn't that cause for more celebration? Who'd have thought at the start, nearly 300 miles with no money? Except it meant nothing unless we did the whole trip.

I was worried about this day. The Peak District, midsummer, the likelihood of another 20,000 backpackers. Food and shelter might be hard to come by. I checked the provisions. We had one orange, two small chocolate biscuit bars, one doughnut looking past it, Sam's dog biscuits. And we had no lift. And my feet were to go naked into the world. Hmmm.

There were consolations. For the first time I could apply the massage oil to the entire foot. I gave Sam a wash down in the bath and massaged his legs. For the latter he liked to spread himself on his back somewhat indecorously. His eyes closed and he fantasised over goodness knows what. I popped him his vitamin pill and offered him biscuits. He took each biscuit in turn to a far corner of the room and ate it.

I liked to think my doorstep manner was improving. I had to gain confidence quickly. As soon as I mentioned I travelled without money, a flicker of alarm ran across many faces. I had to allay that. There was a lot of mistrust about. And I was an obvious target for it.

'Police are looking for a man who has conned his way into several homes claiming to be a penniless writer. The man has so far made off with 13 central heating systems, five Ford Granadas, a stocking full of five-pound notes and three babies . . .' And why should people not think that? Weren't the newspapers full of such stuff?

Practice was making me better, I thought. Except I'd made my pitch unsuccessfully three times in Onecote. Cranking myself for a fourth wasn't easy. And there was the dilemma. However convincing I sounded, the mistrustful world, in that time-honoured phrase, thought, 'Well, he would, wouldn't he?'

I wrote up the diary, breakfasted on black tea and a chocolate biscuit, and soon after 8 a.m. we were ready for the road. I left a thank-you note for Inter-Galactic Chief Hill, checked everything was exactly as we'd found it (no scum on the bath . . .) and pulled on my backpack. The straps were still soaked from the previous day's sweat. Hat and straps. The hotter the weather, the wetter I became.

Onecote's inhabitants were still asleep, their dreams no doubt nurtured by the Jervis Arms grub. The sun was still being kept at bay, but I sensed it awaiting its moment in anticipation, like an audience awaiting the great star's entrance from the wings. Not long now.

We townies had too little relationship with the sun. How often did we plot its character? What did it matter to us, in our air-conditioned offices, our centrally heated houses, our smoked-glass cars? We ignored the sun most of the time, then rushed off to lie under it for two weeks like bacon under the grill.

In this weather I would watch its progress. As we set off in the morning, the sun would be level with my right shoulder, still struggling to be properly awake, slowly gaining strength as it struggled up its arc, wobbling its way to high above my head, where it would gaze at my thinning locks. For a few hours it blazed in its full glory, then dropped down towards my left shoulder, its power weakening on the slow decline to the horizon, pushing out ever longer shadows. Its last words before it disappeared were always the same: 'I'll be back.'

I never tired of this. But then I realised we never tired of the natural world. Quiz shows we tired of, nightclubs, the latest fashions, celebrities. Like back home in Cullercoats, I never tired of the sea.

The previous night in the Unpredictable Arms I'd heard the phrase 'me duck' several times from the crowded lounge, proof we had moved into the east Midlands, the region that had spawned me. We were walking on a small, quiet road, the B5053, towards Warslow. I felt a strange satisfaction to be striding out while most of the country was still deep in Sunday slumber.

Sam's habits had not changed. He still tugged to be squashed by passing artics, he still fought for tarmac as opposed to grass. Not that countryside grass verges were always the better option; the concealed drainage channels meant you could easily turn an ankle.

We approached the Derbyshire border, the landscape changing again. The countryside was prised open like a mussel shell. Drystone walls traced their lines across the hills. Warslow was still snoozing. It had a totem for the best-kept Staffordshire village of 1997.

Since Clifton Kennels we'd spent three nights of de-personalised sleeping, two empty holiday cottages and a scout bunk house. It had left me out of sorts. I wasn't an isolationist. I was social. And nosy. I liked to peep into other people's lives, see what teabags they used, whether they kept the top on the toothpaste, what books were on the shelves. Had Sam and I been on an Arctic expedition, climbing a mountain, trekking across a desert, it wouldn't have mattered. But we weren't. We were here, in Britain. We were close to everyday life. It was just that sometimes we couldn't touch it. That's what being penniless did to you.

North-east of Warslow, we made our first stop at 10.15. Again this was at a crossroads and again I propped myself up against an old-fashioned signpost. I realised why I kept doing this. It stemmed from my boyhood fascination with the Richmal Crompton *William* books. The artist Thomas Henry often drew pictures of tramps, who'd arrive at the well-ordered village and bring chaos. Tramps were often drawn resting against road signs with a scruffy dog and generally dishevelled appearance. That was what I was trying to do. Be one of those tramps.

I munched on half a chocolate biscuit, took a swig of water and went to sleep. How come Sam had had no trouble with his feet, I thought on waking. Because he had the sense to walk on all fours.

Staffordshire brick was now giving way to Derbyshire stone, and as we walked on and dropped down a steep hill, there on the other side was the village of Longnor. It sat up on the opposite hill like a dog waiting for its bone. A grey dog, because that was the stone's colour. We had Longnor in our sights for a good time. When we reached it, the world had finally woken and was buying newspapers with 15 unnecessary supplements.

At the village junction, a road sign read 'Glutton Bridge 1'. I read it again, but it was true enough. In my hungry state, I conjured up the village as a provider of rich chocolate cake, bacon butties dripping with ketchup, oversized spotted dick and custard, steaming Sunday dinners, the Yorkshire puddings piled up like an old tyre dump. Glutton Bridge was not on my map. My fate obviously was to visit it. As Sam and I hurried out of Longnor, I was in a state of some excitement. Up the hill we went. Towards Glutton Bridge.

On the ridge top, we came across a Dutch couple at the viewing point. They were taking in the breathtaking view. I could see only sausage, egg and chips. Twenty-one years previously they'd spent an idyllic holiday at a place called Glutton Grange, which was on my route. Glutton Grange had been run by a Mr and Mrs Holland. A coincidence, see? Holland, Dutch couple . . . Anyway, the Glutton syndrome was growing in strength. 'We thought of calling,' said Stephen, 'but decided against it.'

I had a brilliant idea. It fitted the syndrome perfectly. I would be their emissary to Glutton Grange. I would bring their greetings to the doorstep. I would be invited in and given enormous amounts of delicious food, chilled white wine of the finest quality. There would probably be an attractive woman. 'That's very good of you,' said Stephen. He reached into his pocket and handed me a shiny green apple. To you, just another apple; to me, foodless and pretty hungry, much more.

The apple put a spring in my step as we headed down towards Glutton Bridge and Glutton Grange, passing the Derbyshire border sign. So excited was I, I almost missed it. There in the verge was a very large, very black and seemingly injured crow, grounded and flapping its wide wings to little effect. I picked it up. It pecked at my hand. I had little experience of handling injured birds. 'Stop it,' I said. It pecked again. After a while it stopped pecking and seemed more comfortable. As we walked on, crow grew calmer. Or maybe it was dying. At an isolated stone house, a woman was tending her garden.

'Do the Hollands still live at Glutton Grange?' I asked.

'Yes, they do,' said the woman, and pointed across the valley. 'And there it is.'

Perfect. Sam, crow and I walked on, straight through the village, across the River Dove bridge and up towards Glutton Grange, an eighteenth-century, wide, stone building, double fronted, the approach to which was through a sculpted hedge arch. It was obviously a farm. I thought I saw a man moving in an upstairs window.

Giving the door knocker a good thud proved difficult. I was carrying one book of maps, one green apple, one injured crow and Sam's lead. Redistributing all these made old crow angry again. It had obviously been influenced by the scene from Hitchcock's *The Birds* where the flock shreds Tipi Hedren to bits. It fastened its powerful beak into the fleshy bit of my left hand between thumb and first finger, took several bites, then anchored itself there.

I put down the maps, the apple, Sam's lead. I gently tried to prise the beak free. No go from crow. And it hurt. It hurt me, that is. Not sure about crow. 'Come on, old crow,' I said, 'don't be like this.' It made no difference. I had to prise the beak open like a mussel shell (the day's second mussel-shell simile). A small bead of blood was witness to crow's determination.

I knocked at the door. There was no reply. I knocked again. The same. This was hard to swallow (as my fantasy food was proving to be). Everything had been building to this moment, the pattern of the last hour. And hadn't I seen a man upstairs?

Knock, knock. Nothing. It was all inside, I knew it. The supply of cream horns, chicken and mushroom pies, bowls of hot tomato soup, warm crusty bread, slivers of freshly roasted pork.

I looked round the farmyard. A generator was running. A tractor was parked. A barn had hay in it. Hens jerked about and clucked. A working farm. No workers.

Peck, went crow.

I propped myself up against a shady tree opposite the house. As the man said, all I could do now was wait. The sun was at its height, crow had settled, Sam had stretched out. I fell asleep.

The sound of a slamming door woke me. Stephen and Mai Barnes had decided to visit after all. Holland wanted to be reunited with Holland. We all looked at the house. Stephen, for good measure, knocked as well. 'They'll probably be back in a minute,' he said, though I'd have more conviction claiming Notts County would soon be in Europe.

He seemed uneasy. Had they had a row? Did he want the apple back? Could it have been crow?

After we'd stared at the house for as much as you'd want to, he turned to me. 'Look,' he said. 'This might help you – to buy something.' In his hand he had a pound coin.

I'd now been offered two quid in two separate counties. I could have made a career of it. 'Ta very much,' I said, 'but I decided not to take money off people.'

For some reason I felt guilty. Stephen Barnes put the money back in his pocket. They left. As I would have to, my Glutton dream in tatters.

But what about crow? I couldn't just carry it to Edinburgh. There seemed nowhere round here to take it. 'I'll have to leave you here, crow,' I said. I placed the bird on the front lawn. It would be clearly visible to anyone walking to the front door. The two small beaded eyes looked at me. Crow flapped its wings in a flurry of ineffectuality. I gathered up my things, walked away with Sam and turned back to see its angled black body on the green grass. The sight haunted me for the rest of the day.

We needed regular water on a day as hot as this. I'd worked out a way for Sam to get water from my bottle when the terrain was river- and puddle-free. I filled the bottle's small screw top. At first he ran up to it too excitedly and knocked half the water to the ground. Slowly I trained him to stay cool, come at it slowly and curl his large pink tongue inside the top. Three curls and the top was empty. He was allowed three tops full per session. We were on rations.

We climbed and dropped, climbed and dropped, often through craggy landscapes pitted with ruined stone cottages. There were giddy heights, then we'd plunge deep down into the beautiful Derbyshire dales. Often we seemed to be on top of the world, the peaks rising in all directions, the sun having chased every wisp of cloud from the sky. The hordes of backpacking ramblers didn't materialise out here. Maybe they were further north, at the more popular peaks.

There was one strange contrast in this spectacular landscape: we came past the dramatically ugly Hindlow limestone quarry. This was a ghostly presence which for several hundred yards each side was surrounded by flowers, grasses and shrubs draped in the grey shrouds of the limestone deposit. The vivid natural colours elsewhere were suddenly contrasted with this spectral scene frozen in grey. An added curiosity was the strong smell of liquorice from the fennel plants at the roadside.

We crossed the A515 and were heading up the A5270. I didn't normally munch in transit, but hunger drove me to a small piece of chocolate. Our third stop was propped up against a stone wall of a farm. On the other side the farm dogs got a sniff of us and howled and barked. Had Sam and I not experienced the canine choir of Clifton Kennels in full throat, we might have been thrown.

Another small nap. When I awoke, I saw opposite, perched on a telegraph wire, a serried rank of birds. For the second time that day I thought of Hitchcock's film. Why were so many birds gathered like that? Fifty yards up the road a young couple had also stopped to see the assembly. This was obviously the day of the birds. I had helped one bird. These birds could help me. I walked up to the car.

'Strange, aren't they, those birds?' I said.

'Yes, they are,' replied the man.

'I wonder why they're gathered like that.'

'Yes, we were wondering that,' said the woman.

'I also wondered,' I said, 'are you possibly going through Tideswell?'

They were. I stretched out in the back of the couple's car. I was so pleased with myself I forgot to ask their names. Tideswell was about 17 miles from Onecote. I could push on further, I could break the 20-mile barrier. Ah, those thousands of backpackers I mentioned. They were all in Tideswell. Looking for a decent cup of tea and a currant scone.

I chatted on to the couple, who were from Sheffield, and they dropped us at the A623 crossroads. We pushed on, turning off up the B6049 towards Bradwell. It was late afternoon. Bradwell would do. My feet, dressing-free, had, I suddenly realised, stood the test. 'Yeeeeeessss!' That was me yelling out across the landscape. Because my feet had dogged me virtually from day one. My journey was hardly ever free of foot problems. My odyssey had been informed by my feet. Now came the hint – they were really on the mend. I yanked Sam's lead and strode out for our final miles with a surge of adrenalin.

In the clear air, everything looked pure, vivid. I could smell newly mown hay. I could see, round a wide angle, six tractors like Dinky toys in different fields. I'd have said this was a sentimentalised, romanticised view of nature on this fine summer evening. Except there it was, in front of me. To the right, some way distant, hang-gliders launched themselves off a peak, their vivid white curves drifting down in graceful arcs. I'd find out more about them later. Part of me felt good. But I needed refuelling.

One mile from Bradwell, we passed a large farm. In the yard a chorus of barking dogs tugged at their leads, launching themselves at me. Their trajectories were cut short as the leads tightened, but they would launch themselves again, be jerked back to earth again. The farmer was up in a field loading hay. Something about his body language as I approached told me this would not be my night's shelter. I was right. On we went. I'd eaten little this day. Some days I was having to make do with less than I would have normally consumed in one meal. To cheer myself up, I argued that this was probably no bad thing. It didn't work. There never seemed to be any problem feeding Sam. This probably said a lot about our country. Fat dog walking with skinny man.

The striking stone village of Bradwell was alive with flags, bunting and other decorations, part of the annual well-dressing gala, a strong custom in these Derbyshire villages, and a celebration of water which had survived that commodity's privatisation and creaming off by fat cats. On the main street a series of trestle tables displayed knick-knacks and were manned by that race of elderly ladies who kept charity shops going, and who should be put in charge of the whole country.

I rummaged at one table and a lady said, 'You look very hot.' I nodded. 'You can buy a cup of tea in the village hall,' she added. I told her I couldn't, and why. 'I'll make you a cup of tea,' piped up another lady. 'Come with me.' She led me across the street, showed me the decorated well and took me into her small terraced house.

She was Muriel Mason, aged 67, and this was the home she was born in. Within ten minutes I knew of the death of her husband, the number of children and grandchildren, her mental breakdown, her love of boats and her charity work for the Edale Mountain Rescue Team. 'I sell everyone a mountain rescue pen,' she said. 'All proceeds go to the team. Twenty pence.' She held one up. I reminded her I had no money. 'I'll buy it for you,' she said. She took out twenty pence, put it in the box and handed me the pen. Professional fundraisers would not recognise this behaviour pattern.

Sitting in her small, cosy living-room, I was given a cup of blackcurrant tea, the first hot thing I'd swallowed all day. It was nectar. She disappeared into the kitchen and emerged with half a loaf (sliced), a hunk of Cheddar and a pack of Lurpak. 'I can't put you up,' she said, 'but take these. Try Robert and Alison Frith, who live by the church.' She'd given me good news and bad news in the same breath. For the second night running I was off on a roundabout of potential hosts. Two down, how many to go?

Which Shakespearean characters was it who said 'Do you live by the book?/No, sir, by the church'? Something like that. *Twelfth Night*? I could have made more of this little jest had Robert and Alison Frith put me up. They did recommend someone else (I was getting through this village like wildfire): Jen Smith, who lived at the old staging house by the disused café.

Sam and I trotted off again. Our record number of rejections at one time was four. I had no desire to smash it. I was weary. I wanted a base for the night.

Jen Smith was away, but looking after her elderly mother was her friend Sue, a woman of androgynous appearance and deep voice. She heard me out and invited me in, gave me a cup of tea. The old house was called Lyndale and was cluttered, ramshackle, eccentric. I wanted to stay. Sam went to sleep immediately. Two cats, perched on top of a rocking chair, fixed their gaze on him. Jen's mother, Kate, was sitting and looking at me.

'I just need somewhere for the night,' I said. 'I'm pretty whacked.'

'Jen's away,' said Kate and smiled.

'I have my own sleeping bag, can sleep anywhere, and I'm no problem, but I need somewhere to lay my head, write up my diary.'

'She's away,' said Kate. I realised she suffered from senile dementia. I looked at Sue. The look said, please don't make me go out there again and start all over again.

'You could sleep in the old café,' said Sue. 'No one uses it now, except the gliding club for meetings.' I told you the gliding club would come up again.

I woke Sam and we walked the few yards from the front door over to the café. It was on a corner, and each side had a large plate-glass window down almost to the ground. The pub, the Valley Lodge, was right opposite.

I stood inside and felt a certain empathy with goldfish. There was a sink, a kettle, bench seats round the sides, a counter. On the walls were various hang-gliding posters. Hang-gliding magazines and leaflets were scattered around haphazardly. There was a map detailing the aerodynamics and thermals in the Bradwell district. I memorised it instantly.

I wasn't interested in any of the people walking outside and hoped they had a similar lack of interest in me. I washed and changed, and also washed a top, socks and pants, hanging them in the window to dry.

I ate some of Muriel's bread and cheese. There was Winalot for Sam. I spread out my belongings to mark my temporary territory, removed the cushioned tops from the bench seats and made a bed on the floor. Moderately fed and cleaned, I sat down on this bed. I did not want to just lie down in my goldfish bowl and go to sleep. Food had been in short supply. So too had human company. I wanted to hear people's voices, crack jokes. I wanted to babble on about nothing of great importance, and have people babble back at me. I felt this loneliness tugging at my sleeve over the next hour as I wrote up my diary.

I knocked at Lyndale's front door again. Could I come in and just sit with them for a while? I wanted the house's amiable clutter, the cats, the rocking chair, Sue and Kate.

I had six cats for company in the house. Four were suffixly linked: Octypus, Platypus, Oedipus, and – wait for it – Purpus. These belonged to Kate. Tigger and Oliver belonged to Sue. Oliver had been named after a consultant psychiatrist. Not many cats could say that. Actually, Oliver couldn't say it either. But it was true.

The cats flew through the air with the greatest of ease. They leapt from chair top to chair top like trapeze artists. When they landed on the rocking chair, it swayed like a metronome.

When not airborne, they became subterranean, burrowing under the carpet which rose up in front of them like a miniature mountain range.

All this happened as if it were perfectly normal in this house. Kate spoke to me of her daughter, Jen. Her eyes misted over with affection. When Sue left the room, Kate leant over to me and whispered, 'She's an angel, you know. An absolute angel.'

Sue was a psychiatric nurse, and Kate had been one too. Every few minutes Kate would ask, 'Where are you sleeping tonight?' and I would reply, 'In the café.' Her next question would be, 'Where are you going to?' and I would reply, 'Edinburgh.' She didn't tire of asking these questions, and I didn't tire of answering them.

We all drank tea and watched *A Touch of Frost.* My tired limbs relaxed. Sam had stayed in the feline-free café. The day's exertions leaked from me. I can't now remember a single word I said in the next hour and a half, but they were all vital. I watched the television, the whizzing cats. I answered Kate's two questions.

At ten o'clock I walked back to my goldfish bowl. This sense of exhibitionism was reinforced as I had to switch on the light. I was hungry again. Another cheese sandwich. How did I look to those entering and leaving Valley Lodge? This was Well-Dressing Week, with lots of social and artistic events. Locals might just believe it part of the programme. Tilda Swinton slept in a glass case as an artistic offering. I could do the same (almost). Plus eat a cheese sandwich. My own avant-garde piece was in three sections. Part one: prepare and eat a cheese sandwich (symbolism – the greed of the over-consumptive West). Part two: the removal of trousers (symbolism – the stripping away of pretence by the artist). Part three: the falling asleep (symbolism – the indifference of society to the world's suffering).

I dozed off and dreamed of winning prestigious prizes.

Day Sixteen – Monday, 10 August

Miles travelled so far – 293

The grey lake
Calls out to the grey sky
Which soon will respond

No Room at the Inn – Bucked up by Books – Knocking up Neighbours

None of my washing hung in the window was dry when I rose at 6.30 a.m. I had no alternative but to put on the wet socks; the rest I stuck in a plastic carrier bag.

The only food was Muriel's bread and cheese. I ate some. Knowing the likely heat of the day, I transferred her Lurpak butter from its tinfoil into a plastic carton. I had learned to throw no food away unless it was decomposing or simply walking away on its own feet.

In the clutter of this disused café, half hidden on a table, I came across a carton of Ribena, partially drunk. There was no way of telling if it had been there two days or opened to celebrate Labour's election victory. Nor did I care. I drank it down.

I still had doggy supplies for Sam and gave him some Winalot sticks. There was no mirror, but I managed to shave using the reflective surface of the metal kettle, whose curves turned my face into that of Frankie Howerd. Sue had given me teabags and milk, so there was the luxury of a hot drink to start the day.

I studied the map as I ate. Now we were past halfway, I ventured the occasional nervous look at the journey to come. I also checked the mileage tables, but was choked to learn that Manchester to Edinburgh (and we were not yet level with Manchester) was 245 miles. The journey seemed stuck at this middle distance. I longed for the mileage to drop below 200 and glumly wondered just how many miles above 500 our town-dodging and main-road omissions had pushed it to. The map gave me some cheer, though. Once we were free of Leeds and its environs, the route north was virtually city-free.

Bradwell early risers were treated to the sight of a man doing press-ups in full view of passers-by. He followed this by writing for an hour. My writing routine was now well established. I wrote in the evening once we had found shelter and in the morning before we set off. Each session brought around 1,000 words.

I had my small rituals. I would place directly in front of me the ornate cloth notebook I had brought for the main fountain-pen writing. I had two smaller notebooks in which I jotted ballpoint notes, impressions and descriptions throughout the day. These were placed on one side. On the other side I placed my bottle of Quink. The contents seemed to be vanishing faster than an alcoholic's Famous Grouse, due partly to the regularity with which I filled my elegant Waterman fountain pen (a present from a friend, Pat Riddell) and partly, I suspected, to the sudden heatwave.

I took care with the handwriting now, and regretted the many biro years which had seen it deteriorate. All my writing materials and implements were kept in a strong plastic folder. This was the first thing to be taken out of my bag (held in a special zipped pocket) and the first to be replaced. A fastidious stock check was carried out each time. I could just about handle losing the spare socks or knickers. Not so the diary.

Sam and I bade farewell to our strange night's shelter and knocked at the Lyndale door. Sue opened it. She seemed more remote, guarded. 'I'd rather you didn't see Kate this morning,' she said, full square in the door. 'She will have forgotten all about you, and it's best left that way.'

Stupidly, my pride was hurt. How could she forget all about me? Sue had offered to run me a few miles up the road. My plan had been to ask her a whole load of questions. She was a fascinating character. But the different mood neutered this idea. We drove more or less in silence. I thanked her for the food and shelter, and by 8.30 we'd been dropped off and were striding out through the village of Bamford. The good news was that there were wide grass verges on which to walk. The bad news was that they had last been trimmed by the council to celebrate VE day. Sam disappeared at the end of his lead. Only the tugging reassured me he was still there.

The morning mists blunted all peaks, and although the forecast was good, today's early cloud was more stubborn than the previous morning's. It wouldn't be muscled out by the sun quite so easily.

Our journey took us alongside Ladybower Reservoir. Some locals claimed the church steeple of the flooded village could be seen at low water levels. Others said this was tosh. Sky and reservoir shared the same slate-grey colour. Walking past a great dam always made me nervous. When human-kind took on nature, nature always won in the long run. I didn't want to get washed away in the long run.

For a few miles we were on the Snake Pass, the old, often spectacular trans-Pennine route linking Sheffield and Manchester. We then turned north onto a remote and bleak-looking road that had the courage to traverse the lonely

Strines Moor. Within a few yards this had become the most desolate and unpopulated route since Dartmoor – and without the busloads of German tourists. By this stage the Pennines had reared their humped back. We were only a few miles west of a major city, Sheffield, but for the next two hours we would neither pass nor see a single house. People like to get away from it all, but there are limits. And, in the mist, who could tell whether we were even still on earth? It could have been the Planet Mirch.

Two miles' steady climb up the moor and out of the mists loomed an isolated building. The Strines Inn was perched on the top. It was so isolated I wondered if it had ever had customers, or knew who had won the World Cup. On this hostile morning I was sure they'd welcome a solitary traveller, even a penniless one. I pictured mine host rustling up a steaming mug of coffee to warm the blood.

We were within a few yards of the building when a German shepherd dog – about the size of a German shepherd – bounded from the front door and made such an aggressive beeline for Sam that the poor thing tried to hide up my trouserleg. Framed in the pub doorway was a man I took to be the landlord. In a deep, booming, Yorkshire voice he shouted, 'We're not open yet! The dog lives here. It runs free!'

The definition of 'running free' appeared to be liberty to eat smaller canines. I managed to keep myself between Sam and the hell-hound and began to explain how we just wanted to rest up for a few moments. Boom time again. 'We're not open. The dog'll go for your dog – it runs free! It lives here!'

I noticed all the outside tables had screwed to them metal notices forbidding their use by picnickers. The pub sign included the words 'Open at 10.30 a.m.'. It was 10.26 a.m. One option was to wait four minutes in the anticipation of such a metamorphosis that the mug of steaming coffee would duly appear. Call me a cynic, but I thought it unlikely.

Hell-hound was still at it, and hell-hound's owner was still in the doorway. Sam and I retreated from this hospitality and round the corner took our first break of the day, in an open barn.

My meal the previous night had been bread and cheese. My breakfast had been bread and cheese. At last I had a change. There was no bread left. I had just cheese. I washed it down with water.

After the friendliness of the Strines Inn, the road's character changed. We dropped down off the moor into thick woodland. Occasionally the road opened up and offered views of more woodland on distant hills. The only sign of human life was the odd glimpse on a far slope of a bilberry picker. I quite fancied meeting some people. Flesh and blood.

We walked through several more miles of solitude, into woods, out of woods, up hills, into valleys. By midday the sun had finally given the mist the hot shoulder and was king of the castle. Soon after, we took our second break. I removed my boots and socks and lay on the grass verge.

Maybe something had happened. The entire world's population had dematerialised with the exception of men in Caterpillar boots with purple laces, who were strangely immune to the alien weapon. Best gnaw on the cheese again.

The solitariness was such that I began to hallucinate. After the break, over the crest of a hill and in a remote lay-by, I saw a brightly coloured wagon and on the sides the words 'Sheffield City Council Mobile Library Bus'. I looked in all directions. I was keen to spot the coming rush of old ladies wanting to swap their Catherine Cooksons. No one. In every direction. No people. No houses.

I decided to face up to the hallucination. I approached the bus and knocked at the side door. A woman appeared. I told her what I was doing. I waited for her to vanish in a puff of smoke, or one of those wiggly fade-outs in films. It didn't happen. The occupants of the bus were drinking tea and eating sandwiches. Hearing of my long journey, the woman said, 'You'd best have a banana.'

The banana was real. The people were real. They were on their meal break, and their route included this remote spot. I stretched out in the airy, spacious interior. I felt the calming presence of books all around me. Sue Chambers and Allan

Calvert unscrewed the flask and offered me tea. When I said I was travelling minus any money, Sue said, 'You'd better have a second banana,' and I did. I ate it with cheese. I leaned against the thrillers and love stories, and was cheeky enough to ask if they'd stock my book if and when I finished the odyssey and wrote it.

'A'reet,' said Allan, which was good enough.

After the solitude and the Strines saga, Sue and Allan's hospitality and cheerfulness, not to mention a comfortable Len Deighton to rest my weary head upon, was welcome. Books had come to my aid. It seemed apt. And if I had found the misty isolation disconcerting, the afternoon was to chuck the opposite at me – the longest stretch of urbanism so far.

'How about a lift?' I asked as Allan turned the ignition key and made ready for an afternoon of peripatetic literature.

'Not supposed to,' he said.

'Just a short one,' I said. He had hundreds of authors on board. One more wouldn't make much difference.

'Just this once,' he said, and we pulled away. Our short journey took us across the South Yorkshire border, through the village of Bolsterstone, famous for its male voice choir, and I was dropped near the roaring traffic of the Wortley bypass.

From the Peaks to South Yorkshire – a few miles, a whole galaxy apart. South Yorkshire is a triangle defined by Rotherham, Doncaster and Barnsley. A quick contemporary history lesson is dominated by one fact: this was the main sacrificial lamb of Thatcherism. The South Yorkshire coal industry was the victim of the bitter ideological wars of the '80s, a way of life, a social structure more or less wiped out. At Home Counties dinner parties they might have disagreed over the finer points of Thatcherism's legacy. Parts of South Yorkshire were virtually put to the sword.

We were close to the M1 – another landmark to cross – and, according to the woman in the Wortley village shop, there was a short cut. This same woman provided Sam with such a large bowl of water he could have swum across it.

Somewhere in Britain was a perverse race of functionaries. Their object was, in the cause of some obscure by-law or long-forgotten and incomprehensible dictum, to create maximum annoyance and frustration among the populace. Our short cut was across a park. The park gates were padlocked. This, I assume, was to prevent people from stealing the park. Or, as a functionary might have argued, we have already provided a park. Now you want access to it as well!

There were lots of reasons why, in midsummer, a large, spacious, peaceful park should be locked up. None of them made any sense. I scaled the gates, taking Sam with me. Perched on top, I tried to persuade him to take a leap. He wouldn't. I aimed him at a soft piece of grass and chucked him. He gave me a sour look but was okay.

The park was deserted – often the by-product of locked gates. We walked on through suburban streets, finally reaching the footbridge over the M1 at Pilley. Walking across a motorway isn't common practice. Six roaring conveyor belts of traffic move beneath you, a huge swell of unstoppable noise. I wasn't certain which would be the worse conviction: three years' solitary confinement or the same spell on Pilley motorway footbridge.

It was already four o'clock. My body didn't want to go much further. Come to that, neither did I. As the day progressed, our 30-minute breaks became more vital, more longed-for. The footbridge took us into Birdwell, and our resting place was once again literary – a brick wall at the back of a library. No peaceful solitude, though; it was a scrap of scrubland a few yards from the busy road. On one side the chug of buses and the growing hubbub of the rush-hour build-up, on the other side the steady roar of the M1. I knew where to stop, all right.

There was, inevitably, still some cheese. I removed my footwear. Passers-by stared. I couldn't have cared less. I wondered where we could stay the night. It was impossible for us to get beyond this conurbation today. We were faced with walking through the South Yorkshire urban sprawl, where hulking miners' institutes rotted away like decaying teeth in a landscape of slow-moving canals, slag heaps and scrapyards, a blighted landscape. I was tired. I couldn't face it. Who would put us up? Where would be our sanctuary? Why was there only cheese?

One place name leapt from the map: Darfield, directly on our route. It was the home of a friend of mine, writer and broadcaster Ian McMillan. I'd made no contact thus far with anyone I knew. Propped against the brick wall on the scrubland, surrounded by traffic, with tired feet and body, the prospect of a grim urban terrain stretching away, I weakened. Sam and I would stay one night with Ian McMillan. His great humour would cheer me up. His confidence would inspire me. And maybe there'd be Heinz tomato soup. I rang him up (reverse charge, of course). No reply. He'd be out working. We'd find his house.

We were still five or six miles from Darfield. An old gadgie at his gate told us a short cut. It would mean negotiating a major new highway. But no traffic. We walked in the central lane of this highway. I let Sam off the lead. The vehicles we saw were blissfully driving on the wrong side. The bypass was as yet unopened.

Walking a spanking new highway designed for high-speed travel was surreal; there was a sense of forbidden fruit. The road builders came past in their dumper trucks, the JCBs, always on the wrong side of the road. When they reached roundabouts, they negotiated them the wrong way round. Was this some anarchic desire for illegality, some repressed urge to flout road regulations without fear of repercussions?

What would normally whizz by in a blur passed at walking speed. I was able to study the rivets in the central aluminium fencing, the small raised bumps on the hard shoulder's white border. The road itself was enjoying that short balmy spell. It was built, but not open. It could relax, stretch itself, stare at the sky. Soon this would all be gone. Traffic would thunder over it, fumes would choke it, tons of metal and rubber would press it down, render it threadbare. Its life ahead was one of grim servility.

How free we walkers were. Had we been attempting this still-unopened stretch on four wheels, vehicles with flashing lights would have pursued us and apprehended us. As walkers we progressed unhindered. At one stage I stopped and lay down in the central carriageway. We should try everything once. The drawback was that when I got up again, I realised just how tired I was. And why not? My body had carried me almost 300 miles. How much further, it was asking?

Our advance trip up the new highway left us at Womb-well, with still three miles of hang-dog urban blight before Darfield. We walked them. I enquired after Ian McMillan's house. It was a long trudge up a hill, at the top of which I stopped for a breather and to ask directions from some early-evening drinkers sitting outside a pub. I gazed longingly at the cool, fresh-looking pints. I didn't want to win the lottery, have sex with the world's most beautiful women, or travel on a punctual Virgin train. I just wanted to drink deep from one of those pints.

The amber liquid glinted and winked in the evening sunlight. I swallowed hard. That was because it was hard to swallow. First right, they said, second left . . . the light filtered through the beer. One man took a deep draught, which left a white moustache on his upper lip. Can't miss it, they said. A woman chinked the ice in her lemon and lime. Another man drank. His Adam's apple jumped up and down in delight. Thanks, I said. And we passed on.

To a shocking truth. The McMillan family were away on two weeks' holiday. I sat on the pavement outside their house. The thought of trudging on was, well, unthinkable. 'J'y suis, j'y reste,' as Cantona didn't say. I could go no further than this street. I would badger the neighbours. I did. James Hague was sympathetic, but his partner Elsie Manship was brutally honest. 'I'm sure you're genuine,' she said. 'I just couldn't have a perfect stranger staying under our roof.' I understood. Even though no one was perfect. Ian McMillan's mum lived a few doors down. 'Ian's mentioned you,' she said. 'Normally you could stay here. But my husband's sick, and the nurses are in.'

Three houses down. I was back on the pavement, hunched up into a ball. I returned to James and Elsie.

'How about your garage? I could stay there.'

'It's full of clutter,' replied James. He then added, 'I've got an idea.'

This involved a fourth house in the street, the neighbours opposite, John and Lilian Taylor. They'd got a new garage. 'You could sleep there,' said Elsie, 'and we could feed you.'

Here's how it worked out. House four offered me not a garage but a caravan, while house two gave me food and bathroom and writing space. I got a shower, chips, meat pie and veg, and a sit in front of the telly in an easy chair.

The street was post-war, semi-detached, comfortable, solid. James Hague had been a salesman, and we talked about travelling the country. We also talked films and theatre, me, him and Elsie.

Over the road the massive frame of John Taylor awaited. He was big in that special way Yorkshiremen were big, 59, just retired after 34 years with the Barnsley-based Redfern Glass. His local accent, liberally sprinkled with 'thee', 'thou' and 'thine', had an almost biblical resonance.

The caravan was comfortable. I realised once again I was out of the mainstream. Not since Clifton Kennels had I slept in a house. And even further back, to Clyst Hydon in Devon, since I'd known the inside of a bed. On the other hand, I'd not slept in a hedgerow, a shop doorway, a reception centre. No cause for complaint.

The journey from Bradwell had been long and wearisome. I rolled out and wriggled into the sleeping bag, but couldn't sleep. More of this landscape awaited us. After 16 days on the road, a sense of loneliness had crept in. I thought of my partner Kitty, my son Dylan, thought of a normal life.

And I thought of poor old Barnsley, and its Cinderella image. Ian McMillan was born and bred in the town. His liveliness, imagination and humour had done much to counter the stereotype (he'd been resident poet at Barnsley FC too). But somehow it seemed symbolic that when I studied the Michelin map again, out of all the towns, villages and cities, I could find only one example of a place name misspelt.

They'd missed the 's' out of Barnsley. And they'd done it twice.

Miles travelled so far — 313

In the sluggish canal
The new haiku
Refuses to flow

Foot Saga Finale — Sam's Mini-Crisis — A Barn for a Bed

Sleep was feverish. We'd pushed hard the previous day. I woke at 6 a.m. Through the caravan window, the copper coin of the sun quivered low in the sky. I quivered low too. My sprightly enthusiasm was gone. I wanted to stay in bed. The thing I least wanted to do was walk another 20 miles through this terrain.

We'd slogged it since Tedstone Delamere in Herefordshire. The drip-drip effect, the daily grind of finding food and shelter, of travelling 20 miles. There'd been no sex, either. My insoles needed running repairs. They were wet through with sweat, and seemed as permanently damp as my hat. I borrowed some adhesive from James to fix the insole backing. Glue and damp don't mix much.

I thought about people who had turned me away. I realised that those who had taken me in had had more open faces. Open faces, open houses. I relied on goodwill, and in modern Britain it was often in short supply. Lots of people were afraid. But of what?

Sam was sleeping a great deal. I wondered about having him checked by a vet. His pads seemed all right. I bathed his runny eye. But I knew little about dogs, and worried what effect all this was having on him. 'I'm knackered, Sam,' I said. 'How about you?'

John Taylor cooked me an English breakfast. Two hot meals in succession was a rarity, and I wondered if I was turning soft. I devoured the egg, bacon, beans, buttered bread. I gulped the mugs of tea. It was like pouring it all down a chute.

At last we were pulling away from the great Manchester octopus to our west. It was a small victory. All progress was a small victory, every stretch of road negotiated, every county boundary, every river or motorway crossed, every village passed through. All became a part of our unwinding odyssey; all were rooted forever in the great trek.

Caravans had begun to play a big part. I'd always seen them as ugly blisters on the country landscape. I'd always thought they signified a dull way of life. I'd never had much dealing with them. But then I'd stayed away from churches, too. And foxhunting. Ditto. And boy scouts. Ditto.

John Taylor had a deep voice that seemed to come up from the bottom of a pothole. It reminded me of the long-forgotten northern comedian Al Reed. John rarely looked me in the eye. Retired, still in his fifties, he was building his own garage. What did retired people do for the next quarter-century or so? Writers, who didn't really work, didn't really retire either. As the painter Lowry once said, most people were only happy when they weren't working. Artists were only happy when they were. So I must have been happy that morning in Darfield, Barnsley.

John told me that a chiropodist lived over the road. One more would make the hat-trick. It was too good an opportunity to miss, a chance to annoy a fifth house in the street in the space of about 12 hours. I knocked on his door and cheekily asked for a gratis consultation. I'd come to realise that people didn't mind honest cheek. Better than deception.

Derek Johnston gave it to me straight from the hip.

'If boots needed insoles, they'd have come provided with them.'

Right, what about the socks?

'You need proper walking socks, not those fancy purple things.'

The boots?

'Those soles and heels are too hard. The boots don't absorb enough of the impact. The originals were softer. You should have insisted on them when you had them done.'

Would I survive? Would the feet?

'Slowly get rid of the insoles. Don't go mad and you'll probably be all right.'

And he was gone. Minus fee.

John's wife Lilian, rarely glimpsed by me, had left some sandwiches. There were more from over the road at James and Elsie's. I'd been in so many houses, a farewell street party was almost in order.

John told me of some footpaths to get us towards Great Houghton, and with the sun hot and climbing, we set off. For the first time I was able to free Sam from his lead. The lead had become an umbilical cord. Its severance gave Sam freedom, but also broke the link. He zig-zagged here and there, but every few seconds he glanced back to assure himself of my continuing presence. I was better able to study him from a distance, his beautiful white and orange pelt, his tail swishing back and forth like a fly whisk, his ears hanging down like tinkers' pouches.

It was not an inspired morning's walking. The countryside had a defeated look. We passed more sluggish canals. Always there was the faint rumble of motorways which criss-crossed this terrain. At one place we came across giant earth-moving equipment scampering over a lunar landscape. More roads on the way.

At the end of the bridlepath, the direction was unclear. We'd happened on a grim-looking terrace, isolated in this emaciated landscape. I tried knocking on all doors. Ferocious dogs threw themselves at doors and windows; one large dog bounded from the back and threw itself at Sam. There were no people, only the sense of desolation, hostility. There is a thing in literature called pathetic fallacy; maybe that was me. Maybe the sense of Great Houghton as a village of soiled brick just reflected my own state.

We sat down on an area of grass off the main street. We weren't due for a stop, but so what? A large woman, with a brood of kids hanging off her like tassles, passed. I asked the way to Hemsworth as I massaged my bare feet. She had a broad Scottish accent and laughed out loud when I told her I was heading for Edinburgh. 'If yev got bad feet, laddie,' she said, 'piss in a basin and soak them in it.' I realised the importance of optimism. Stay upbeat. Things would happen. Something did happen. I picked up my backpack to find it covered in dog shit.

The busy road to Hemsworth had a grass verge which had recently been the focus of the South Yorkshire 'Let's Dump Litter' festival. A detritus of discarded Coke and beer cans, broken bottles, sweet and crisp wrappers, cigarette packets and other rubbish crunched a distinctive symphony underfoot. And while I'm being a moaning sod, a word about the public footpaths. In theory there were many. Some had been ploughed in by farmers. Elsewhere the signs stated merely 'Public Footpath', with no hint of its destination. Imagine motorists' fury to see ahead of them a huge sign stating simply 'Road'.

We walked on till midday, the sun relentless. At last we were seeing some open countryside. As if in celebration, on a bridlepath near Hemsworth we had a brilliant escort, a shimmering cloud of butterflies rainbowing the path ahead. They hovered at eye level for several moments, then curved off towards Sheffield in a whirry delight.

Sam was panting like a steam train. His tongue hung from the side of his mouth. It reminded me of grocers in the old days, showing my mum the slices of ham. Would that be enough, madam?

My bag pressed the sweat into my back. My hat was hot and damp. We were on the busy A628 and stopped under a shady tree at Ackworth. Our water was gone and Sam's panting was moving up a gear. I felt I could drink most of the Lake District without a burp. We paused at the cool-looking Ackworth Garden Centre. A row of garden fountains gushed down one aisle. Cool water gurgled up from each fountain. Sam began moving along the line. He drank his fill at the first fountain, then moved to the next. I wanted to join him. The only way was on all fours. I got down.

We moved along the line of fountains, Sam and I. We drank from about six. Customers looked at us. Staff, too. Our tums filled up with cool, clear water. Sam's capacity seemed limitless. As long as he kept going, I kept going too. I expected him to glug like a waterbed. He'd taken on more water than the *Titanic*. We left.

The temperature was well in the 80s. There was no wind. Our water bottle normally lasted all day. Now we were needing to refill it constantly, hydrate constantly. Was hydrate a word?

We headed on towards Pontefract, and I knew the sun had got to Sam. Where normally he tugged on the lead, he lagged behind. His panting was deep and painful. His eyes, normally wide and bright, looked like they'd been closed by a Mike Tyson straight left. There was no alternative but to carry him the two miles into the town, a small, panting bundle, a hot package of heat exhaustion. I put him down on the outskirts. He walked a short distance but then simply came to a halt under a shady tree. He looked up at me. No more, Pete. Please, no more.

We pitched temporary camp. I fed Sam several caps full of water and some apple from Darfield. It was a busy piece of road opposite a garage, but no matter. I removed my boots and socks and made a pillow of my bag. Sam was an overheated engine. He needed to chill out; the thermometer needed to drop. Half an hour in the shade and his laboured breathing had ceased, his eyes had come back. 'We're past the hottest part, Sam,' I said. 'That old sun has done its worst today.'

And fortune smiled on us at the Shell garage opposite, where we went for water refills. The cheerful assistant asked where we were going. I told her. She shouted over to the van driver buying petrol.

'You're passing the A1, aren't you?'

'Well, yes, I am. Why?' asked the young driver.

'Drop these two off. They deserve it.' And she burst out laughing. The driver had no option. As we drove away, I yelled from the window, 'What's your name?'

'Jenny Duggan,' she yelled back.

'I'm writing a book, Jenny Duggan, and you'll be in it!' I shouted.

'Just make sure you get to Edinburgh!' she yelled back, and waved as we pulled away.

The lift was doubly good. It took us three miles through an urban landscape (Pontefract), and we passed another landmark. We were in North Yorkshire, after which came the north-east. After which came Scotland. Said like that, it sounded easy. One more thing. The lift whizzed us across the M62 – one more motorway bit the dust.

We jumped out at the A1 slip road. Much of my history could be plotted via this road. Its whole length was soaked in association. Most of the people I knew lived near it: family, friends, lovers past and present. Ask me to name people near main roads and I'd offer a meagre few. They were scattered along the A1 like flies on sticky paper. Name a junction; I could go off and have a cup of tea with someone.

But I'd never walked next to it. It felt almost embarrassing to be on such intimate terms. I was used to whizzing past at high speed. I was overcome, like waiting in a crowd to see a celebrity hurry past. The celebrity pauses and talks to you. It's all too close, too sudden. That was me and the A1.

Sam and I passed along in this state of embarrassed intimacy, past the giant cooling towers. Two miles we walked, in a car not even time for a CD track. For us, 40 minutes. We left on the Brotherton slip road, crossed a bridge and picked up the A162, which slowly diverged from the A1 like two open scissor blades. It was 14 miles to Tadcaster, a town we wouldn't be seeing that day.

It had been a mixed day. Good for food, dodgy for liquid. I was grateful that the sun was easing itself down towards its hidden armchair. Sam had weathered the crisis, his sagging mouth firmed up, his eyes much wider, his walk almost returned to its normal jauntiness. We walked on, the thrum of the A1 slowly weakening.

Early evening, we reached the A63 crossroads. Running alongside was a string of pleasant-looking suburban houses, plonked down on this great flat plain of York. Even at that moment, I told myself, they were all getting excited at the prospect of an itinerant arriving unannounced. Which would be the lucky one? I knocked at a bungalow. A young woman suggested I tried Lodge Farm, a quarter of a mile west.

The farm stood on a lowish ridge, with a long, gently rising drive. On the drive I passed horses, sheep, ranch-like fences. The cluster of farm buildings offered no people. Nor the large yard. There was a tractor. More livestock. No people. At the farm's rear, half-hidden behind an encircling stone wall, was a large, three-storey country house. At the front, in a small plot of land, an incongruity: a bungalow that belonged not here, but up a suburban cul-de-sac with a branded wooden sign outside saying Shangri-La. Next to the bungalow was a 30-foot-high barn with pointed roof. Its open front had layers of hay and fine views down to the road. I wanted to sleep in that barn. I wanted to wake in the hay, preferably with the sound of a cockerel. There might be warm, new-laid eggs close by, the clucking of hens.

I checked the bungalow. No people. I went to the barn and climbed up several 'steps' of hay with Sam. In my bag were two black bin liners. I stretched these out and removed the articles from my bag. Muriel's butter, now in a container, had turned to custard. Its dripping grease had blessed various items of clothing. A small pool of grease gathered at the bottom of the bag. I was not pleased but Sam was. Melted butter seemed his favourite dish. He licked everything: brolly, camera, socks. He licked up the pool in the bag. He licked the container itself. Had I taken the top off, he would have licked the whole thing dry. A dog and butter? While Sam licked, I ate. It was cheese. Our Darfield food supplies had now gone. We were left with the predictable mix – dog biscuits and cheese. And one apple.

After this cleaning and eating, I wrote, my first-ever 1,000 words penned in a hay barn. Then I stretched out and gazed at the open landscape, the vast sky whose blue was slowly darkening. Only one thing was wrong. The hay was not the soft, springy stuff I remembered; it was packed tight into giant bricks, and about as flexible. Sharp bits protruded and went in the wrong places. Had the combine harvester done for frolicking? And where was the farmer? Would he return any moment with cart-loads of more hay bricks? Would he chuck me out? I stretched myself on the bin bag and fell asleep.

I was woken 15 minutes later by the suburban sound of a lawnmower. A youngish woman was mowing the Shangri-La lawn and looked slightly knocked back to see me emerge from the barn. Have you noticed how quiet it goes when a lawnmower stops? Or a vacuum cleaner? It's a soft, marsh-mallow-type silence, and it lasts just a few seconds before normality is restored. I felt it at that moment when the woman stopped mowing.

'I was just resting up,' I said, and told her of my journey. 'I was wondering if I could sleep there. I'm quite safe and carry no matches.' I spread my arms to affirm my safety standard rating.

The woman looked me up and down, like you might a rug in a sale. 'I'll have to phone the farmer,' she said. 'We just rent.'

'I'll be in the barn, then,' I said, and returned to the lair. It was eight o'clock when I heard more voices. She'd been joined by her husband. The woman's name was Jennifer Ballantyne. Her husband, a maintenance engineer at Leeds University, was Ian. The farmer, a Godot-type figure who never appeared, had said okay.

I was invited in for a cup of tea. Then I was offered sand-wiches. Not long after that pork and beans appeared. Soon after that my washing was whirring around in the machine. Soon after that Ian and I were on the Internet. And I was a happier bunny.

'This is a lovely spot,' I said.

'We're moving to New Zealand,' said Ian. It always seemed strange to me, people moving halfway round the world, but lots did. 'There's nothing left for us here,' he added. Via the Internet they'd tracked down every emigré from Hawick (his home town) to New Zealand over the last ten years. Thousands of miles to find people from Hawick?

The move had problems. Daughter Kerry, 18, wanted to stay put. It was unresolved.

'What's the name of your books?' asked Ian at his computer screen. His search engine, Yahoo, failed to find any of my obscure publications. It failed to find me in lists of poets. It failed to find my work in newspapers. 'You are a writer, aren't you?' asked Jennifer. We all laughed. A few minutes later she said, 'I thought you had no money?' and held up a shiny ten pence piece found in my combat trousers before washing. I remembered. I'd scrounged it in a shop for a phone that wouldn't make reverse-charge calls. My son Dylan hadn't been in, by which time the donor had gone. We all laughed again. It was like that film *A Shadow of a Doubt*. I could never be absolutely certain that people trusted me. Just as they could never be certain whether they should.

At 10 p.m., after a whizz round the web sites, with trousers, T-shirts, socks and pants washed and dried, I walked back to the barn. Ian and Jennifer trusted me enough to invite me for porridge the next morning.

At last, in the dark of the barn, I had a chance to use the journey's white elephant – the head torch. I slid into the sleeping bag and pulled the elastic fitting over my bonce. I swished the beam of light this way and that like Luke Skywalker. I read several pages of my diary. I sought further justification for bringing it by shining the beam out of the barn to check the possible approach of wild, rabid animals. There was also the matter of the barn roof, where poisonous spiders might just have been waiting to swoop. All these vital tasks the torch was able to complete. Sam lay on the hay and ignored it.

Below, half a mile down the slope, the occasional pin-prick of light indicated a car on the road. I stretched out on the hard hay and slept fitfully. At three in the morning Sam decided on a spot of loud barking. This triggered the sheep off into orchestrated bleating.

For all that, I would not have missed the first night sleeping in a barn since my feckless youth.

Miles travelled so far — 333

Pursuing the horizon ahead
Behind us another
Is keeping pace

A Walking Machine — Mortimer Fan Club — Pavilion of Dreams

I was waking ever earlier. Five o'clock, for heaven's sake! The beautiful pale dawn viewed from the barn was turning from salmon pink to eggshell blue. The two giant trees were murmuring to one another in the breeze. The sky was clamped down like a giant lid.

In another two hours a lot of people would wake and begin worrying about their jobs, their marriages and growing old. I felt great. Five a.m. Sam and I got up and walked down to Shangri-La. Ian was feeding a horse called Norman through the fence.

His porridge was ace. He seemed embarrassed to be doing the cooking. He was tall, fit-looking, shaven-headed. Jennifer had long, thick, auburn hair and an open, attractive face. Their big move-to-come padded after their thoughts all the time. 'You've got to give it a go, haven't you?' he asked.

'I was scared about doing this,' I said. 'Being scared is often a good sign. Means you're not in a rut. Part of me still is scared.'

Ian asked how many words I'd written in the diary. About 36,000.

'Blimey,' he said. 'I could never do that. I haven't written a letter in 20 years.'

'Well, I'm no good at engineering,' I said. We ate the porridge.

Jennifer said, 'Anyway, New Zealand is only one day from England by plane.'

165

'Yes,' I said, 'and Edinburgh is only one month from Plymouth by foot.'

I must confess I felt quite pleased at having come up with that.

They offered me a shower and gave me some sandwiches. I would be on the road by 6.45 a.m. I checked the hay barn carefully, and packed all my belongings. And I cast off one set of the cushioned insoles – a major moment. My feet were slowly hardening, becoming self-sufficient. I could still feel the layers of dead skin, like foam, but the crisis was over. They were on the upwards part of the cycle. Suddenly I loved my feet.

We took our leave of Ian and Jennifer. In contrast to the previous morning, my spirits were high. With Sam in tow, I strode out through the open, flat landscape of the Vale of York. I was strong, fit, lean, fast. I could walk forever. How could I possibly have felt so drained? How could I have contemplated packing in? The very idea! Everything was fine. It was brilliant. My strides were ten yards at least. I was walking at the speed of light. Nothing could stop me.

Except the small village of Barkston Ash, which we reached after 90 minutes. We had walked five miles while many people had yet to struggle from their pit. The weather was overcast and it was coming on to rain. This didn't matter a jot. I sat barefoot at the roadside, Sam by my side, the brolly propped up above us. I had a small sandwich. Sam had a doggy chew. We slept. On the next stint, a rabbit popped up in front of us like bread from a toaster. Sam almost jerked my arm from its socket. Cuddly wee chap that he was, I realised he'd have torn its throat out.

We walked through Towton, with its rows of stone-faced houses masquerading as all stone. The Rockingham Arms bore the sign 'The Best Fish and Chips in the World' – with the word 'probably' written small. On the village noticeboard was an announcement that a ginger cat had been found, 'very friendly and noisy'. Not many cats were noisy.

We were now north of Leeds – no major cities in our path. York lay to the east. If we tacked west we would also leave to the east the large conurbations of Teesside and Tyneside. Unlike in the urban sprawl of the Midlands, our need to duck 'n' dive was minimal. The rain stopped, replaced by a fresh breeze. After the previous day's heat, this was the bee's knees.

I'd checked Sam. He looked fine. As I was to discover, he wasn't.

It was a long haul up the A162 to Tadcaster. On the outskirts, two fit-looking 'mature' walkers approached. They were as lean as string beans. Every Wednesday for 20 years Brian Crapper and Alvin Bell from Selby had stridden out on long Yorkshire walks. They'd lost a certain footpath. Did I know it? They were doing a 12-mile walk. How far was I going? More than five hundred miles. Gosh!

They were astonished. So astonished they returned five minutes later and took a photo. So astonished they came back a third time as I sat against a tree in the John Smith brewery carpark. This time they kindly gave me a sandwich and folded out their OS map to show me a public-footpath short cut. How I'd have loved to have carried OS maps. But I'd have needed a trailer.

All day the rain was to come and go, unable to decide what it wanted. We walked through Tadcaster town. It was famous because of its brewery, and the brewery knew of this status. Which is why it stood in sturdy northern dominance. And why it had the outrageous cheek to embrace within this dominant northern architecture a chimney which could easily have been a minaret in Samarkand. And, what's more, it got away with it.

We passed through the town and up on a minor road towards Wighill. We were suddenly on silent, deserted country lanes dotted with cool, clear puddles, through which Sam walked and from which he often drank. His drinking was accompanied by extraordinary noises twice the size of him, like a snorkel diver testing the equipment in shallow water. These gurgles, followed by the act of drinking itself, lasted several seconds. Sam seemed oblivious to the fact he was making them.

The landscape was now steam-iron flat. Vast cornfields stretched away, surfaces as smooth as yellow baize. The crops looked plump, ready for harvest. After another stop at Healaugh Grange, we left the road for our friends' footpath. Soon we were plunging waist deep through a field of corn. My waist, that is. Sam became merely a rustle somewhere at my feet.

Few people had travelled to Edinburgh this way. We'd stayed east of the A1 to avoid the gravitational pull of Leeds and Bradford. Now we needed to box clever and recross the same road before it nudged us towards Teesside and Tyneside. By the time the A1 became the A1M we would be west of it. We had crossed the final motorway. Zig-zag about in Northumberland as much as you like, you'd be in no danger. Rare among English counties, it was totally motorway-free. But Northumberland was still a good way ahead.

We endured our corn capers and rejoined the road. At a crossroads, we came on a small habitation called Bilton. Bilton was inhabited entirely by ghosts. There was no sign of life in any of the houses clustered around this crossing. I checked all the doorbells (a man has to pass the time some way). Many were cobwebbed over. The entire (albeit small) population of Bilton had been abducted by aliens, and no one had noticed! They'd had the humans. I decided they wouldn't get the apples. I scrumped about a dozen from a garden. They were green and small and hard, and were later to exact revenge.

This was to be an 11-hour, 24-mile day. Such statistics would have been unthinkable 18 days previously in Plymouth. I was a different creature. The Plymouth Mortimer belonged to another species entirely. Inferior, of course.

We crossed the B1224, heading up towards Green Hammerton junction. I'd looked at the map. The village of Whixley seemed a natural stopping place. I liked places with an 'x' in their name. Apparently there are five football teams in the English league thus blessed. Do you know them? Before Whixley there was a small event of no significance to anyone except myself. For the first time in more than 300 miles and 18 days we walked over a railway crossing, at Lattal.

Some places on the journey seemed wrong. Whixley, despite its 'x', was among them. I asked about shelter at various places, without any luck. One person suggested the pub. It was shut. Another didn't open the door. One woman appeared at her upstairs window and said slightly sniffily, 'I don't think people do that kind of thing round here.' At the main bus stop, a gang of teenagers slouched about in baseball caps and trainers. They gave Sam and me some lip, which decided it. Whixley was not for us.

Except it was. In a way. It was already later than our normal stopping time, but we pushed on. A mile from the village, my anxiety meter began to tick. I needed to get settled, a place to write and sleep. The later the hour, the louder the tick.

We passed a rather fine cricket ground. The pitch was encircled by a fence, and close to the road was a blue and white wooden pavilion. What I especially noticed was the side door. It was ajar. This was Whixley Cricket Club. I had not been inside a village cricket pavilion for more than 20 years. I pushed open the door. The pavilion was deserted, with that strange mixture such places have – partly impersonal, partly home-spun friendliness.

There were two changing-rooms, home and away, a scoring box, complete with the number tiles, a main social room with sink and running (cold) water, and some benches. On the wall ten stumps were racked up, and on a row of hooks in the home changing-room hung a huddle of umpires' white coats. On the table in the main social room was a four-pint plastic container of milk, which slowly, and without fuss, was turning to butter. I found some teabags, but no way of heating water. There were some mugs and a bottle of that sickly orange juice you diluted.

The pavilion walls were thin wood only. We had shelter, frugal though it was. There was a large, flat table where I could write my diary while the light was still good. There was no electricity. Our strange list of sleeping places would now include a cricket ground. There were three outer doors, and none of them was secured. In Whixley, all doors had been closed to us. At their cricket club, all were open.

By the time I'd written the diary, Sam was already fast asleep. It was only 7.30 p.m. What if someone came along? What excuse did I have? Turning up for net practice? In an urban area, an unlocked cricket pavilion would have been stripped bare in days. They'd have had the lot: bails, coats, rancid milk, sickly orange juice. Here it was untouched.

I needed to sort out bedding. Rolled up under a long trestle table I found a bulky length of coconut matting, some sort of surrogate pitch. I dragged this heavy item into the rear room (which I'd worked out was the warmest, given prevailing winds), releasing as I did so a million spiders and beetles. I folded up the umpires' coats for a pillow.

Inside the pockets were sets of bails, plus sets of counting stones to mark each over. This small discovery touched me. I turned the bails and stones over in my hand. They symbolised a sports world galaxies away from the one we were increasingly exposed to. I thought of the umpires at these games, solid, trustworthy men with large red faces and stout midriffs.

The pavilion itself was also far from the new culture. Its atmosphere was more Corinthian than Sky Sports. Probably they had jumble sales, fundraising events. With a bit of luck their efforts would raise a thousand quid, or just over one hour's work for some Premiership football players.

I laid the black bin liners on top of the matting to discourage the creepy-crawlies, and laid the sleeping bag on top. Plumping up my 'pillow' was only partly successful. There were no towels, but I rooted out a small tea towel to do the job. As I opened my toilet bag, the strong whiff of peppermint revealed a tube of toothpaste improperly fastened, with smears of green mint liberally spread about.

The light was beginning to fade as I laid into my meagre rations: one small sandwich, plus a scrumped apple or two, all washed down with the sickly orange juice. Had it not been for my rambler friends, there would have been no sandwich – the ones from Jenny Ballantyne had gone much earlier.

The pavilion was growing cold, and my body had sent an urgent memo for some hot food. By eight o'clock both Sam and I were in the sleeping bag and involved in the little-known spectator sport of watching the sky grow dark. The wooden building gave the occasional creak as the sky's turquoise blackened. The odd car passed on the road, and on the table in the main room the sour milk thickened just that little bit more.

My wild, optimistic mood of the morning had been tempered somewhat. Sam was asleep. Dreaming of what? In my own case, the shortest odds were on mince and dumplings.

Day Nineteen — Thursday, 13 August

Miles travelled so far — 357

On the pavilion board
Easily reached
A record score

Cheesed Off — Walking Alone — Keeping it Cool

In the middle of the night I woke with a start. Sam and I had been rumbled! A bright light was shining directly through the window.

I knew what it was. SAS searchlights. The place was surrounded. Any moment the loudhailer would say, 'Step outside the building with your hands in the air! The place is surrounded!'

Whixley did not take kindly to illegal invasions of its cricket pavilion.

I sat up in bed. Resistance was obviously useless. I looked out.

Someone had hung the brightest, shiniest, biggest moon

I'd ever seen right outside the window, then fitted an extra bulb. It bathed the entire room in tinfoil. No SAS.

I tried to snuggle back down. The pavilion was cold. Possibly no one had ever been in it at 2.45 a.m. Despite the coconut matting, the surface was hard. No position remained comfortable for more than 15 minutes; there was a need to reposition regularly. And Sam was in need of affection. I pulled him closer to me in the bag and whispered in his little pink ear. I felt his heart beat. It was like the beat of a moth's wing. The pavilion creaked and groaned and, like me, waited for the first rays of dawn. It probably creaked and groaned every night and had long given up hope of an audience.

By the time I dragged my body from the bag at six o'clock, my mood was downbeat. I was truly Dr Fickle. The spirits on this trip went up and down quicker than a trampolinist. I felt alienated, devoid of human contact and warmth. I felt sorry for myself. Cold, hungry – and a breakfast of rancid cheese. I wanted to get up, set off. Walk into a pub when I wanted to. Buy a hot pie when I wanted to. What did a proper bed feel like? Crisp sheets, warm blankets, clean pillows?

I stood up in the middle of the pavilion and in a loud voice said, 'Just stop bloody moaning!' I sat at the table. There was still a small segment of sandwich to accompany the rancid cheese. Two small sour apples. Sickly orange juice. That was a four-course meal, for heaven's sake. And hadn't I had a hot drink at Lodge Farm, only 24 hours previously?

Possibly what I needed was simply to stay still. But not in a draughty cricket pavilion. Maybe Sam needed to stay still too. The wee fellow looked tired. His mouth hung open in the way mouths do when their owners are plumb tuckered.

I dragged the coconut matting back to its original location. I put everything as I had found it. I gave Sam his vitamin pill and massaged his feet. My feelings towards the pavilion were ambivalent. It had been a cold night, but the pavilion had beckoned us in from the road and offered us shelter. Also it seemed to represent something that was important. The pavilion breathed the very love of cricket. On the wall was a yellowing press cutting, undated. It told how Captain Stuart Witham had scored a record 185 for Whixley. I went into the score room. For a few moments I handled the numbered tiles that the scorer would hang on hooks.

By seven o'clock we were back on the road. And I was talking to Sam. 'We need to take time out, Sam. We need human contact. Oh, we need, Sam, we need!'

Walking on the bobbly, tufted verges, we headed up towards Boroughbridge on the B6265. We were in the face of a strong breeze. At our first resting place I propped myself up under a tree and drifted away for a quick dream about Typhoo teabags. Actually I didn't. Dream, that is.

We'd walked about six miles and passed Marton on our left when we came across an attractive gatehouse. Sometimes I just saw a place and rang the bell. I saw this one. And rang the bell. What I really wanted was an attractive, sympathetic woman to invite us in and give us hot tea and hot buttered toast. In this case, that is exactly what we got. Her name was Eleanor Hewitt. She was as welcome to me as a blood bank to a vampire. I spread myself on her large, soft settee, nodded to tea, nodded to hot toast and raspberry jam. Sam nodded to a giant bowl of dog food. It was a big stone house, and would I like to meet six-year-old Greg, who was himself a nifty writer? I nodded. How about Essie, the springer spaniel/Border terrier? Bring them on! Bring them all on!

In this house, over a spell of 25 minutes, I renewed my membership of the human race. I would be one of those 'before and after' examples. Walking in through the front door, hang-dog, dispirited, slumped shoulders. Walking out, zappy, wappy, dappy, and a spring in my step – boing!

And it wasn't just the tea and toast. Eleanor had friends further north on my route. Would I like their addresses for possible shelter? They lived in houses. With beds! I grew giddy at simple thoughts, like an easy chair, a carpet, a bed-side light. Had I not been so English I would have cuddled Eleanor Hewitt from sheer joy.

A transformed man walked on. I smacked my lips. The raspberry still lingered. The hot tea had pulsed through my body. Depressed, me?

My abortive attempt to stay with Ian McMillan had stiffened my resolve. All my night stops would be with total strangers; there would be no easy options. But I realised in Boroughbridge that I would walk past the front door of some old friends, Tim and Jude Tribe. For two miles I became, in turn, defence and prosecuting counsels.

PROS: M'lud, I put it to you, this is a case of cronyism, an old pals' act. Another case of not what you know, but who you know. Mortimer is shamelessly exploiting his contacts to take the easy option. Make him fight for every stop, I say.

DEF: M'lud, we are not asking here for overnight shelter. My client wishes merely to call on and say hello to old friends. Not to do so when he passes their front door would appear rude in the extreme. Does my client not deserve this small bonus?

JUDGE: I rule in favour of the defence counsel.

The Tribes' old stone house was bang in the middle of Boroughbridge but had managed to nick down a small lane, scurry round a corner and make itself totally secluded.

They weren't in. The door was answered by son-in-law Jamie Wright, a naval medical officer visiting with his wife Verity and their two young children.

I was just passing, I said, on a 500-mile walk. Can I come in?

Who told you to do it, he said (the military mind). He'd once been dumped in the Arctic on a survival mission.

No one, I said.

He gave me some tea. His daughter Poppy was instantly attracted to Sam and helped give him a bath. We dried him with fluffy towels and he turned into one.

There followed an important piece of serendipity. Jamie was reading Homer's *Odyssey*. I flicked through the pages, reviving the power it had held over me first time around. How was I to know that those few moments would influence my entire, well, er, odyssey?

When Jude and daughter Verity returned, my journey was to take a significant shift. Jude, with years of medical training, looked at Sam and said, 'That eye isn't right.' She took a closer look. 'That eye needs seeing to,' she added, and then, 'There's a vet next door.' How lucky I'd been on my trip. Chiropodists and vets were always next door, up the street, ready and waiting.

Enter Christine McCormack. Her verdict was damning. Sam had developed an ulcer in his eye, with a membrane growing across (later evidence suggested insecticide from the waist-high cornfield). He was also totally exhausted. Sam shouldn't go another foot. And right there and then, fresh from his bath in Boroughbridge, Sam's odyssey was finished.

I looked at him. He looked back. Guilt consumed me. I'd cleaned his eye regularly, massaged his little legs, popped his pill, checked his pads. And turned him into an exhausted wreck. 'I can give ointment for his eye,' said Christine, 'but he needs a lot of rest, now.'

I wasn't only guilty. Part of me was envious. Sam could stop, put up his feet. Sam could go home. No one would point a finger at Sam. Sam has done great. Well done, Sam. And me? I had to go on. Samless. I looked at Sam and wanted to be him. I wanted to sit here and, like Sam, wait for owner Sarah Davidson to drive down from Tyneside and pick me up.

The sensation was brief. I slapped myself and pulled myself together.

Great Sam. His wee legs had carried him 370 miles. He'd waddled on, day in, day out. King Charles spaniels were not the world's greatest canine explorers. They didn't pull sleds, rescue snowbound mountaineers, go on expeditions. Many just snoozed in front of fires. Cheer for Sam.

Three chiropodists and one vet down. How many more good-natured professionals would be called upon to waive their fee?

I made arrangements for Sam's return. It was an end to something. I'd known this journey only with Sam. I'd not gone to sleep without Sam, woken without Sam, walked without Sam. I'd talked endlessly to Sam. I'd won most of my arguments with Sam. Sam had been a focal point with people I met. My arm muscles were flexed to counter Sam's lead tugging.

The Sam saga had seen me more than two hours in Boroughbridge and behind schedule if I was to make Eleanor Hewitt's friends at West Tanfield.

'I'll give you a lift,' said Jude.

I stood staring at Sam on the settee.

'Just go,' said Jude. 'That's the best way.'

I just went.

Jude ran me up close to Ripon. Only when I got out of the car, waved her off and began to walk up the A6108 did the realisation hit me. I was walking alone. Yet I was lucky. What if Sam had fallen sick 200 miles further south? What if there had been no vet nearby, no Jude Tribe to spot the eye?

With no Sam to talk to, my thoughts turned elsewhere. I kept thinking of Homer's *Odyssey*. His journey had been longer. He'd faced mythological beasts not common on the B6265. And he'd had someone else to write the book.

But I had decided in advance to call my journey an odyssey. I'd met someone reading the *Odyssey*. And in the book Odysseus (or Ulysses, as the Greeks called him) had found himself in all sorts of scrapes. Usually the fates, gods, or what you will, had protected him. He'd come good against one-eyed monsters, seductive sirens, storms at sea, enchant-resses. They'd looked after him because of his own courage. I realised how often fate had been on my side. Meeting Geoffrey Boucher in Tavistock when I was ready to quit, David and Teresa in Ilminster, who'd persuaded me to rest. Knocking on a door in Shaw and finding chiropodist Sheila Carter behind it, with vital consequences for my feet. Happening on a Boroughbridge vet at just the right time.

Sometimes journeying from Troy to Ithaca, Odysseus had been punished by the fates when he'd been impatient or plain daft. Mainly, though, they'd protected him. It may sound whacky to you sitting in your armchair, but the road to West Tanfield suddenly had Damascus potential. I'd had the courage to attempt this journey. So the fates were looking after me. I suddenly felt a huge link to Odysseus. I was a junior partner, if you like. It wasn't religion. But suddenly I felt less alone on the journey.

This wasn't relevant in normal life. Don't go down to the corner shop for a jar of marmalade and expect the fates to watch over you. Do something extreme, push yourself to the edge. The fates weren't interested in the mundane. And I'd had small punishments too. I'd been impatient, plain daft. If this all sounds like tosh, I can only say do it. Something that pushes you to the edge. Find out. I had lost a dog. And found the fates.

I turned to the next page of the Michelin map book. And look! In the top corner, the southern reaches of Tyneside. My home. The fates were also helping me adapt to my Samless state, giving me a diversion. Yet so used was I to having Sam at my side, I almost expected passing motorists to slow down and shout from the window, 'Where's the dog, then?'

I passed the tidy village of North Stainley with its idyllic but strangely duckless pond. Jude Tribe had topped up my meagre food rations and on the next stop I had the luxury of an entire sandwich, plus a lump of cake. I woke and, in the first moment's panic, thought, where's Sam? Oh, yes. Forgot.

My mood ebbed and flowed. Elation. Sadness. Strength of mind. Loneliness. Finally I (and I realise I was so used to writing 'we') reached the village of West Tanfield, which spanned the River Ure.

Eleanor Hewitt had given me two addresses. Alison and Andie Gruber lived in a gloriously cluttered Victorian terraced house. I mean cluttered, too – furniture, animals, kids. Dogs, cats, rabbits, hamsters, two of their own children and seemingly a hundred or so they fostered. I arrived in the rain, managed to squeeze past various human and non-human species to a seat in the kitchen and watched Alison cook some sausages.

'I'd put you up,' said Alison, 'but Andie goes on night shift. People would talk.'

I was rather attracted to the idea of people talking.

Andie worked at RAF Leeming. And the sausages were for me.

'And you're travelling with no money?' asked Alison. I nodded.

'So everyone else supports you, and you just take the money from the book?' said Andie. I nodded again. Lovely sausages. Jimmy the cat looked up at me. Chester the collie rubbed its fur against my leg.

Their young son Tom directed me through the allotments to option two, Prospect House. We arrived at the back door. It was 300 years old and was owned by Dawn and Jedd Coul. Jedd opened the door in a pair of baggy shorts he must have nicked off Don Estelle.

Prospect House offered good and bad news. 'We can put you up,' said Jedd (good). 'Sleep in the garage' (bad).

I could see over his shoulder. Prospect House itself looked enticing, a real, well, prospect. He led me down the path and into the windowless garage. It was like a removal firm's storage area.

'Where would I lay my sleeping bag?' I asked.

'I'll clear a space,' said Jedd. I got my first glimpse of the floor.

'I have to write up my diary somewhere,' I said.

Jedd set to again, hacking his way through the jungle. Another small space appeared, into which he put a small table and chair. Jedd went. I turned slightly to one side and knocked something over. I was in a well-stocked junk shop, an in-transit furniture van. It was 7 p.m. I wondered if I was in here for 12 hours.

Let me tell you where Jedd went. To clear a large field of horse shit in preparation for the school sports day the next morning. Let me tell you what he found when he eventually returned from the long session of shit-shovelling. He found the writer he'd left for the night in the windowless garage sitting drinking with his wife in his lounge, in his house. And the writer was to sleep in that house.

Dawn had come into the garage while I was clearing space to enable my writing arm to move through 20 degrees. She looked around and said, 'You can't stay in here! Come up to the house and have something to eat. And I'll clear the spare room for you. You can sleep there.'

And so I entered Prospect House, with its spacious kitchen. Dawn led me along the upstairs corridor with its beams and its creaking floors and threw open a door to reveal a delicious-looking bed, plump pillows, crisp sheets, a duvet. 'Have a shower,' said Dawn. The hot soapy water ran all over me. I rubbed myself with things that smelt nice. I emerged pink and clean. She fed me with piping hot lasagne.

'I need somewhere to write up my diary,' I said. She took me to a quiet back room, a table covered with a rust-coloured chenille cloth. What a day of changing circum-stances and moods this had been. My pen flowed easily across the page. Dawn brought me coffee. I drank it and thought of Sam.

The news from Boroughbridge was that Sarah Davidson had already picked up Sam. He was back home. I thought of him whizzing back up north, on some roads he would have walked with me. Sitting on the car's back seat. He was, apparently, making a good recovery.

How peaceful and beautiful this cottage was, its low oak beams, its large, airy rooms. Dawn and Jedd were both teachers. Each morning Dawn drove 45 miles in one direction, Jedd 37 miles in the other. Then back in the evening. I thought of those perpetual motion magnets. Together. Apart. Together. Apart. Dawn was expecting their third child, but also expecting redundancy any time from her Ilkley school.

The kitchen had a large table which could have doubled as a tennis court. Eight chairs were spread around it, and in the centre a jar of giant sunflowers threw open their arms. A large Aga quietly hummed its mantra. The doors and ceiling were natural slatted wood. The kitchen had three doors, one as wide as a motorway. Previous owners had built an ugly rear extension minutes before the building was declared listed. Their Herculean labour was in restoring it.

Dawn Coul. I found myself saying the name many times over. It had great serenity. Dawn Coul.

And so my glass of wine. A glass of wine would be no great shakes to most people. At that moment, sitting on a soft settee, clean, fed, the memory of my rancid cheese meal in the draughty cricket pavilion still fresh, it was Nirvana. I felt the cool glass in my hand, the chilled fruitiness in my mouth.

I needed my nightly foot massage, an activity which fascinated Dawn and Jedd's six-year-old daughter Rosie. She stared hard as I gently rubbed the oil into my feet. Could she do it to her feet? She'd no sooner done it than she shoved her feet into my sandals and stomped around the room shouting, 'It works!' Soon afterwards she went to bed, Jedd returned from his dung shifting and I raised my glass to him. Cheers!

And who was I, I suddenly thought. Just one bloke, travelling the length of the country with no loot. And what did that mean? It could mean sleeping on cold concrete, or sitting on a soft settee with a glass of wine.

During much of my time in Prospect House, I instinctively looked round to check on Sam. His absence came and went, like a toothache. It was eleven o'clock when I went to bed – late for this trip. Sitting up in the plum bed, I read the daily newspapers. I was normally a newspaper addict. How out of touch I was on world events. My universe was a line of arrows heading north.

One small piece of history made its mark. I discovered that my niece Hannah had on this day given birth to a baby girl called Chloe. Baby, mother and father Martin were doing well, and here, on this strung-out marathon trek through Britain, I'd become a great-uncle.

Miles travelled so far — 376

Staying close to my heel
Nothing now but
My shadow

Squirearchy Rules — The Army's in Town — Getting the Bird

What delight could compare with waking in the small hours with a severe attack of diarrhoea? For a man of iron guts, it was almost unknown, but then I realised it was due to the excessive number of scrumped Bilton apples I'd consumed. Those aliens were getting even. What would be their next move?

In the morning I rose again, less urgently. In the soft luxury of Prospect House's bathroom, I opened my washbag. The first thing I pulled out was Sam's little bottle of vitamin pills.

The moment threw me. I unscrewed the top and took out and handled the pills which Sarah Davidson had broken into small pieces. I pictured Sam, his head up, as twice daily I popped him his rations. A huge black space took up residence inside me. Nothing would affect me as much regarding Sam's absence as that unexpected sight of his pills. I had to make some small gesture. I ate one of the pills, then put them back in the bag.

'He travels fastest who travels alone.' I'd forgotten who'd said that but knew my walking speed would probably now increase minus Sam and his meanderings. The increase would be marginal, though. Compared to the way most people get from A to B, my own speed was laughable. So what? Where were they all going? Why hurtle around in tin boxes? I had never much been a car freak, and had not owned one for many years. I preferred life without, and found all that male talk about gearboxes, reconditioned engines and torque wrenches bafflingly uninteresting.

But my alienation from the car had grown more extreme on this trip. From this perspective, the car culture seemed a blind one. Economic forces were pushing it, but towards some kind of oblivion. Vested interests ensured ever more cars came off the production line and onto the jammed roads. People were knighted for manufacturing them, whereas they should have been beheaded. Cars had to be tamed. Reined in. They damaged us in more ways than we knew. We were addicted. It was sad.

I hadn't seen much of West Tanfield, said to be 'steeped in history'. Anything steeped was either history or false teeth. Just as anything desiccated was coconut. The village was a squirearchy. The pub, the bistro, the shops, the garage and many houses belonged to one man, Chris Bourne-Arton, who himself lived in the village. My own philosophy was the less you owned, the better.

Understandably, there were few 'For Sale' signs. Plenty of other facilities, though. The village radiated out from the central roundabout alongside the river. It boasted a post office, a gunsmith, two churches, a furniture-maker, a large village hall, a bowling green, tennis courts and a 1350 Marmion tower, a gateway to a long-disappeared manor house described as 'a haule of squaried stone'. I looked up that word 'squaried' in my two-volume *OED*. No sign of it. The tower was a fraud. A good fraud, though. In 1513 Catherine Parr's granny had owned it. It had fooled people down the centuries.

I ambled around the village before breakfast. As I walked back, a van pulled out of a back lane. Staring from the rear window were two King Charles spaniels. The double pain.

Back at Prospect House, I asked Jedd whether we were yet in the north-east. He spluttered into his Chivers. 'Certainly not! The north-east starts at Stokesley! This is North Yorkshire!'

West Tanfield was affluent, well ordered. It could have featured in some of those rural escapist advertisements. There were some problems, though. His lordship – as it were – had recently turned one of the two pubs into a bistro, leaving the locals, now unable to nip in for a quick 'un, a bit miffed.

I sat close to the great warm beast of the Aga for breakfast and prepared for my first full Samless day. Rosie challenged me to a game of knuckles. She looked at my backpack, now ready for the road. Could she pick it up? She tried. No luck. As I was about to leave, she gave me a parting gift – a Rockie chocolate bar. All children on my odyssey made a big impression. What impression did I leave on them?

West Tanfield had pampered me. I'd lost Sam but my fortunes in other ways had improved. And there was more. Tim and Jude Tribe had said on the phone they'd like to drive up and buy me a couple of pints, some pub grub. Where would I be the next evening?

I had no idea. I'd phone. Reverse charge.

Dawn gave me some miniature chocolate bars. These would prove a godsend in the days to come. Also sandwiches. In the bathroom, I stood on the scales. Eleven and a half stone. I didn't know what I should weigh – as if there was such a thing as an ideal weight – but felt I had lost about half a stone. I wondered where weight went when you lost it.

Rosie was also fascinated by my boots. She observed closely my slow daily ritual: criss-crossing the long purple laces, binding them round the top of the boot, fastening them up tight. This was always a moment of some *gravitas* in the morning, an act to concentrate mind and body and mark my intent. Rosie knew this.

My habit had been to talk to Sam regularly on the road. I decided to continue, to keep his presence alive. Let them lock me up, if they wanted to.

Walking out of West Tanfield, I felt, possibly for the first time, that I was now in charge of the journey and not vice versa. Human contact, after so many isolated nights, had been like a transfusion.

It was a fresh morning. To the east, the Cleveland Hills were a misty blur on the horizon. I stuck to my plan: 90 minutes walking, 30 minutes resting. Two factors were helping my walking speed. First, the Samless state. I no longer needed to indulge his roadside olfactory adventures. The second was my increased fitness. In those 90 minutes I could now walk five miles as opposed to four. This may not sound a dramatic increase, but it was.

I'd not even considered a morning lift. My feet were on the mend. Motor cars were less relevant to me. I walked up towards Bedale on virtually traffic-free small roads. There were many crossroads with no signs, and I had to shout to several farm workers for directions.

This North Yorkshire countryside was a pasture and arable mix, the hill dotted with sheep like drying cloths. In the air was a rich manure smell. Walking was becoming meditation on the move. My mind was learning to travel in a way it never could have behind a car wheel.

I passed through the village of Crakehall, which had a Museum of Badges. Someone somewhere must have woken up one morning and thought, 'I know, I'll start up a museum of badges!' Where was that person now? I tried hard, but couldn't generate enough enthusiasm to go and have a look.

On the spacious village green they were preparing for a fête. It was a reassuring English spectacle as inhabitants set up trestle tables, the cloths billowing in the wind. People were walking in with boxes full of stuff to sell. Unless it was radically different from every fête and jumble sale I've ever been to, those boxes would contain (among other things) old records, copies of *Black Beauty* and *Little Women*, toast racks and one-bar electric fires that didn't work. I was tempted to hang on, but the opening seemed a long way off and, anyway, what could I have bought?

I'd examined my feet that morning. Each foot still had a thick layer of beige-coloured dead skin. This was half detached, flapped slightly and resembled Jabba the Hutt's mouth. It looked dreadful, but once you got over that, it wasn't too bad.

Near the village of Patrick Brompton, smudged rain clouds were charging across the hills towards me. For once I took early action. The brolly was out. I pressed its button and it instantly flowered black. At this sight, the clouds lost interest. The rain ran out of puff and never arrived.

These villages were unknown to me. Yet I'd travelled within a few miles of them countless times on the A1. Some travel narrows the mind. At the north end of Patrick Brompton was a building called Rebel Cottage. What could it mean? I knocked. No one home. No one in the street to enlighten me either. The rebel's cause remained unknown. The village church bell counted out midday as I walked through. Time to pitch temporary camp outside the village at the corner of a freshly harvested cornfield.

The menu on this morning was almost cordon bleu. One sandwich, one apple (not sour), one small chocolate bar, water. All food now tasted delicious. All food was precious. I lay back and put Sam's journey into perspective. He'd travelled 300-plus miles from Plymouth to Boroughbridge. His legs were little longer than a pipe cleaner. His journey was done. My task was to finish it. For him. And for me. And for anyone else who might have been remotely interested.

Midday. I'd walked ten miles. Good going. Walking was becoming truly natural for me. Like watching telly for other people. Or sitting in a traffic jam. I walked through Scotton, a village unsure of its identity, not knowing whether to hide away or make itself known, and headed towards Catterick Garrison, Europe's largest army settlement. (How did they know things like that? Had they asked simply everyone else?) I was thinking about all those soldiers when I passed a sign saying 'fish 'n' chips – 150 metres'. I didn't know they made fish and chips that long. Must be to keep the soldiers' strength up.

First impressions of Catterick were grim: long wire perimeter fencing, on top of which, looking for all the world like giant heated hair curlers, were plonked rolls of barbed wire. It got better, though: long, sweeping stretches of well-trimmed grass dotted with fine oaks and other trees. A green and pleasant land no less. I walked through the garrison for half an hour, during which time I saw only one uniformed soldier, on sentry duty. In this peaceful landscape it was difficult to think of making preparations for war. But maybe that was the intention. To fool whoever our enemies were at that particular time. We'd need to ask the Americans. Only the street names harked back to futile death: Kitchener, Smuts, Haig, Somme.

Each day I would wake to a cheery new statistic – the number of days passed. In the morning the new total would excite me. This was day 20, and until early afternoon I played with the novelty of this new number. As the day proceeded, the statistic, like French bread, began to go stale. By late afternoon I was impatient for the new number, though I would have to wait until the next morning. And so the process continued.

On towards Richmond, Yorkshire, as opposed to Richmond, Surrey. The town peeped its grey stone face above the trees on a far hillside ahead. Were I a travel writer, I would here toss out one of those fascinating facts that almost save some travel writers from boredom. I would tell you that in its 900-year history, the walls of Richmond Castle have never been breached. But you could find that kind of thing in a guidebook.

Richmond was both no-nonsense Yorkshire and aesthetically pleasing, and the best way in was to walk. Across the stone bridge, you saw the trees cascading down to the River Swale, then climbing the bank to the spacious square dominated by the giant obelisk that could have been a pencil factory's landmark. I had once been to a pencil factory, actually. In Keswick, Cumbria. Probably better than a badge museum.

Richmond teemed with visitors. Coaches stood in close line like some repeating wallpaper pattern. And there it was again, my 'town syndrome'. It was a symptom of being penniless.

Tourists were drifting in and out of pubs, licking ice cream, glugging Coke, ripping at hamburgers. I wasn't hungry. It was the principle. They could do it. I couldn't. Exclusion.

I had spent a solitary morning. A few shouts to farm workers apart, I'd spoken to no one. It was mid-afternoon. I'd walked about 18 miles. The first sizeable village north of here, according to the map, was Gilling West. That would be my target for the night. What would Gilling West have in store? I had no idea. I never had any idea. I simply got somewhere. Tried to sort things out.

The afternoon had turned hot. Two miles further north, I passed a large stone house, heard voices in the garden and peeped over the wall. A group of people were looking uncommonly festive for 4.30 in the afternoon. Would they fill my water bottle? They'd give me a cup of tea as well. And allow me a surrealist conversation. The cottage overlooked the large estate belonging to Lord and Lady Zetland (more squirearchy). I'd happened on a double celebration. Ian Sperring was 56 that day, his partner, Dorothy Radford, was 50 the next. Here's the surrealism bit.

'Where were you heading tonight?'

'Somewhere round Gilling West.'

'Ask for the farmer Hughie Bird. Tell him the Mermaid and King Rat sent you.'

'The Mermaid and King Rat?'

'That's right. Tell Hughie Bird the Mermaid and King Rat sent you.'

'Very well. Thank you for the tea.'

I walked on. Gilling West rose up before me in a hillside huddle after another mile. The village was less than two miles west of Scotch Corner (on the A1) and I'd never even heard of it. On the village's first lamp-post a poster advertised that weekend's cricket match between Lord Zetland's XI and Gilling West CC. I pictured red-faced sons of toil bowling to aristocrats. In the White Swan was an announcement of a local having his head shaved for charity. I could do that. But who would notice?

The landlord pointed me towards Hughie Bird's Mill Farm, one mile distant. It was to prove one of my more memorable stopping places. Enter farmer Hughie Bird, 60 years of age, lively, laughing, welcoming me like some long-lost relative. That very day he was celebrating 35 years of marriage to his wife Joyce. What was the celebration to be? She was off to bingo. He was off to the pub. He was celebrating getting in the crops, too: barley, rape and wheat, all ahead of time.

He lived in a real farm. That is, the inside didn't look anything like farmhouses looked in advertisements, IKEA or Habitat catalogues or films about talking pigs. There were cows outside. And sheep. And dogs. And a big muddy yard. And various outhouses whose secrets I was to discover.

In the kitchen sat Elsie Liddle. Elsie 'did' for Hughie. And rushing past in a whiff of aftershave and a flash of hair gel was Hughie's son, gearing himself up for a night on the town (Richmond). In the countryside, most teenagers were invisible.

'Mermaid and King Rat sent me.'

Hughie roared with laughter. He shoved a mug of tea towards me, and a door-wedge piece of pork pie.

'They said you might put me up.'

'I might as well,' he said. 'Take the caravan.' And he roared again. I told him what I was doing.

'You're looking very fit,' he said. I told him I felt it. Hughie rapidly followed it by one of the *non sequiturs* I'd get used to.

'Times are hard for farmers, you know.'

Townies had views about farmers the way they didn't have views about sewage inspection officers or gents' tailoring assistants. One view was that government policies, BSE and so on had crippled them, that they'd been treated with huge unfairness, that they were a political football and were being bled dry. The other view was that they were loud and perpetually whingeing bastards who'd fed sheep's brains to cattle, were dosing their animals on dangerous and unnecessary amounts of antibiotics and deserved all they got. Discuss.

'They were in the local pantomime, you know.'

'Who?'

'Mermaid and King Rat.'

I rang Tim and Jude Tribe, told them of my location and arranged to meet them later in the White Swan. Why didn't Hughie come too?

'I will. And so will Elsie. Won't you, Elsie?' Elsie, who hadn't said much and seemed a bit shy, said yes, she would.

'Mind, Hughie, I can't buy you a drink. Or anything else.'

'Are you really travelling with no money?' he asked. I said I was.

'But you've got credit cards, that kind of thing, as standby?'

I shook my head. He roared with laughter again.

'I'll buy you a pint, all right!'

The big farmhouse, like most, had functionality as first priority. Rural chic was far behind. I had the chance of a second shower in two days. In the shower I washed my top, socks and pants, then wrung them out. Elsie took them off to dry.

My small caravan was close to the farmhouse in a little walled field. Mill Farm had a fine setting. On all sides the countryside rose gently or sloped away, rich and green. The sheltering trees murmured in the evening breeze. I'd had a quiet, uneventful day. I'd walked 21 miles to the village and another mile to the farm and my body had not screamed in anguish.

Showered and changed, I sat in Hughie's big farmhouse living-room and wrote up my diary. Occasionally he would plonk a mug of tea in front of me, but generally he left me alone. Like I'd have left him alone for the milking.

Afterwards, I retraced the mile to the pub. Tim Tribe was outside looking out for me, meaning I didn't have to walk in penniless and alone. What a nice thought. I paused at the entrance.

'I'm not used to this anymore, Tim,' I said.

I was a regular pub drinker at home. It had been almost three weeks since I'd been in one. I was able to walk in. I was able to order a pint as if it were totally natural. There was no pressure for me to leave. I had to plead my case with no one. The eyes of the regulars did not fix on me beadily. I stared down at the foaming pint of beer. It was all mine. The whole glass full.

'Order some food,' said Jude.

I picked up the menu. 'You don't realise what this feels like,' I said. 'I'll have gammon, chips and peas.'

I drank two pints. I polished off the food. I was talking with people who knew me and had done for 25 years, people who had common reference points, mutual friends. It was as if, for a short time, I'd slipped back, as if the long odyssey was just a figment, a recurring dream. There were two planets. The one I normally lived on, with links that Tim and Jude knew. And the last three weeks from Plymouth, with links that no one could know.

I looked at Tim and Jude. What kind people. How come Tim had lost no hair?

After the meal, we walked down to Hughie's local, The Angel. I had told them about Hughie, his exuberance, his wit, his friendliness. But Hughie was different now. He had become morose, and seemed bitter. Light and laughter had given way to dark and scowls. What had happened? He'd made light of the world. Now it sat on him and squashed him.

The reason he gave was a dispute with a neighbour which had flared. The deeper reason, I realised, was the insecurity of the modern farmer. Their suicide rate was the highest in the land, their anxiety enormous. They woke to the cockerel and the fear of the bank manager's letter. Hughie's paradise could also be his nightmare. The other Hughie would return the next day. Which would survive longer?

The Angel evening was strange. Pints kept thumping down on the table. The bar was full. I had drunk beer for years. It was part of my culture, a way of life in the north-east. Now it felt like a poison. It polluted me, was alien to me. In three weeks I had grown away from it. I had lived a simple life on the road. I had been mainly alcohol-free. Why did people drink in such enormous quantities? Why not just one, or two? The pints kept coming. I couldn't drink any more. Didn't want any more. How many had I drunk? Five?

Six? They sat in my stomach and felt uncomfortable. I had to leave the pub. It was ringing with laughter. The more they drank, the happier they got. Not me. Not right then.

I walked out with Tim and Jude and said my farewells. Hughie was still inside. The beer had mellowed him. But he was still Hughie Mark II. I preferred Mark I.

I walked in the silent darkness back to the farm. The stars guided me along the small road. I could hear only my own breathing, my own footsteps. I wanted to be rid of what I'd been pouring inside me.

It would go in its own time.

The stars pulsed their cold light and the looming hedgerows led me on to my small caravan. I undressed, and heard the farm dogs bark at my scent. I wriggled down into the sleeping bag. I'd anticipated this night as a luxury. How strangely it had turned out. My reactions to what I thought was familiar had become unpredictable. As I drifted away, and felt the poisons running inside me, the two contrasting faces of Hughie loomed before me.

Day Twenty-one – Saturday, 15 August

Miles travelled so far – 393

Through the forest trees
The sun moves with me
Rests when I rest

The Sunless Life – The White Lands – Town Without Pity

All night the alcohol flowed silently through my veins. I woke feeling dog rough at seven o'clock. My reaction was to be up and away. I had a wash of sorts, dressed, pulled out the small retractable table and, without a total rush of creative adrenalin, wrote up the diary. At the farmhouse, Hughie had said goodbye to the Black Dog. He was again cheery, energetic, keen to show me his farm, his life.

'Stay this morning,' he said. 'I'll make up your lost miles.'

He wanted me to. And I wanted to. I'd paused nowhere since Clifton Kennels, except the Sam stop at Borough-bridge. I needed to stop, fix my gaze. And I wanted to know more of the complexities of Hughie Bird.

'Lead on, Hughie,' I said. We had tea and toast, then set off to discover Mill Farm. Close at heel were the two farm collies, Jen and Bo (the latter, with its different-coloured eyes, named after David Bowie). Elsie had dried and folded my clothes into a neat pile. I don't know why but this bucked me up enormously. Clean clothes were good for me.

There were 90 milking cows but stalls and machines for only six at a time. This made for marathon milking. Why not invest in a bigger shed and cut down on the three hours twice daily?

'Who could invest in farming right now?' said Hughie, and threw up his hands. He lived, breathed and slept the farm. It surrounded him, was part of him. He couldn't shut an office door, take the commuter train home. It was his strength. And could be his nightmare.

The milkmaid was a lively slip of a woman called Cathy McGeogh, who in 16 years had grown to know each cow by name and loved the work. 'Worth her weight in gold!' said Hughie – not quite the bargain some people might have been. She looked as if she'd be about six stone dripping wet.

Everyone remembers branding sessions in Westerns, that sizzling sound, the wisp of grey smoke. The reality here was the exact opposite. Not heat but cold. The branding was freeze-dried.

Hughie's cows give out around 1,000 litres of milk a day. Later, I nicked a bit for my cornflakes. Natural, untreated, unpasteurised. Brilliant.

The cows were waiting in the outer byre for milking. Cathy led them in individually. They were like patients in a doctor's waiting-room. Each time Cathy came through to the byre, I expected her to shout, 'Next!' They entered the shed in that heavy, dreamy way cows have. They stepped up to the milking position like people stepping up for communion. There they stood, a sombre, solid line of backsides, tails twitching like a row of dials in a cockpit.

The milking machines made a Heath Robinson hiss-tick, hiss-tick. At times a cow would slip on the unnatural (for them) concrete. Slip too far and they'd do the splits – the reason for the leg manacles hanging on the walls.

Cathy was also The Inseminator. This sounded like the latest Schwarzenegger role. It meant she was in charge of the freeze-dried tubes. Hughie pulled a thin rod from one, the tumbling dry ice giving a strange science fiction feel. I was looking at a future Friesian-Holstein. A new calf had been born that night. Calves learnt to walk fast, and life with mum was short. Within 12 hours the two were separated. Forever.

A boyhood memory of watching Notts County involved the heaving mass on the Spion Kop. Always somewhere a match flared. Never a second without. The image came to mind seeing the cows massed post-milking in the concrete pen. Not a second passed without one shitting. Nothing produced shit like a herd of cows. They were unstoppable shitting machines. Splat, splat onto the concrete. One there. Now there, now there. And each day Hughie Bird had the (literally) Herculean labour of sweeping out this vast yukkie spread into the sinister, silent pit at the bottom of the yard.

He led me through a shed door to an extraordinary sight. We were in a windowless shed, 125 feet long and 40 feet wide. There was a dull, lowish light, a humid atmosphere, a sense of being sealed from the world. The floor was totally carpeted in a writhing mass of two-week-old chicks. Stretching the length of the shed was a series of moving feeder lines – shallow trenches sprinkled with grain, plus a moving conveyor belt of hanging water baskets like some miniaturised scenic fairground ride. I was in an intensive farm broiler room. This room was life in its entirety for these chicks. They would live here from day one to six weeks, then be taken to Wales for slaughter. Two days later they'd be sitting plump on the supermarket shelves. They would never see daylight, nor be aware of the sun's existence. Nor would they know what natural wind was, nor grass, nor natural running water. They would not know there was day and then night. They would know only this shed, their delivery lorry. And death.

Hughie took a pride in maintaining the shed. 'If the birds weren't happy,' he said, 'they wouldn't grow properly.' The shed was clean, warm and efficient, but not primarily geared towards the chicks' happiness. The temperature, the ventilation and the feeding process were regulated automatically, as if some unseen technological 'deity' oversaw the whole thing. Later, when I saw the film *The Truman Show*, it put me in mind of this shed.

The shed's soft, soporific atmosphere, the lowered light and the humidity contrasted with the constant chirruping of the chicks. They were gathered as if at some huge protest meeting or political rally, a potency of numbers that suggested a mass movement.

We walked through the moving carpet of 9,000 chicks. Hughie's keen eye was looking for casualties. One chick was caught between the supports of the water-carrier belt. Another was trapped in the feeder lines, only its head visible as a mountain of grain piled up behind. A third chick just looked beyond it, stretched out. Some chicks Hughie rescued. With others it was a quick movement, like wringing out the dishcloth – one twist of the neck, and dead.

'So,' asked Hughie, 'do you think they're badly treated?' He'd made the shed as clean and habitable as possible. The chicks faced no thirst, no hunger, no predators. But they were born and died without knowing the natural world, which seemed to transgress some basic law. I looked at the heaving mass and thought how one day all this would return for its vengeance on the human race.

How would I feel, buying my next supermarket chicken? Yet this was a normal part of Hughie's world. Had I worked in it, it would probably have become normal for me. Sometimes first impressions are more important, though, before we conveniently adjust to things being 'normal'.

Hughie closed the door on the shed. Back to the sunlight

and the wind. Once the door was shut, not the slightest sound came from within.

Back in the cow byre, Cathy was dehorning the new calf. Ted Hughes wrote a brilliant poem on this process, so I'll defer. Cattle gathered *en masse* could cause serious damage with their horns. A special paste burned into the roots prevented further growth. Hornless cattle. Sunless chickens.

'Stick your hand in her mouth,' said Hughie, and I did. The bottom felt solid, the top was warm and gummy. 'Cows don't have any top teeth,' he said. 'A cow can't bite you. But don't try the same thing with a horse!' And he roared his infectious laugh.

We clomped back to the farmhouse in our wellies. Joyce, who'd gone to the bingo the previous night, made a big pot of tea.

'Did you win?' asked Hughie.

'Yes, I did,' she said.

'How much?'

'I'm not telling you,' she said. When he walked out of the kitchen to hang up his coat, she leaned over and whispered, 'It was £200, but I'll let him sweat a bit before I tell him.' She gave me a cheeky grin at this shared confidence.

Elsie returned from the village and the four of us sat around the big kitchen table. Joyce cooked a monstrous pile of bacon. There was fresh bread, scones, butter. Every time we attacked the pile and it grew less, more rashers appeared. We ate, chattered, laughed. The tea was endless too. Hughie was a mixture of the serious farmer and the unrestrained, childlike story-teller. He'd recount an anecdote with huge glee, then pause. He held up a bag of rape seed the size of a bag of coal. '£150 – just for that bag!' he said. 'It's crazy.' Everything he'd harvested that year would be fed to his own cattle. About one hundred acres' worth. 'No money in selling it. It's serious.'

At such times his face took on the pained look of a child whose lolly had been snatched away. He was naturally infectious about his work. It pulled him high up. It dragged him low down. And he'd done me proud at Gilling West, fed, sheltered, entertained and educated me. I'd miss him.

This village was another crossroads in the journey of accents. North Yorkshire, Teesside and County Durham seemed to create a cocktail here. And sitting around that large table, with endless bacon and endless tea, seemed at that moment to be the whole world and everything in it.

But about 150 miles of open road still awaited me. I pulled on my trusty boots. I'd bought these Caterpillar boots second-hand (or foot) three years previously at a Manchester open-air market. They'd stood me in brilliant stead.

The above paragraph probably makes me the only figure to endorse a product publicly without sponsorship or advertising contract, nor any financial benefit. How free that makes me feel.

Had I asked, I'm sure Hughie would have driven me to Edinburgh. But I was no longer interested in grabbing every lift I could. I wanted only to make up lost time (my Edinburgh target being four weeks). A car was no longer a substitute for feet. Feet won.

We drove north, crossed the busy A66 and headed up towards the County Durham border. Hughie knew the occupants and seemingly the entire history of every house we passed ('that farm sold its cattle because . . .'). Mile after mile we drove, and still Hughie's encyclopaedic knowledge continued. I thought of the average townie, who didn't know the neighbour four doors down. We went through the Barnard Castle area – but why were almost all the buildings white? 'They belong to Lord Barnard. It's a condition of tenancy you paint your buildings white.'

This was the age of New Labour, Cool Britannia, the Spice Girls. Yet some things were unchanged. I'd experienced the forelock-touching culture three times in two days, country landowners with vast acreages. It was a system seemingly impervious to all influences. On the surface the status quo seemed peaceful. Did it matter who owned what? I saw no peasants wielding flaming torches, running up the hill screaming, 'Smash the system!'

I'd never had the inclination to own much. One small terraced house was more than enough. Owning loads of properties would only have made me miserable. Were the landowners happy? Were the tenants? These seemed the important questions.

Hughie, being Hughie, took a diversion. He was keen to show me the strangely named Four Alls pub and restaurant at Ovington. This was an old, thick-beamed building, but where did the name come from? No one seemed sure, but apparently there were three Four Alls public houses in England. On the wall in the bar was a framed Victorian colour print. It included not four but five 'alls': a painting of a soldier ('Fight for All'), a judge ('Plead for All'), a vicar ('Pray for All'), a farmer ('Pay for All') and Victoria herself ('Govern All'). It was a perfect example of superior Victorian patronage, but only partly explained the name.

Hughie wasn't finished. We stopped again by the striking Winstone Bridge spanning the River Tees, the wide sweep of water marred only by the streaks of detergent some nice person had discharged upstream. 'They say someone once flew a biplane under that bridge,' said Hughie, but he knew no more. I checked at the local cottage. They knew the story, yes. Details? Alas, no.

My Hughie Bird time was almost over. He dropped me at the dizzily high village of Woodland. Twenty miles to the south was the distinctive landmark the Jockey's Cap (named for obvious reasons), a regular site of burning beacons. I waved Hughie goodbye. Back he went to his fine-looking Mill Farm, its 9,000 incarcerated chicks, its 90 cows, its £200 secret bingo prize, its endless cow shit, its financial nightmares, its precarious future.

And on. I expected to walk about 14 miles that day. It was already afternoon, and I struck out for the Wear Valley. The alcohol affected my natural walking rhythm. I walked faster – an act of purification. The route took us into County Durham and past the spread of Hamsterley Forest. One choice was the road directly through, but the day was bright, sunny and clear, great sweeping landscapes of unspoilt countryside were there for the seeing, and the dark forest interior didn't appeal. My road did occasionally wander off into sections of forest, but always emerged to the wide panorama. The roads, little more than lanes, were silent, deserted.

I was now to start the crossing of the three great north-eastern valleys, Weardale, Teesdale and Tynedale. The best, most natural way to explore them was to head up each individually. I had to cross them the other way, over the ridges. The contours would rise and fall, rise and fall. I'd be like an ant walking across a corrugated metal roof.

For the first three hours of rise and fall, I passed no hamlet. There were no road signs to Wolsingham, the next town. Most of the roads were not shown on my map, and at each isolated crossroad I needed to plot my route by the big wobbly sun which happily for me hung up there, blazing away in the sky all afternoon.

On top of a ridge I finally spied Wolsingham in the valley below. The small town hugged close to the River Wear, which from here was invisible, bordered each side by thick lines of trees. It gave the impression of a giant bendy toilet brush. It was a spectacular sight. What I didn't know was that Wolsingham would do everything in its power to resist my visit. Those friendly fates I mentioned had decided to have a bit of fun at my expense, but how was I to know?

The road turned and twisted down the valley on a long-winded route to the town. On a hilltop stile a public footpath was signposted. Much quicker, surely. Wolsingham was about two miles away. I followed the path across the top field. Gradually it grew fainter. Then it disappeared. I kept going by instinct, whatever that was. Soon the route became a hazardous obstacle course. I needed to leap a succession of streams. Someone had conveniently placed several barbed-wire fences in my way. Just in case I found scaling them too easy, they'd pulled and tugged at their securing posts till they wobbled like loose teeth. This gave the act a certain *It's a Knockout* sense of the absurd. The plunging route then dropped into a thickly wooded area which became as impenetrable as atonal music. The town disappeared from view.

I'm not sure how it happened, but I found myself in the middle of eight-foot-high, very thick, very stinging nettles. The town had gone, and the sun followed it. Blotted out. The route was both impassable and impossible. I back-tracked, only to find that the same considerate person had, in the interim, managed to place several more barbed-wire fences in my path. I say 'path', but there wasn't one.

In the distance I could hear the laughter of children. For some reason this made me feel I was in a ghost story. I was hot and sweaty. I needed to toss the bag over fences before scaling them. Sam was lucky he'd got out. I was wearing the loose Indian trousers. At each barbed-wire-fence scaling, I feared snagging them. All directions seemed to end in impene-trability. I had a terrible vision. Years later, they would find my skeleton in here. Somewhere in my bag would still be a tiny piece of rancid cheese.

I finally came to a fence on the other side of which was a goods yard with a line of lorries. Lorries meant a road, which meant an exit. I scaled the fence. I explored the yard and found the exit. It was via a pair of eight-foot-high gates, which were seriously padlocked.

I scaled the gates. I wobbled on top, and threw down my bag. At that moment a ridiculous notion came into my head and there, on top of the eight-foot-high gates, I burst out laughing. I visualised a police officer spotting me on top of these gates and shouting, 'Oi! Just where do you think you're going?' To which I would have replied, 'Edinburgh!'

I jumped down, walked down the track, found a small bridge and entered the Weardale town of Wolsingham. No town on my journey had resisted me so strongly, had so wanted me not to be there. What did it have against me? Its resistance was reinforced when I tried to make two reverse-charge calls to my partner Kitty and my son Dylan. I needed a reassuring voice. Neither was at home. Wolsingham chuckled again.

I had the same feeling as at Tetbury, as at Whixley. To quote the most-used line in US cinema, 'Let's get outta here!' It was already evening, the next village up the valley,

Frosterley, was three miles distant, but no matter. 'Let's get outta here!'

The valley road to Frosterley offered several farms. I tried at three locations for shelter. The reception was, well, Frosterley. At the first farm they smiled as they informed me it was no go. At the second farm, I again walked through a yard in which were chained various ferocious dogs. As at Bradwell, they leapt towards me until restrained by their chains. This restraint only drove them to more ferocity. Their barking continued through my abortive conversation with the unshaven man who answered the door and viewed me with great suspicion. He looked as likely to offer me shelter as to inject rabies into his dogs – though from their behaviour they might already have had it.

The third house had gone to a lot of trouble removing itself from the world. It was a cottage, and the path to the front door was so overgrown and entangled I expected a sleeping princess at the end. The cottage seemed to have huddled into itself and pulled a dark cloth round it.

I knocked at the door, knowing even as I did so that the door was destined not to open. At the second knock a shrill female voice shouted, 'Who is it? What do you want?' The voice was jointly defensive and aggressive. It belonged to some being of secured locks, bolted windows, sunless rooms. I shouted my apologies and left.

Would I have to sleep rough? Not the end of the world, but it meant no food morning or evening, problems writing the diary, waking cold with the prospect of a hungry 20-mile walk to come. It meant not only physical deprivation but psychological too. I wanted someone to make me welcome, afford me shelter. I hated the alienation, the rejection.

The evening light was beginning to fade as I trudged into Frosterley. Again it was Saturday night, again the world was cranking itself up in its search for pleasure. Ten million people were preening themselves, gazing at their mirror reflections as they prepared for all the excitement and pain that might be 'out there'. I was 'out there' already. And I wanted to come in.

Experience had taught me to look for caravans; they gave me shelter but reduced the sense of territorial invasion to the donors. I'd slept in very few beds. But then I'd slept in no gutters either.

Frosterley was a long, strung-out village, and I was virtually through it when, at the western end, I spotted Bridge End Cottage. This seemed to be in a game of hide-and-seek, off the main road and crouching down alongside the Wear, its head just peeping up. Next to it, also joining in the game, was a caravan.

Now imagine this. Two couples are having a pleasant Saturday night. The men go off for an Indian take-away, leaving their wives to do the preparations. They return and find, sitting on the settee, drinking their wine, an itinerant, a gentleman of the road, an uninvited guest. Nor will the guest soon be gone. He is staying the night.

It could have been the plot of a Harold Pinter play. But it was me. In Frosterley. I rang the bell of the cottage, which was built on a steeply banked stretch of the river. The lady who answered looked surprised, but was without hostility. I threw myself totally on her mercy, explaining my plight. It seemed to amuse her. 'You'd better come in,' she said.

I clomped in. Clomped is the only word. The cottage was warm, comfortably furnished, calming. I was in my big boots, the pack on my back. Try as I might, I found it hard not to clomp.

The woman's name was Joyce Crozier. Sitting on the settee was her sister-in-law Joanne Crozier. There were four Croziers in all. At that very moment, husbands Ron and Barry were high-tailing it from Consett with the chicken korma. There was a splendid golden retriever, Amber, who sniffed the remnants of Sam on me.

The cottage was upside-down. You walked in the main door, then went downstairs to the bedrooms. I sat on the soft settee and breathed deeply. These were the moments, those few delicious moments, when rejection was replaced by acceptance, when I wanted to squeal with pure delight. For a few hours at least, no trials awaited me. No uncertainty. What's more, I was offered a glass of cool white wine. Ta.

I got some curry as well. Ron and Barry returned and opted for charity rather than indignation. I was in the north-east, my own stomping ground. I deserved a good reception. Barry Crozier, who worked for Tyne-Tees, recognised me. I recognised him. How strange that felt. I'd grown accustomed to anonymity. Part of me felt I was cheating. The other part was more pragmatic. It meant the caravan was mine for the night.

I'd come from cows and chickens that morning. And arrived at pigeons. Joyce and Ron were keen racers. Pigeon racing was a traditional north-east sport but, like whippet racing and leek growing, its hold seemed to be weakening, with less attraction for the new, computer-literate generation. Sky Sports showed no interest. Could it survive?

The Croziers had built their own cree. The word 'cree' did it an injustice. My image of a pigeon cree was something botched together from old doors and pieces of wood, stuck on a piece of wasteland and viewed from a passing train. The Crozier cree was five star. It was a Hilton cree. Wherever pigeons gathered in the world, they would talk in hushed tones about the Crozier cree. It was a two-storey structure, had a pantiled roof, treated wood, a series of connecting rooms, was centrally heated and had been specifically designed for different purposes (Sauna, sir? Jacuzzi?). It was interior designed, clean, airy and probably had room service. Maybe a water bed on demand. The pigeons flew hundreds of miles to get back to this cree, and who could blame them?

That very day, the Croziers had won first, second and third prize in a 150-mile race from Leicester. I imagined their pigeons released in the Midlands. Let me home, they'd shout. And no stopping them. Pigeons averaged 40 miles an hour. They could reach speeds of 100 miles an hour. Set them loose 700 miles from home and they'd still make it. All with those little wings. How did they do it?

Nobody knew. Except the pigeons, who were keeping it under those puffed chests. At the same time a pigeon was both serene and pompous. I would have been too. I thought of them travelling naturally up the country, like I was. They only took four hours to journey 150 miles – that would be eight or nine days for me. If they'd set off from Plymouth, they'd have been in Frosterley in less than half a day. I'd been at it for centuries.

As Ron Crozier put it, 'Whenever or wherever you release a pigeon, no matter how quick you jump in your car and drive, the pigeon will be home before you are.' And that's without an integrated transport policy, fuel subsidies or anything. The pigeon just flies. I kept thinking of all those pigeons, always destined to beat humans for speed, and probably not being much bothered about it.

Potholing apart, pigeon racing might have been the world's least likely spectator sport. No one seemed interested in sponsoring pigeon racing. Which newspaper had a pigeon-racing correspondent? Which bookmaker offered pigeon odds? Meanwhile, the Rons and the Joyces raced their pigeons purely for pleasure, which was what the essence of the sport was. Their chests swelled with almost as much pride as the birds' to tell of their victories.

We all stood in the cree as the pigeons cooed and nodded their heads constantly, as if agreeing with specific points of argument. They possessed some secret beyond us. One day they might tire of giving us pleasure and simply not return home, and the world would be left with empty crees, Hilton or otherwise.

I went off to my caravan at 10 p.m., too tired for my initial plan of hanging on to watch the opening *Match of the Day* of the season. It was the right choice. Newcastle were rubbish.

I oiled and massaged my feet, the sound of the cooing pigeons in my ear. What big, daft, clumsy things my feet were for carrying me from place to place. But they were all I had.

Miles travelled so far — 419

On the moorland top
The snow polls trembling
In the August wind

Free the Mortimer Two — The Empty World —
A Touch of Italy

The day ahead was likely to be my most lonely and desolate
so far. I'd be heading directly north into an exposed wilderness. My only companion would be the wind, and my own
thoughts. I didn't mind this. Being solitary in a solitary
landscape was okay. Alienation fed on the presence of other
people.

Up and out of Weardale I'd travel, through the Derwent
Valley, and end the day somewhere in Tynedale. For the
22nd day, and probably the 60th time, I pulled on the big,
bad boots. I was up early, and so too were Joyce and Ron,
who made me tea and toast. Imagine how much free grub I'd
had on my trip. How much hospitality.

I'd written my diary and was on the road before 9 a.m.,
striding the back route to Stanhope, close to the river. I was
now used to my penniless state, gave no thought to having
money in my pocket, and accepted that all food and shelter
needed to be begged, borrowed or stolen. This didn't make it
easier, it was simply that I took it as (for the time being) my
natural state.

My rations once again were virtually gone. I had two
mince pies (from Jude Tribe), one small chocolate biscuit
(from West Tanfield) and an apple (from Mill Farm). I knew
that at a pinch I could see through the day on these.

I'd toyed with the idea of a less remote route, travelling
through Allendale. This would have added seven miles to the
journey. Nothing to those in their Astras or Cavaliers. Too
much for me.

Stanhope was one of a string of small towns as you moved up the increasingly remote Wear Valley. Emphatic signs of the north-east were now more in evidence; several cars had miniature black-and-white number nine shirts swinging in their back windows. On each side of the road into Stanhope, various circular flower beds were set into the sloping grass verges. Each bed had a concentrated blaze of individual colour, like a series of giant open paint pots. Outside the Pack Horse Inn, the local football team had just got changed and were clomping about nervously. In the square, the sign 'Stanhope and Weardale Co-operative Society' belonged both stylistically and in philosophy to another age.

I still had one set of insoles. These were riding up badly. No matter how many times I flattened them, their irritating wrinkles came back. My feet, I realised, were talking to me. They were telling me the time for any false supports had gone. It was time to free the Mortimer Two!

I sat down in Stanhope and removed the insoles, placing them in a side pocket of my bag. Even at this late stage, the act made me nervous and my first steps were wary. There was no pain. In three weeks, the feet had come full circle. They had been tested, bruised, blistered, bandaged. They had somehow kept going. They had got me here. Now they were free. And walking on.

The road north from Stanhope was Crawley Side Bank, a route steep enough to graze your nose. These gradients no longer exhausted me as much as they'd once done. I was puffed for three minutes, not four. The town soon fell away, and after I crossed a cattle grid, ahead of me was virtually nothing, just wild, desolate moorland.

A sheep had squeezed through the bars of the gate at the cattle grid and was now isolated from its moorland mates. It had no reason to have done this, except the innate stupidity of sheep. And, of course, it wanted to get back, but couldn't. I opened the gate and invited the sheep to return. Naturally, generations of sheep evolution saw it do something else. It ran to the other side of the road and tried to squeeze through the bars of the other gate. It got stuck. I pulled it out. It had only to walk through the gate. It ran off the other way. I pointed to the wide-open gate, indicating the simplicity of the act required. The sheep did nothing. Its wool trembled slightly in the keen wind. I gave the sheep a wide berth and got town side of it. I ran at it as fast as I could, arms outstretched, making the loudest 'wheeeeooooorrrggg!' sound I could. From sheer terror, the sheep ran through the gate and rejoined its mates.

The road continued to rise steeply onto unfenced moorland, marked only with the striped snow poles. In all directions except back to town, the terrain was treeless, peopleless, buildingless, a desolately beautiful sweep of shuddering gorse bushes and endless bare ridges over which the west wind whistled. On a far horizon, moderately protected by a clump of small trees, was a huddle of buildings. For half an hour the huddle grew closer, a three-cottage terrace 1,300 feet up, isolated from everything else in the known universe.

I was rarely nervous knocking at isolated houses. When there were hundreds of them, I was daunted. Two teachers, Rose Clark and John French, answered my knock. They'd moved here three years ago from Leicester (probably too many pigeons). Living in such an isolated spot seemed absolutely crazy, and I warmed to them immediately. I warmed to them even more when they gave me tea and toast.

The terrace was called Weather Hill Cottages. 'Which spelling of weather?' I asked.

'As in bloody awful,' said Rose.

The cottages had once housed railway workers. The North Pennines experienced its own mini-Klondike with the nineteenth-century lead mines, when this wild terrain would have teemed with activity. A few miles west were loads of ruined miners' cottages. Yours for a snip.

Opposite Rose and John was a one-man quarry. This being Sunday, the one man was doing something else. Just the rusting corrugated sheds shuddering in the wind, diggers and grabbers like immobile giant insects, the gouged-out sandstone exposed like an open wound. And the wind, puckering up its lips into a thin whistle.

The tea and toast had been doubly welcome. The route was still rising, the temperature falling. On and up, increasingly desolate, no signs of humanity. I talked loudly to myself, an act of some embarrassment when silently past me came a group of dedicated cyclists, heads down into the wind, such a low gear engaged that the pedals seemed to revolve ten times per yard. Their gaudy, shiny lycra, their slow silence, their bowed heads passing gave a surreal sense to the whole scene.

By the time I'd reached 2,000 feet the wind was numbing my left cheek as effectively as Xylocaine. The wind buffeted me. I staggered like a drunk. I could almost reach up and pull down the cloud. I imagined it raining. If I produced the brolly, I could well become, involuntarily, the Weardale hang-gliding champion.

As a distraction, I ate a mince pie. The wind whipped away the crumbs like sparks from a circular saw. Up and up, until finally the road levelled out and I was walking the ridge top. The cold was beginning to numb all of me, and this vast, sparse landscape was making Dartmoor seem the over-crowded tourist trap it was.

I was due a stop and found a round stone sheep shelter. I huddled in and ate the apple. My teeth were chattering like those toy wind-up ones. It was to prove the shortest break of my entire trip. This was August. This was a time for balmy breezes, a time for suntan lotion, sleeveless tops. In a thousand places people were stretched out on beach towels like corpses in the morgue. They were peeling off sunburn. I was in a sheep shelter, getting hypothermia.

I got walking again. Mercifully, the road began to descend, and I broke into a trot.

'Hup! Hup! Hup! Hup!'

I had no idea why I shouted this, except that with the backpack jerking up and down I must have felt like one of those macho soldiers out on an endurance run. This was probably the closest I'd ever get to the army.

I kept on running. To the east I saw Derwent Reservoir glint its grey eye at me and, probably for the first time in my life, I ran into another county. I was in Northumberland – the final county before Scotland.

By the time I reached Blanchland village I'd stopped running. Blanchland hid itself in the Derwent Valley, a shy place which only revealed itself, and its pale sandstone face, in those final moments before you reached it. After the endless expanses of the moor, this seclusion was doubly strange. Townies drove out to gawp at its time-warp appearance. Blanchland had decided exactly what moment in its history it liked best and stopped all development then. For all I know, behind the small windows in its rows of pale stone houses, the entire village population was browsing the Internet. The impression, though, was of something different.

Thirty miles east of here was my own home. I felt its gravitational pull, the sense of homesickness, and knew I needed to get north as soon as possible. I rang Kitty from Blanchland, and her voice made the ache greater. People with cameras, anoraks and ice creams wandered through the tiny village. I could scarcely bear to look at them. People in leisure pursuits always depressed me, here even more so. A sweet smell of wood smoke pervaded the village. So what? The Lord Crewe Arms was said to have its own ghost, a White Lady. I had no time to make her acquaintance. Away, away.

I climbed steeply on the B6306, and as the miles fell back, my depression lifted. I was heading towards Hexham, leaving the Derwent Valley behind, the road dropping me down into Tynedale. It was 5.30 p.m. I'd covered 21 miles, and Hexham was still three miles distant. I didn't fancy those three miles. Not till the next day. And just as Weardale had, for a long time, closed its shutters against me, so Tynedale flung them open immediately.

Another half-mile, close to the village of Slaley, I spotted a fairly functional farm cottage and, in an enclosure at the rear, a caravan. I knocked at the door of the cottage. It was answered by a big man with dark hair, a thick moustache and a Mediterranean appearance. I stated my case. Could I sleep in the caravan? Sure. As simple as that. 'Go and sort your stuff out, then come back to the house,' he said. When I returned, on the kitchen table appeared a plateful of mince, potatoes and cabbage, plus a mug of tea so large I needed a navigator. Hot (or rather cold) in pursuit came a bowl of trifle.

The man was Ernie Auriemma, an estate worker for Linnels Farm. He was of Italian descent and lived here with his wife (and trifle creator) Vivien, 18-year-old son Andrew and their 21-year-old daughter Claire. If I'd been on this farm in 1464, I'd have been in the middle of the battle of Hexham. Me and Henry VI. In 1998 I got hot food, a bowl of trifle, then the offer of a second. I accepted and gulped it down.

'You were hungry,' said Ernie. I'd learned to live with hunger. In the affluent West, eating was often more about lifestyle than about hunger. For me it was a vital fuel. And I'd changed my habits. I'd learned to ration when needed. I'd mastered the discipline (for the first time) of eating just a teeny amount, saying, 'Right, that's all there is for the moment,' and not arguing about it. Not for this trifle, though. Loads of that.

Full bellies and empty souls. That was what a lot of us had for much of the time.

Sometimes I just arrived somewhere and it seemed no bother. Like here, Linnels Farm. After they'd fed and sheltered me, Vivien and Ernie said, 'Hang on here, or go to the caravan, whichever you like.'

I was tired, but fancied the company. I sat around in the living-room for an hour or so. On the settee Andrew sat clutching the remote control. His whole body and mind was focused on the Sky TV indy-car racing. I wondered if he knew I was there.

Miles travelled so far — 440

At the wood's edge
The final tree
Is also the first tree

In Paradise — Same River Twice — A Tramp at the Ritz

One of the strange effects of walking 20 miles a day penniless was waking in the small hours in a state of confusion. I looked around the caravan for Sam, only slowly realising he was safely back on Tyneside. At the same time I was looking for my son Dylan, whom I hadn't seen for almost a month. I slowly floated to reality's surface. I looked from the caravan window and heard the trees rustling in the dark. Where was I? Ah, yes. I fell asleep once more, and woke again at six o'clock.

Often I arrived somewhere for the night and only the next day realised how tired I had been, how the fatigue had lessened the impact of my surroundings. Often I spent the night or evening in a strange state, dreamlike, half oblivious to my surroundings.

On this morning I lay in bed and rearranged the previous night's jigsaw. I remembered Ernie mentioning he went off early on his rounds, and I'd nodded dumbly. Not good enough! I was a writer! I needed to be there with Ernie! I needed to see! I jumped from the bed, dressed, a quick splash, then up to the house. Okay, Ernie, let's go!

And how had he ended up here? His Neapolitan father had been a POW at nearby Haydon Bridge. He had fallen in love with the enemy and after the war brought over his Italian sweetheart and they married.

What about that strange surname? Ernie had had to invent a mnemonic for it, otherwise no one could remember it. 'Just say, "All Us Red Indians Eat Mince Meat Alone,"' he grinned, so I did, and it worked.

He was a big, gentle man, and he gave me another reservoir of tea before saying at 7.30, 'Come on, I'll take you to Paradise.' I fancied paradise. I perched on the front of his quad bike and off we went on an eight-mile journey, during which he checked on around 450 sheep.

We drove to the barn, he opened the door, and catapulted out were the two collies, Jess and daughter Molly. Two velocity facts on mum and daughter. Molly was the fastest dog I'd seen anywhere. She'd been shot from a gun. In motion she was more a blur of black with an impressionistic smudge of white. Jess, on the other hand, was the world champion at running backwards. A limited category, admittedly, but impressive nonetheless. She would position herself in front of the moving quad bike and reverse at high speed. The object was to keep Molly out of the bike's path, though I suspected by now the original motivation had been forgotten. Jess simply got in front of the bike and went backwards. For much of the time Molly showed no inclination to stray into peril. There was also a third pooch, Dougal the Airedale. Dougal looked like a toy dog on wheels. He had a gammy leg, which he'd hitch up and carry like a handbag.

Paradise opened up in front of us. Paradise was 44 acres of pastureland ringed by thick and tumbling woodland. It was invisible from any road, a natural amphitheatre, a Site of Special Scientific Interest on which no chemicals or fertilisers were allowed. There was only one way in and you'd need Ernie to find it. You could have frolicked naked in Paradise and only the military satellites would be witness to it. But the enclosed serenity of the place, its calming influence as you simply stood, belied its history. It was exactly here that the two sides had hacked away at each other during the Battle of Hexham.

At the risk of sounding fatuous, I liked Paradise. The first sheep checked, we trundled on, through woods, up and down muddy tracks. Jess and Molly perched on the quad bike like two book ends. In one wood Ernie said, 'We brought a herd of cows through here. They took fright and ran. Took a gang of men a whole day to round them up.'

We passed lots of history too. A holly bush where Jacobite families left secret messages for the 1715 uprising; a 400-year-old bridge spanning Devil's Water; and, beside the bridge, Linnels House, the second in the country (after Cragside, also in Northumberland) to be lit by electricity.

Every morning Ernie checked these 450 sheep scattered over several locations, then went home for breakfast. He gave me some, and on the table Vivien had left me some sandwiches, which were especially welcome as supplies were almost gone. There was a pure luxury too: a bar of Belgian chocolate.

I'd become more philosophical about food. Since Boroughbridge and my brush with Homer's *Odyssey*, my sense of the journey being 'overseen' had left me feeling that while the fates might see me go hungry, they'd not let me starve. Not as long as I stuck to my task. But I was growing tired of sandwiches. The mince and spuds had reminded me just how good hot food could taste, and just how much bread I'd digested these last weeks. Bread – and cheese. They'd become over-familiar.

I took my leave of Ernie with the rest of the house still asleep and dropped down the two and a half miles to Hexham. All the people I'd met and stayed with were inextricably linked in my mind, never to be separated, all part of the odyssey's pattern. Yet none of them had the slightest idea the others existed.

Crossing the River Tyne in Hexham was a symbolic moment. I'd been walking in Northumberland for some miles, but the 'real' Northumberland to me was always north of this river. I waited for the county, England's fifth biggest and least populated, to open its arms to me. I wanted to drink in its wild countryside, its great loneliness, its Cheviot Hills, echoed in the melancholic Northumbrian pipes.

Hexham had its abbey, its market-town feel, its setting in the rich Tyne Valley. And its monstrous chipboard factory belching its noxious fumes from the Stygian complex of pipes and machinery. A Hexham prayer: Oh, Lord, may the wind blow north-east and carry the foul stuff away!

I walked along the busy A69, then north on the A6079, the link road to the A68 to Scotland. Under a spreading chestnut tree in the village of Wall, I lay down and went to sleep. My instinct was often still to tether Sam at such moments, or to check on him when I woke.

I'd left the three great rivers, Tees, Wear and Tyne, behind. Yet I was to cross the Tyne again, a few miles up at Chollerford. How come? Because up here you get good value for rivers. Two Tynes for the price of one, North and South. For the rest of the day I'd be pursuing the North Tyne upstream into deep Northumberland.

The name 'Wall', of course, was as in 'Roman'. People thought the Romans had built it to keep out the Picts and the Scots. But neither was around then, and, anyway, the wall was an offensive, not a defensive, structure, used by the Romans to launch raids northwards. There was a second wall further north, the Antonine, but its history was brief. Hadrian's Wall had survived. So, too — to create the book's least convincing link — had my feet. They were stronger and firmer every day. The soles and heels felt like Formica.

As my natural bits strengthened, the man-made began to give out. The two pairs of purple socks were slowly disintegrating, and the zips on Dylan's bag were packing in. My boots were battered, but intact (non-sponsors please note). My hat was still damp, and tired.

My walking speed had increased to three and a half miles an hour. Twenty miles a day now caused no problems. My body felt lean and fit, my lungs as clean as a freshly scrubbed sink. I was a walking machine, while much of the world went sickly about its business.

Passing Tyneside was a fillip. The next milestone was the border. And then Edinburgh. I dared to think that my target was just about down to two figures. Ninety-nine miles? In other circumstances, the prospect of walking a hundred miles would have appeared an impossible one. Perspectives change.

I followed the North Tyne another eight miles to Wark (pronounced 'Waaaark'), a village whose pub was called the

Black Bull or the Grey Bull, depending on which day you were drinking. It had a huge horse chestnut tree, a petrol station from the '50s, old stone cottages, and its name reminded me of a very good dialect joke.

Doctor to patient: Now tell me, can you walk?

Patient: Walk? I can hardly waaaalk!

I hope you can work it out. Or walk it out, as Northumbrians would say.

Up the North Tyne valley I went. I'd stopped twice that day, eaten Vivien's sandwiches and allowed myself the indulgence of nibbling the Belgian chocolate. By mid-afternoon I was hungry again.

On the road to Bellingham, I passed a small stone cottage, heard a radio playing and knocked on the open door. I was going to ask for tea. When a slightly alarmed woman answered, I changed my mind. 'Is this the road to Bellingham?' I asked, knowing it was. But it also wasn't. Or rather, another one was as well (tch, get on with it, man!). The woman pointed to a small, gated road 50 yards on. 'Take that one,' she said. 'It's beautiful. People think it's private. But it's not.'

The unfenced road climbed steadily. Sheep noted my progress carefully as the land fell away behind me. On a far ridge stood a sturdy double-fronted cottage. Washing billowed on the line. It was the way children drew cottages, wrapped up by the sky. The view south (I was to learn) was 30 miles – all the way to Consett, and possibly even the Indian take-away.

This cottage was called Ealingham. Or, as I would come to think of it, Tumfull. Some places I *had* to knock at. Tumfull was such a place. The thought of walking past never entered my head. The door was opened by a slim, dark-haired woman, Julie Walton. I could hear whooping and shouting from within. As soon as I told Julie about my journey, she said, 'Come on in.' I knew she would. I just did.

It got better. Her husband Thomas appeared and said, 'I recognise you, you're Peter Mortimer, the journalist and playwright.'

Then four children appeared. It was Rachel's 14th birthday. Greg would be 13 in a few days. On the same day Julie would be 40. Then there was Lindsay and Jake, and a black guinea pig called Ernie (not Italian), and a large table on which was piled more food than I had eaten since Plymouth.

'Eat as much as you like,' said Julie and waved a hand. These were not six words I was familiar with. What I ate was as follows: two giant lamb stotties with lettuce (the meat direct from the farm), some home-made drop scones, some cream cake made by Julie, and a large bowl of blackcurrant crumble and cream. And I drank five mugs of tea.

While I ate, Thomas reappeared. I'd told him I was looking for somewhere to stay around Bellingham. He had news. He had fixed me up for the night, absolutely free, at the Riverdale Hall Hotel, where his relatives worked. Riverdale Hall was among Northumberland's finest hotels. A large, beautiful stone building with grounds sweeping down to the river. It had its own swimming pool, cricket pitch, *en suite* rooms. It had food dishes you sometimes couldn't even spell.

I was a man who'd grown used to barns, caravans, cricket pavilions, a man who'd been forced to grow philosophical while gnawing rancid cheese, a man for whom hot water had come to represent luxury. Now I was to sample luxury itself. The real thing. My head swam. And, if I wanted, at the Riverdale my body could follow.

'Come on, dig in, plenty more!' This was Julie. The children were hungry (what an ironic word!) to know all about my trip. I walked where? I slept in what? I ate a dandelion? A hundred dogs? Two whole cows? In a café window? Really? Wow! Why was my hat damp? Bandaged feet?

And suddenly I was fuller than I had been for three weeks. For 54 years. My stomach had shrunk to accommodate my reduced intake. Now it had been stuffed fuller than a salami skin. I had forgotten people ever got this full. Would I be able to stand? Would I ever be hungry again? Would I get out through the door? Would I ever forget Tumfull/Ealingham?

And a luxury hotel to come. All this because I had heard a radio playing in an open doorway.

I thought of what awaited. Crisp sheets with creases sharp enough to peel a potato. Small sachets of shampoo that everyone stole, then never used. Tiny tablets of soap you couldn't get into. A television you could switch on and off in bed. A plastic kettle whose flex was too short. A transparent shower cap for people with hair. An extension number if you wanted your shirt laundered. How could all this be? I was broke through Britain. It was the reticent Thomas Walton. He'd just gone off and done it, announced it, and that was that.

Walton – a familiar Northumberland name. On this day the accent had become distinctively Northumbrian too, with that rolled 'r' that revved like a motorbike. It was said to have originated from the speech defect of an early Duke of Northumberland, which his subjects felt obliged to copy. Just like painting the houses white.

Rachel walked around in my hat. Greg said the journey was 'cool'. Thomas sat and watched. I had to go.

I waddled away from the Waltons. I trundled off from Tumfull. I had overeaten at Ealingham. My mood was high. The early-evening sun was miles below. In the valley bottom lay Bellingham. Lazy curls of smoke escaped from chimneys and hung in a faint blue cushion. The village snoozed like a peaceful cat. Along one skyline ran the north Cheviot Hills. The landscape had opened up for me and spread itself in delight. I was overcome with the desire to laugh. My peals of laughter rang out through the hills; they somersaulted and roly-polyed in delight. Like some irrepressible spring, the laughter rose up in me and bounded out like a trampolinist (mixed-metaphor time). The hills were alive with the sound of laughter. Gosh – that phrase could catch on.

For the third time that day I was to cross the River Tyne, on the wide, old stone bridge just outside Bellingham. How different it was to have your footsteps dogged by a river than by a motorway. By the way, the 'g' in Bellingham (like in most Northumbrian place names) is soft, as in Roger.

Just along the river stood the ivy-clad Riverdale Hall. The proprietor, John Cocker, a bright and cheerful-looking man, greeted me. He showed me to my room in the annexe (the main building was full). 'Just come along when you want,' he said and left.

I stood in my luxury hotel room and threw my battered bag on the bed. I removed my clumpy boots, my clothes. They looked liked they wanted to apologise for their appearance. As I stood in the shower and opened the small sachet of shampoo, I panicked. What if this was all some ghastly mistake? What if the room wasn't free? Did they realise I had no money whatsoever? Had Thomas Walton got his wires crossed, simply fixed me up with accommodation? Would a large bill await me? As I alarmed myself, I found the small wrapped bar of soap. It was difficult to open. Had he really said free of charge?

I made myself a cup of tea. The kettle flex was short.

I put my paranoia on hold. I did some washing. I filled the bowl with hot, soapy water, rubbing the soap bar furiously to produce a lather and bubbles. In this I washed my top, socks and pants, then hung them to dry. Millions and millions were spent on advertising and marketing detergents. And really it was as simple as this.

In the reception, my fears were laid to rest. 'Anything you want to eat, just order it,' said John Cocker. 'Compliments of the house.' Two ironies now presented themselves. Often on my journey I had dreamed of good food. Hunger had often gnawed at me. Never once had I thought it feasible I would be in a posh hotel and offered a free run of the menu. You want it? Order it.

The second irony was even funnier. I couldn't eat a damned thing. I was as full as a gun. Fit to burst. I had simply to point, price no object. Yet the menu was as much use to me as paper wellingtons. I thought back to that first day on the road to Tavistock, Sam and I stopping at the luxury hotel for water. The sudden shock, seeing the diners, smelling the roast beef, realising the invisible bubble that was around us. Here the bubble was popped. And I was pooped. Venison, pheasant, fish in wine sauce, duck à l'orange, trout with plums. 'Nothing for me, thanks. Maybe I'll have a pint.'

'Feel free,' said John Cocker and disappeared.

Did the hotel owners have hidden motives? Possibly. I was moderately well known in the region. My credentials hereabouts were okay. And they knew I was writing a book. Against that, the Riverdale was hardly down on its luck. And I never saw John Cocker again. No hard sell, or even a soft sell. Yet I had grown used somehow to the anonymity, had come to feel my journey was genuine. I was not some celebrity. I had no gimmicks, and often had to battle for the food, the shelter. Just me. No researchers. No 'team'. Not even a dog anymore. And nothing was set up. The book is how it was. The world is mainly run on deceit. All writers, painters and artists try to find *some* kind of truth. And if they don't, they should pack up and do something else.

I drank my pint in the hotel bar. A sign read 'Free Swim for Every Diner'. I imagined customers diving in between mouthfuls of sole meunière. Above the impressive fireplace, an array of cricket cups gleamed their bright silver. The village team (which played here) was doing well, second in the first division, West Tyne League. Maybe some time they should play against Whixley. Through the deep bay window I could see the French boules pitch, the children's swings hanging down from the many trees, the cricket pitch, and the North Tyne below.

I was the tramp at the Ritz, the scruff at the Palace, the hobo at the Hilton. The hotel was full of cheque books, credit cards, mobile phones, leather wallets. Neatly ironed clothes hung on coat hangers. Bathrooms had shelves full of posh aftershave and deodorant. I still had some Belgian chocolate.

Thomas Walton walked in the door. He'd come down to see me for a quiet drink. 'As you could see, I don't get much of a word in edgeways with my family.' I realised he was quite a shy man. He talked about the farm, how he ran live-music nights at the pub in the remote village of Greenhaugh. He'd read some of my reviews. Obviously a man of taste.

I'd written up the diary after the shower and enjoyed the drink, on my own and with Thomas. When he'd gone, with the light dying in the sky, I wandered down the sloping lawn. How idyllic it all was. Yet something wasn't quite right. What was it? I finally nailed it down.

This was a beautiful, comfortable, well-appointed hotel. Not a chain but family-run. My only previous hotel night had been in Plymouth, where I'd been aware that the next day I'd be setting off into the unknown. This had unnerved me greatly. Now the opposite was true. Over the days and weeks I had become used to being the itinerant, used to arriving at places unknown, unexpected, unannounced. My hosts were always unprepared. What interested me was how they handled it. Each night was a special night both for them and for me, one we would not forget. In the Riverdale Hall, I was absorbed with barely a ripple. I was part of the normal process, the throughput of people. My stay would be trouble-free. All things were here for me. This is what the hotel did, day in, day out. People passed through here as smoothly as along one of those moving corridors at airports. I was another of those people.

How could I have expected to respond to luxury in this way? But within Riverdale's stone walls, I realised I had changed on my journey. Often on the trip I had dreamed I was wallowing in luxury. Now I was wallowing. And wallowing was an unnatural act.

Miles travelled so far — 461

High on the moorland
Only the wind
And the sucking of my sweet

Swallowed by Forest — Another Country —
The Chill Begins

The sense of having undertaken a great journey was growing in me. It wasn't great in the number of miles – air passengers would whizz the distance in less time than the featured film.

But to me it felt like true travel, an unbroken journey through the length of the country.

Travel wasn't sitting in a tin box at 30,000 feet, eating a rubber chicken, with your headphones on number three for easy listening. That was merely moving from A to B. The faster the journey, the less the sense of real travel. Those who 'travelled' most often appreciated it least. Witness harassed businessmen at airports. Where was their sense of wonder, the excitement? They were too busy with mobile-phone negotiations as they waited in the first-class departure lounge. All travel should be an adventure.

These were my thoughts that morning as I woke in the warmth and comfort of the Riverdale Hall Hotel. I would seek no more lifts. They had fallen away naturally. They had been necessary to protect my damaged feet, and for some of the journey I'd sought them greedily. Now I liked the unbroken chain of walking on foot. I began to appreciate those Indian mystics who crawled every inch of a pilgrimage to be in touch with the earth. Walking had become a spiritual as well as a functional activity.

Breakfast saw a mixture of holidaymakers, shirt-sleeved travellers and business people. I did not know it, but this was to be my last hot food for three days. I did the breakfast menu proud. Egg, bacon, sausage, tomato, fried bread, cereal, grapefruit, fruit juice, toast, marmalade, two pots of tea. I passed on the prunes. I was within 100 miles of Edinburgh and suddenly my series of five-mile stints during the day were having some relevance to the total. Subtracting five from 473 had little significance. Five from 90 much more so.

When I said goodbye, the receptionist handed me a round of sandwiches, an apple and a small chocolate bar. Having at least some small amount of food reassured me. Like the poor man always keeping a penny in his pocket, I tried to hang on to an orange, a biscuit, even, heaven forbid, a lump of cheese.

My clothes had dried overnight and I set off through Bellingham, which, despite the coming of the nearby Kielder Reservoir with its water sports, remained sleepy. The village still smelled wood-smoke sweet, the main-store window was still an eccentric mix of the happenstance. I called briefly to see the grave of The Long Park (a gruesome tale), and wondered at the oddity of the fenced gun in the centre, taken from Fort Taku in China in 1900. I assumed it was part of our glorious Opium Wars.

It was a long incline towards Otterburn on the B6320. On the top of a ridge stood a barn. It was exactly like countless stands I'd seen at division four games when, as a youngster, I'd trekked nationwide to follow Notts County. As I passed the barn, I could smell the Bovril, the acrid tobacco of the old men's pipes (old men still went to football in those days), hear the dull thud of the ball, the echoing shouts of the players around the thinly populated corrugated grounds.

I knew we were getting close to Scotland. The midges arrived. A squadron flew in and assembled in front of my face. They looked like stirred tea leaves, and were totally unimpressed with my aggressive swipes. What did they want of me? How did they travel exactly the same speed as me? What did they think about all the time?

The road rose steadily for four miles. I'd seen very little traffic and I was to see even less as I turned left onto an isolated highway. I was now to walk ten miles, during which distance I would pass only three houses. This cannot happen in Surrey.

The silence I was to experience was powerful enough to be a noise in its own right. Often my silences on this journey were relative, with a low background noise of distant traffic, or even the occasional car. Here I was usually many miles from the nearest road, and there were no motorways. Something about this experience affected me deeply. It was a sense of isolation and solitariness against a vast natural backdrop, and it put matters into perspective. On this terrain, in this silence, my own life was simultaneously a tiny part of things and also vital. I was high in the Pennines, mottled moorland all around. The 'roads' were gated. Livestock here had preference over motor transport. To the west, on a distant hillside, Redesdale Forest spread its dark green beard. Forests were to play a large part in my journey on this day.

Soon I happened upon the first of the three habitations. It was called, unusually, Sundaysight, but why? I knocked to find out. Divina Wallace answered the door. With her husband she reared 1,000 sheep here, across 2,300 acres. She'd tried to find the root of the name herself, but without success. She produced a book of Northumbrian place names. We pored through it. No luck. 'The house has been here 200 years,' she said, 'and there are ruins of more buildings up in the field. They may have something to do with it.' Lots of isolated buildings in the north had strange names. Elsewhere I'd come across Showtime and Seldom Seen.

By now the road had become a rough track, pushing its primitive way through the gorse moorland. No clue of human life in any direction, no vehicles, nothing – until I spotted in the distance habitation number two. Neighbours of Sundaysight, if you like, except the stereo volume was unlikely to cause problems.

This was Keepers Cottage at High Green, still referred to on some maps as Pitt Houses. It was a bizarre sight in such a remote spot. Within its fenced garden waddled a gaggle of geese. A miniature windmill turned its sails in the breeze. Polly the mongrel lay and dozed, and at a wooden outside table sat seven-year-old Corey, who must have plotted my approach from way back, like that famous scene in *Lawrence of Arabia*.

Wee Corey lived here with his grandparents, Dorothy Fahrendorf and her German-born husband Lother. They'd moved two years ago from the Walker district of Newcastle, made famous on the Animals track 'Gonna Send You Back to Walker'. I didn't feel anyone was going to send this trio back. It was difficult to imagine two more contrasting places than Keepers Cottage and the lean, undernourished, hard-bitten Walker. How did they get there? Why? I never found out. How come people didn't tell me everything, instantly? I did get tea and chocolate biscuits, and Dorothy said simply, 'We love it here,' and smiled. Well, that would do. Polly dozed on.

I was lucky enough to experience rush hour at Keepers Cottage. That is, a Land Rover passed. This was Jane Wilson; she lived a few miles further up, at the third habitation.

It took me an hour's walk on the tracks to reach Jane, but by the magic of the printed word I can take you there immediately. Jane was a rare-sheep breeder with her husband Roger and the house was Gibbshiels. I got another cup of tea and an apple. The irony struck me; I seemed much less likely to starve in a wilderness than in a jam-packed town.

How would a townie like me adapt to such remoteness? None of the three houses' inhabitants seemed bonkers. In fact, they appeared to be very balanced. I was used to nipping to the pub, the corner shop. I defined human beings as social animals who often couldn't stand the sight of one another. As a writer I spent a lot of time in isolation. When I came away from the writing, I liked people, noises, laughter. Yet on this trip it was people, noise and the rest which had depressed me. Solitude had strengthened me, the wide, open countryside. Towns had filled me with gloom. Was it because I was penniless? Was I becoming more solitary, more anti-social? I still yearned for people, still found the lonely, unpeopled nights the most difficult times. My nature was not hermitic.

Sundaysight, Keepers Cottage, Gibbshiels – what a good, demanding walk. And each could provide tea and biscuits for the hardy rambler. Ten miles, three lots of refreshments. They should get together. (Mortimer, just leave it alone.)

After those ten miles, I had another six to walk through Redesdale Forest before reaching Elishaw and the A68, which would take me up to the Scottish border. Or the English border, depending on how you saw it. Forest stretched away across every hillside on those six miles. Often there was a lawnmower strip where the felling machines had been at work. Elsewhere a single strip of forest was bordered by a shaven gap, a punk haircut next to a skinhead one.

The track climbed and dipped, climbed and dipped. How come the UK was said to have the lowest tree count in Europe? Had the counters missed this lot? At times the trackside trees had been felled, giving a feeling of space. Elsewhere I was in serious forest, 40-foot conifers close-packed, rising steeply at each side of the narrow track, all sun gone and just a strip of sky above, a slice of light ahead.

The day was changeable – sun, cloud, some wind – but I was spared rain. The path was shale, which made for hard, unstable walking. A week previously my feet would have succumbed. Now my step was firm, and the miles trailed away behind me.

For a few miles I joined the Pennine Way and made contact with a group of walkers. They'd almost achieved their 250-mile trek from Edale to Kirk Yetholm. Had I done it? Me? No, no, I wasn't doing that walk actually . . .

Taking this track cut out as much of the A68 as possible, but there were so few roads of any distinction in this part of Northumberland that for the final nine English miles I was nudged back onto the main highway. Change of terrain, change of mood. It was not only that the odd curlew was replaced by the regular artic. For an entire hour I walked past Catcleugh Reservoir. Once you reached a landmark, you felt you'd done it: a border post, a crossroads, a certain building. Been there, done that. For an hour I got nowhere. Still the reservoir.

And another thing. After the reservoir, the road rose and twisted up towards the border point, Carter Bar. You could follow the traffic up. A big lorry passed. Five minutes later it was still curling up that road, still in England. By this time I'd walked around 20 miles, much of it on rough terrain. My body was crying 'Stop!' but my soul wanted to sleep that night in Scotland. I thought of sending my soul ahead, leaving my body here for the night. I'd eaten my sandwiches, and as we climbed the temperature fell.

What else could I do but push on? Best foot forward, followed by worst foot. It was six o'clock when Carter Bar appeared. This was little more than two lay-bys, each with a hunk of raised rock onto which the country's name was sculpted. And a mobile refreshment van. There were no toilets, however much many Scots' first inclination coming the other way would be to piss on England. Somehow they'd recently spent £250,000 on this site. Actually I quite liked its low-key feel. No McDonald's, no furry tartan toys, no piped pipes. Just the view into Scotland, a series of small mountains spread out before you. They were like cakes rising in the oven. In any circumstances this would be a wonderful sight.

Imagine for me, a penniless wanderer on the road for 24 days and almost 500 miles. My limbs were tired, the cold was beginning to seep through my clothes. None of which mattered at that moment, that first glimpse of Scotland. Into my mind flashed the moment when I'd stood on the south coast and looked out across the wide bay at Plymouth. Now this.

I marched up to the mobile snack bar and addressed the bespectacled young man. 'If I were to tell you I had travelled penniless all the way from Plymouth to get here, would that be worth a cup of tea?' I asked.

'Och, aye, it would,' he replied in a sing-song Scottish accent. That accent lifted my mood. That accent, plus the hot tea he put into my shivering hands, was like spinach to Popeye, like a charge of electricity to Frankenstein's monster, like the magic sponge to Alan Shearer, like ammonia salts to the fainted lady, like . . . that's enough.

'Hey, man – brill!' I laughed out loud, whooped. People stared at me. 'What's your name?' I asked the provider.

'Stephen Hogg,' he said.

'It will be immortalised,' I said, and drank deep of the heat which coursed through my body. I left him to his wagon, shaking slightly in the wind, marched across the border and saw the very first road sign to Edinburgh – fifty-eight miles. Fifty-eight miles! A quick stroll up to the end of the street, a walk round the block. A legless chicken could do it. A one-legged man going backwards. Fifty-eight miles! My own route, on the small back roads, would, I knew, be longer. But even so. In three days (I calculated), Edinburgh could be mine.

Straight after Carter Bar, I left the main road and turned down the A6088. The traffic vanished so rapidly I suspected everyone knew something except me. No traffic, few buildings, as we dropped from the summit.

Let this be writ in Scotland's favour. The very first buildings I came to by the roadside gave me shelter. These were Fellside Boarding Kennels, isolated in the unpopulated terrain. Unlike the Northumberland stone buildings, these looked more squat, more functional, and again I was to be among dogs, though far removed from the hounds of Clifton. This was where the dogs checked in for their annual holiday, leaving owners little choice but to go off to Lanzarote, Corfu or some such destination to fill in the time.

The kennels offered a rare old crew of dogs – dogs no bigger than a piglet, other dogs the size of a small horse – all in the care of two ardent canophiles (is there such a word?), Bernard and Joy Whiteley, who'd moved here a few years ago from Lancashire. Dogs were their business and their passion. They looked after holiday dogs, but they had their own pack of huskies housed just up the lane. On the next morning, when I'd have more energy, I'd come close to these remarkable pooches, appreciate their unique nature. In some ways my day had imitated the huskies' – Bernard and Joy raced them over the very forest tracks I'd walked.

At this time of the day I was often knackered, shamefully

unreceptive as a writer, not up to the job. The Whitings offered me my final caravan of the odyssey, a small affair little bigger than a currant bun, which rocked in the wind like a bairn's cradle. Bernard also gave me a cheese toastie, which I devoured rapidly, and a cup of tea. They asked me about my journey. I answered on autopilot. They showed me the bathroom. I plunged my hands in hot water. Heat was good. I retired to my small caravan, wrote up my diary, prepared to extinguish myself for the night. I'd walked 23 miles. My fuel tank was low.

Bernard knocked at the caravan door. 'Fancy a pint, then?'

Actually, when I thought about it, I did. But where? I looked around the wild landscape. Hardly a building in sight.

'Bonchester Bridge,' said Bernard. 'Only six miles.'

That was it, you see. There was tiredness. But greater than tiredness was the need for human contact. The call came. I responded. Plus it was only the second time in more than three weeks I'd been invited into a pub.

'I've no loot at all,' I said. Bernard shrugged his shoulders. Company out here was probably rare, even the penniless kind. He was a biggish, dark-red-haired man with a laconic sense of humour.

Bonchester Bridge was on my route. It seemed like travelling into the future, six miles I would do again the next day. It seemed like cheating, like I shouldn't have been on that road except when walking it.

The Horse and Hounds was an old, low-beamed, quiet pub. Bernard bought the pints and lingered at the bar, as is many men's wont. 'Bernard,' I said. 'Sitting down would be nice. In the circumstances.'

I couldn't find anyone Scottish. Bernard was English; his mate Martin, who joined us, was English; perched on a stool at the bar was an English public-school type. The barmaid was English. Bernard read my thoughts.

'This border area isn't very well known, but English people are beginning to find it very attractive. People tend to think of Scotland as Edinburgh, or the Highlands and Islands, but it's beautiful round here, just look at it.'

Lots of English people had fled into Scotland in the later Thatcher years, hoping for less barbarism over the border. I thought how perceptions of the Scottish character had changed over the last two decades. The English then saw the Scots as a florid-faced race of drunken, chanting football supporters, or groups of tediously loud males on long train journeys, roaring their objectionable way through a mountain of beer cans, and insulting other passengers.

But Scotland had acquired a dignity, an identity. It had lost its sense of inferiority and gained a cultural one. It was now left to the English to wonder who they were, to rant at Europe and foreigners, and to fortress themselves inside their own narrow world. Scotland had come of age.

I felt myself melting into the seat, as if the tiredness was slowly dissolving my body. I had sat down and fancied staying there for a decade or so.

'Have a malt whisky,' said Bernard. How come he could always read my mind? Part of me felt fit and healthy, up to everything. Another part, just below this level, felt itself slowly emptying, draining away.

'We're actually in Roxburghshire,' said Bernard. 'No one can spell that, so we just say the Borders. I used to live in a terraced house. I couldn't stand the noisy neighbours. I love it here.'

People in my terrace often suffered from a noisy neighbour. It was me.

Bernard also worked as a care worker, but I suspected his best care was for those huskies. They could survive 50 to 60 degrees below freezing. Their hollow fur was especially adapted for cold extremes, and at night their noses dried up to protect them.

One of the least popular people among husky folk was Scott of the Antarctic (how come no one ever used Scott's first name?). For efficiency at the sled, he cut off his huskies' tails, robbing them of vital night-time insulation.

Two hours rolled its uncomplicated way in this pleasant pub. We drove back under a vividly clear sky, the stars like silver beads in such pollution-free sharpness. For the second time I was passing over my route for the next day. I'd have covered it twice before I walked a yard of it.

A cold wind rocked my small caravan that night. I felt snug in this small settlement in the middle of this unfettered terrain. I was asleep within minutes.

Day Twenty-five — Wednesday, 19 August

Miles travelled so far — 484

Round the historic ruin
Two generations of sheep
Chew into the future

The Mega Dogs — Round-up Time — Barn Number Two

Bernard walked the dogs early, and there were lots of them. I'd thought of joining him, but woke up in my little sleeping bag and thought again. The 23 miles the previous day was the most I'd walked. But was I tired physically or mentally?

Maybe I yearned for some stability, an end to the relentless daily change of landscape and people, a need every day to adapt to the new. Maybe I was at the other end of the spectrum to being in a rut. Instead of being solidified, I had no form at all, an eternal shape-shifter.

The lower temperature caused some problems and solved others. There was no longer any problem with space to pack the spare clothes. I just wore all of them.

I rose, walked up to the house, washed and stood in the kitchen. I ate a slice of dry bread. I felt alone. Was I not welcome here? Did I take my welcomes for granted? Was I becoming a parasite, crawling my way through the nation's generosity?

Bernard walked past the window with a brace of dogs. Joy was busy doing something elsewhere. So why was I standing here like a self-indulgent prat? Give the man a hand. Since the great creosote session on Dartmoor, I'd done little singing for my supper. This was a chance.

I ran out the door and offered to help with the dogs. Bernard's face lit up. In an instant the atmosphere changed. 'Ever walked huskies?' he asked.

No. Huskies have 28 valves, 500 horse power (dog power?). Huskies are turbo-charged, twin-booster rockets. I was given the leads (the reins?) of Shalk and Patchy. Bernard pointed me down the lane. I was pulled forward as if by a supercharged Ferrari. Each husky has a pulling power of 500 lbs and I had two of them. All a human can do is hang on and hope for clemency.

I whizzed down the lane. With two huskies and a pair of roller skates, I could have been in Edinburgh before you could say Pedigree Chum. As long as they pulled together, there was hope. Then Shalk wanted a pee. Patchy wanted to go on. I was the circus strong man, two horses pulling in opposite directions. My arms and their sockets were about to end a lifelong relationship.

Eventually, when the two had had their fun, they returned to the kennels to be replaced by a brace of boarder dogs. No contrast could have been greater. Poppy and Suzy were two elderly Labradors. They had seen life and now wished merely to reflect on it, a post-prandial stroll, a leisurely stretch of the legs, two sedate, dignified ladies for whom the world could turn slowly. They trod their gentle way down the lane, occasionally turning their brown eyes to look at me. With the huskies the leads were as taut as a Stradivarius string. Here they were as loose as a skipping rope.

Later, I saw the whole husky pack. Many of the beautiful dogs had piercing blue eyes which looked into your inner-most thoughts. I imagined guiding eight huskies, pulling the special rig over an icy forest track. The rigs had no steering, only the human voice to guide them. It was what huskies were built for. Not sitting on a fireside rug all day. Huskies had happily resisted human domesticity, yet some people still bought them as pets. Huskies had better things to do. Go and buy yourself a poodle.

The dog time lifted my spirits. Doing things always did. I had toast and cereal, tea, and said my farewells. I then headed back on the Bonchester Bridge road I already knew too well.

The road continued to drop, the countryside becoming tamer, more gentle. A fierce wind whistled from the west, through the distant vast acreage of Wauchope Forest, still a part of the Kielder complex. Not for the first time, there was a pebble in my boot. Not for the first time, I convinced myself it would go away of its own accord. I shook it this way and that, I exiled it to a non-provocative area of the boot. Always it would return to continue its provocation. Deep down I knew that in this war between the elephant and the flea, the flea would inevitably win. Its attacks were minor but consistent. It employed attrition. And each time it attacked, it seemed slightly larger, sharper. All wriggling and shaking were useless. I would need to remove the boot. When I finally shook it out, the offending item was no bigger than a full stop.

I was on the A6088 but for the first few miles scarcely saw a car. On the opposite side, near nothing at all, in a forest of weeds and with a sense of neglect to suggest no one had given it a second glance, no had paused in decades, was a tumbledown barn. Its front door had long forgotten how to open. Its useful life had long passed into memory. The empty road stretched away in both directions. The poor edifice cried out for some attention. And there, almost pathetic, as if in some self-deluded way the building wished to see itself as something more than a forgotten irrelevance, was a sign on the door: No Parking Please.

Further on the road, and home only to grazing sheep, was a ruined church with a plaque, the place where in 1388 James Earl of Douglas assembled his forces to invade England, an invasion culminating in the Battle of Otterburn and, much later, in the Sassenachs' revenge of the poll tax. Some Scottish 'A' roads were single track, just as some English 'B' roads had proved to be race track.

By this stage my socks were moulting. I discovered more

and more purple tufts in the boots. The socks themselves were almost see-through.

I walked deeper into Scotland and became philosophical. Walking was the oldest, safest and slowest form of transport known to humankind. For all these reasons it needed more respect. What technology was needed to improve walking? Very little. How many lives had been lost over the centuries from head-on collisions between walkers? None. How many people became overstressed through walking? None. How many through plane and car travel? Millions.

As I was musing, I caught sight of wild raspberries at the roadside. They were my favourite fruit. The good press went to strawberries: the Wimbledon fashionability, that certain sense of 'Englishness'. Raspberries were made fun of, used to describe rude noises. Dictionaries of quotations ignored them. I loved them. I popped some into my mouth, felt the fruity, tangy flavour explode. How could anyone prefer those bloated, overweight strawberry things? For several hundred yards they grew in profusion. I popped 'em in, emitting little squeals of pleasure. I loved the taste, but also needed the calories, the vitamins. All I had left were a few precious squares of Belgian chocolate. For all I knew, these raspberries could be my day's food.

I passed through Chesters (whose one-time vicar was said to have penned the song 'Rule Britannia' – hardly the most popular choice hereabouts). It was tiny, as was Bonchester Bridge, providing me with a reminder of how unpopulated Scotland was. Not much smaller than England, yet one tenth of the population. A billboard in Bonchester gave the lead story in the current *Hawick News*: 'Parking Blitz at Sandbed.'

In the blink of an eye I was through BB and climbing again. Mountains were visible in all directions. Most were rounded and cuddly-looking. The exception was the craggy Rubers Law, which would dominate the horizon for several hours, firstly to the north, later to the east, rising to more than 1,300 feet with its distinctive frills of heather.

A sudden surprise: on a straight road near Denholm, a Land Rover pulled alongside me. In it I could see the smiling, ruddy face of a farmer. Who was I? Where was I heading?

He was Andy McReady from Upper Toft Farm. He and his son (also Andy) were about to round up 251 sheep in one field and persuade them to go through a gate, over a road and into another field. I fancied seeing this. The tussle would take place on the nearby brae (I was settling into the lingo). I had a grandstand view.

The flock of sheep was a moving, shape-shifting cloud. A changing, swirling entity, then still, then moving again. Against the sheep were two men, one Land Rover and three dogs. Initial success was none. The sheep, whom I'd considered ridiculous, succeeded in making humans, dogs and machines look ridiculous. Several times they seemed controlled, in the right direction. But then a trickle of sheep, like water through the weakest point of a dam, would leak away, the leak became a torrent, and the chance was gone. Or they simply ran round and round in a circle, like some giant animated Catherine wheel, going nowhere. At ever faster speed. The collies, Tim, Midge and Glenn, broke up these catherine wheels and forced the sheep to regroup. Slowly the canine trio, aided by man and machine, nudged the huge errant cloud towards the gate, through which the sheep were eventually squeezed, like toothpaste through the tube.

Once on the small road, the sheep were reluctant to go through the second gate. They ran up both directions at once, only to be defeated by two powerful forces. The collie Tim showed remarkable intelligence, running past the sheep on the stone wall's blind side, leaping over and facing them down. The sheep that ran the other way faced a man wearing purple-laced boots, combat trousers and a damp Indian hat. They surrendered. Both fleeing flanks were slowly nudged through the second gate.

This was great fun. I think Andy McReady enjoyed having an audience, too. I asked for any farms ahead which might give me a cup of tea, and he gave me directions. I walked on another mile and a half to Whitriggs Farm. When

Betty Whitriggs answered the door, I proclaimed, 'You have to give me a cup of tea because Andy McReady said so!'

There was not only tea. Betty laughed, invited me in, sat me down in her welcoming kitchen and served up a Scottish beef sandwich from their own herd, with biscuits to follow.

Not for the first time on my journey, a husband was to walk into his own home to find his wife chatting away with a total stranger scoffing his grub. Jim Whitriggs, like his wife, was quite advanced in years, fit, healthy-looking, nattily dressed in a distinctively tweedy, rural way. The farm had been in the family for 50 years; 500 acres had cost £9,000. And did I know, asked Jim, that a previous laird hereabouts had squandered more than a dozen farms on gambling? English, I assumed.

Jim spoke so quickly and with such a strong Scottish accent that I found myself clinging to its coat-tails. I slurped down the tea, swallowed the delicious beef. North of the border the weather had changed considerably. The tea was my central heating. There was no sweat on my hat. Sitting in the farm kitchen, I suddenly felt in the real Scotland. And not a haggis or sprig of white heather in sight.

On to Denholm, on the junction of the A698 from Hawick to Kelso. In the centre of Denholm, on open land, stood an extraordinarily rococo monument to a man called John Leyden. If the day hadn't by that time turned cold and blowy, if I hadn't been getting a bit tired, I might have been arsed to find out who he was.

On to the B6405, then the B6359 (this sounds a bit like the man in the Monty Python guest-house sketch), small, quiet, forgotten roads. On a far hillside, scattered sheep looked like a join-the-dots puzzle. Was this a forgotten area, or was most of Scotland simply forgotten in the rush for Loch Ness, Edinburgh and the like?

I'd picked out the curiously named Lilliesleaf. I'd sleep there. With such a name it would be wonderful. I always expected everywhere to be wonderful. Places to me were often more real in the imagination than in their actuality.

I walked into the small pub, the Cross Keys, late

afternoon. Again a few locals looked at me. Small communities were sometimes suspicious initially. Large communities ignored you entirely. Which was worse.

The landlord suggested St Dunstan's Farm, 200 yards up the road. I walked through the farmyard and knocked at the door of the main house. It was answered by a man with a large, ruddy face as shiny as a red balloon. Did he have anywhere I could sleep? I explained my situation, my journey.

'Ah'm hevvin' ma tea,' he said. 'Ye'll be waitin' five minutes.' He looked me up and down, and closed the door. In the next 20 minutes I had ample time to study every aspect of his farmyard.

Finally, he emerged. I could sleep in his barn. And, I wondered, did he have anywhere I could just freshen up a bit? I'd been on the road all day. The farmer's name was Walter Inglis. I'd always wanted to meet a farmer called Walter (*The Archers*, you know). He pointed to a cold tap in the middle of the yard. My bathroom.

I was hungry again. It was the cold, it ate up my calories.

'Ye can hev a cup o' tea at seven i' the mornin',' said Walter. 'Noo, ah hev to gaun te work.'

None of this filled me with unfettered joy. To cheer myself up, I asked how far it was to Edinburgh, wondering if it was less than 40 miles. 'Edinburgh?' said Walter. 'Ye'll be talkin' mair than 50 miles fra' here.'

It was six o'clock. A long and cold and hungry night lay ahead. I walked to the large, open-fronted barn, settled myself in some hay, took out my diary and began to write. An hour later I looked up. Walter was looking at me. When he saw me looking back, he went away.

As the sun dipped and the dusk felt its way in, the temperature fell. Scotland in late August was a different proposition from Devon in late July. I had no food, a draughty open barn, a thin sleeping bag. I decided to be pushy.

I walked back to the farmhouse, knocked. Walter's presence filled the doorway. 'It's pretty cold out there,' I said.

'After walking all day, a cup of hot tea would be really welcome. Or anything. And could I possibly borrow a small towel?'

Walter nodded and said nothing. The door closed. Ten minutes later he appeared at the barn. He had a bucket half full of warm water. He had a pink pillowcase for a towel. He had a round of dry bread with a single slice of luncheon meat inside. And he had three cold sausages. And a mug of hot tea.

'Wuv had a lot o' break-ins,' he said, as I tucked in. 'Wu hev te be careful.' I sensed he'd softened slightly towards me, and nodded in appreciation.

'Ye'll be writin' a book, then?' asked Walter. I nodded again, and bit the head off a sausage.

'Fra' Plymouth, ye say?'

Another nod. He looked at me with a mixture of caution, curiosity and disbelief.

'Aye, well,' he said, and went away.

I finished the food and drink, plunged my arms into the bucket of rapidly cooling water, washed, and dried myself with the pillowcase, which tended to redistribute water rather than remove it.

I searched through my bag for any spare clothes to put on. None left. I took out the black bin liners, again stupidly not realising I could insulate myself in them rather than just lie on them. It was still only 7.30 p.m. Elsewhere people were preparing to go out, settle down to the telly, emulsion the ceiling or fiddle their tax returns. I was lying in my inadequate bed, in an exposed Scottish barn, slowly digesting my cold luncheon meat and sausages.

Miles travelled so far — 506

Rain hits my brolly
Slides to earth
Further north than planned

Me and Sir Walter — Back to Crime — Well Dug In

For the first part of the night I was warm. Eventually the cold found a way in. By the time the cockerel crowed to wake up the world, he was redundant for me. I was wide awake.

I allowed myself the luxury of a lie-in till 6 a.m. I felt the long sleep had done me good. As well as the cockerel crowing, the sheep baaed, a nearby horse neighed. Noisy place, Scotland.

The hay mites had invaded the least likely places. Scrawling a few biro notes in the small notebook, I obliterated several dozen with the pen's end.

I was wearing most things I carried in the bag. I searched the hay for the remnants and came across a lovely brown egg. This cheered me greatly. I was certain Walter would have mellowed overnight. I imagined a great big fried breakfast sizzling on the range, just waiting for me.

I decided to wash alfresco. I stripped off, filled the bucket from the tap, set it on a tree stump and, in this wind-swept place, threw the cold water all over me, to the accompaniment of my shrieks and yells. A white pony in a nearby outbuilding neighed in unison. I was one giant goosepimple. After dressing, I sought out the pony, stroked her head, felt the warm breath from her nostrils on my cold, tight skin.

Once again I was on Walter's doorstep. I held up the egg as the door was answered by his wife, Elizabeth. Walter and Elizabeth. How sixteenth century.

'An egg!' I said. I could hear vibrating in the air the two unspoken words, 'for breakfast!'

Elizabeth took the egg and we both looked at it.

'Er, Walter said something about a cup of tea?' I said, egg visions disappearing.

'Och, aye,' said Elizabeth.

I decided to be pushy again. Necessity dictated.

'I'll be walking more than 20 miles today,' I said. 'It's fairly cold and I have no money or food. Any small thing would be appreciated.'

'Och, aye,' said Elizabeth again and closed the door. It led into a porch, then a second door at right angles. I'd failed to see anything of the interior, the only location where I couldn't describe a single chair or table.

The decision had obviously been taken. No crossing the threshold.

Elizabeth reappeared with a large mug of tea, and another round of dry bread luncheon meat sandwiches. I thanked her. The door closed again.

I sat on a stone in the yard and drank the tea. Ten yards away, five cats and a dog were looking at me. Perhaps they expected scraps.

Before setting off, I sat in an outhouse and brought the diary up to date. Walter walked past, came over, asked what I was doing. I showed him the diary, which by this time contained more than 50,000 words. He leafed through it, repeating in a low voice, 'Very good, very good . . .'

I knew absolutely nothing about him and his life. As if in some symbolic gesture, he gave me details of two short cuts on the day's journey. This seemed a satisfactory conclusion to our somewhat strange relationship. I shook his hand, he left and I carried on with the diary. Later, as I walked out through the farm gate, the pack on my back, I had the distinct impression that, somewhere, Walter Inglis was watching me.

For the first time I hadn't shaved, due to a combination of fierce wind, exposed farmyard and no reflective surfaces to speak of. I realised I now felt part of the landscape, rather than a figure passing through it. My features had weathered in sympathy with it; I had immersed myself in it for so long, my walking rhythm was in tune with its own rhythms.

How would I react to pasty-faced urbanites? How would I feel piled up with popcorn in the multiplex? I realised my penniless odyssey would have been impossible via large conurbations. Only the culture of the countryside was capable of sustaining this lifetime urbanite through his journey.

Two small reflections on rural travelling: first, those round black-and-white poles at dangerous corners. I remembered them as sturdy metal. Or had they always been pieces of moulded plastic as flimsy as nail clippings? And drains on country roads. Many were choked solid with weeds, uncared for over years. Next time there is a flash flood put down to an act of God, someone should ask if a bit of boring routine drain maintenance might not have prevented it.

I headed off on this cold, grey morning wondering what else my odyssey had in store for me. What would Walter and Elizabeth have made of their visitor as they tucked into my brown egg? How about my other temporary hosts? I'd probably never know.

Walter's first short cut was after walking through the strung-out village. It took us over a small wooden bridge and along a quiet, leafy path, cutting a corner off the road to Midlem, a white-painted village perched on the hillside. It looked Mediterranean on approach. This was belied later by its giant focal oak tree and its ornate village pump (which didn't work).

The rain came to befriend the wind. I took out the brolly – eventually. The brolly suffered the same philosophy as the pebble in the boot: resist till the last moment the bothersome duty of extracting it from the bag. By the time I relented I was usually half soaked. My relationship with the brolly was ambivalent. I needed its protection, but cursed its tendency to turn itself inside out in the wind, resembling some grotesque invertebrate, some monstrous silver-limbed crab. The metamorphosis would come with a sudden, frightening crack. I found myself tacking this way and that to prevent the horrible inversion, which usually I couldn't.

Cars were still a rarity on the small, quiet roads bordered

by tall banks of rosebay willow herb and spanned by bridges only ten feet long. Walter's second short cut swung me away off the road for several miles and would drop me into Galashiels, the last real town before Edinburgh. It would, he said, take me past Abbotsford, the home of that Jeffrey Archer of his day, Sir Walter Scott.

I headed off the road in the wind and rain. The deeply rutted tractor tracks were rapidly filling with water; the track climbed into an increasingly remote shelterless terrain. I wondered about old Wally striding out here, pondering the next plot twist to *Ivanhoe*. Did he carry a brolly?

After two miles being blown hither and thither, I took shelter in a corrugated barn, its sides trembling and rattling. It was now 48 hours since the last hot meal (Bellingham breakfast). I had a badly bruised orange, the luncheon meat sandwich, two shortbread biscuits and the remnants of the Belgian chocolate. The full stomach of Riverdale Hall seemed long distant. I ate what was edible of the orange, swigged the water and from the barn corner watched the great grey mass of the sky.

Then it was back to the track and along a ridge top, an open target for the elements. Finally the track dropped and became tarmac; scattered buildings appeared. The brolly's crab impression was in full swing.

Passing a building belonging to Napier University, I wrongly concluded I'd reached Galashiels itself. On the ring road, a council worker in shimmering dayglo yellow jacket pointed me to the old railway line which had been converted into a cycle and pedestrian path. Follow that, he said, to the heart of the town.

The heart was still three wet, mud-stained, tired miles away. I was not over-jolly, which maybe explained my anti-pathy to such fashionable paths, lauded by conservationists as a safe innovation for walkers and bikers. They were perfectly flat. Perfectly straight. And perfectly boring. You moved through a green tube sealed from the world proper. The walls of hedgerows and other greenery kept the path from anything remotely of interest. At times came sounds of people, vehicles, life, but there was nothing to be seen. The green movement had swallowed this confidence trick and had allowed cyclists and pedestrians to be shunted away from the real world so motorists could carry on their destruction. Why not stick the motorists in a green tube? Let the rest of us enjoy the real world! Why marginalise us?

By the end, I was some sight. Muddy, exhausted, bad-tempered. And in Galashiels I perpetuated a long English tradition. I stole from the Scots. Twice. Theft number one was in the Co-op supermarket. I pushed my trolley, on the lookout for the easily swallowed. This was called 'grazing' in the USA, and supermarkets were wise to it. Almost all items needed careful opening, difficult under the cold security video's eye.

I plumped for a Granny Smith's apple. All right, hardly the Great Train Robbery. I took surreptitious bites as I trundled around, a mock interest in other foodstuffs. I stuck the core behind an instant coffee jar and walked out, muddy, dishevelled, conspicuous. Did they have X-ray cameras revealing the stolen contents of stomachs?

I needed warmth and rest. In the central library, I stretched out in the reference section. I was surrounded by normal, dry people with money in their pockets. I picked up *The Scotsman* and read of the ongoing debate between editor Andrew Neil and Ross McWhirter on the concept of being Scottish. What of the concept of being hungry, tired and cold? My eyelids drooped. I drifted away to the soft rustle of newspapers, the occasional whispered tones of the assistants. I just wanted to stay there forever, that was all. I nibbled my final shortcake, shoved the last remnant of dried bread into my mouth, let the heat and rest partially recharge me.

I wanted a cup of tea. I wanted it more than unbridled sex, or promotion for Notts County. I could get cups of tea in the country. Towns floored me. The man next to me was reading a fishing magazine. I would ask for tea in the tourist information office.

I stood in the queue, waiting my turn. Everything was neatly packaged and Scotticised, the maps, the souvenirs, the key rings, the cuddly toys. An American couple in front were enquiring about accommodation, the man's voice as loud as his checked trousers. Two elderly ladies wanted to know about the theatre. The assistant looked fresh from a customer-relations course which provided a self-adhesive smile to be worn at all times. She was neatly dressed and she neatly answered all enquiries without once faltering. Had one of the Undead come in with an enquiry, she would have smiled on and answered it. It was a busy office, and she was on her own. The thought of this bedraggled, muddy individual asking for a cup of tea was suddenly ludicrous. I asked about alternative routes to Edinburgh, avoiding the A7. She suggested two. Tealess, I walked out.

On the way out of Galashiels, I committed larceny number two. A greengrocer's wares spilled out onto the pavement, including oranges the size of coconuts. I picked one up, stuffed it in my top and kept on walking, again expecting the hand on the shoulder, the hot breath in the air, the words 'You're nicked!'.

What excuse did I have? None. Except that the benefits to me were substantial, the losses to them minimal. And what if everyone made such a value judgement? I had no idea. And, anyway, by this time I was out of town, secreted behind a bush and halfway through the orange. As I bit into the juicy flesh, I thought, whatever happened to Abbotsford? Had I missed Walter Scott's neat pile?

The rain had eased, but the wind's lungs were still full. My first planned diversion was via a public footpath through Hartburn, eventually returning to the A7 at Stow. It looked on the map only marginally longer, but much more peaceful. The fates were looking after me. As I turned off, they told me to check with a householder at the junction. 'That route's no good at all,' he said. 'It takes you right out of your way, is high and exposed and when you get to Hartburn the footpath's impassable.'

I returned to the main road. I'd travelled 12 miles in the morning. Edinburgh was about 30 miles away, and I wanted to make it the next day. The A7 was busy but scenic. Every step now seemed to bring my destination closer.

Diversion number two was from Stow itself, on a small road running parallel, emerging at Fountainhall. But I was destined to take no diversions. There was a hiss of brakes. A giant lorry had pulled up alongside me. A passenger door swung open. From halfway to the sky the driver leaned out. 'Edinburgh?' he said.

I laughed out loud. I remembered those early abortive attempts at lifts, the thumb swinging, the endless vehicles passing, my poor tenderised feet. And now here. I'd not given lifts a thought for days. The driver's smiling face beamed down. I had only to jump into his warm cab. My journey would be over in an hour. I could be back in my own warm bed that night.

'Well?'

Unbidden, he had arrived. I'd like to think my partial weakening was in response to his unprompted generosity. There was also the fact I was knackered.

'Take me four miles,' I said and jumped in. His cab was the size of an average recording studio. I looked round for a sunbed. His name was Brian Feeney and he was from Livingston. I told him of my odyssey, my need to arrive in Edinburgh on foot. I enjoyed the lofty cab. The world scurried beneath us. We looked down on pedestrians' bald spots, the creased tops of trilbies and, in cars, shapely, disembodied knees.

Brian Feeney was a bubbly man who himself often relied on lifts when carrying trade plates. He pulled out some bourbon biscuits. 'Take them,' he said. 'The sugar will give you energy. If I'd got any more grub you could have had that. I've not been paid yet.'

His generosity, plus the fillip of the four miles, lifted my spirits. Galashiels to Edinburgh was 32 miles. I'd walked several and, with the lift, reckoned I was now around 24 miles away. I strode out. I needed to be nearer.

My mind now concentrated purely on the walking. The wind flapped at my green grandad shirt. I strode on. I eventually came to a road sign saying 'Edinburgh 18'. I wanted to kiss it, to take it home. I was below the 20-mile mark. I ate three bourbon biscuits immediately.

Physically, I was drained from the cold, the lack of hot food and drink. Psychologically, I was fired up, and for the moment the latter won out. I felt my body grow chilled as the wind flapped the shirt like a flag. I wouldn't stop. Not even to put on my top. I wanted to be within 15 miles of the capital, from where I would launch my final assault.

Near the hamlet of Heriot, huddled on a distant hillside as if for protection, I called at the isolated Hangingshaw Garage, filled my water bottle and asked the owner, Vernon Nelson, of any possible shelter on this road. 'You'll find nothing at Heriot,' said Vernon in the manner of those horror films where travellers were warned off spooky places. 'Try the Dug Inn a few miles up the road. They have outhouses.'

Vernon was a trusting man. He went off to fill my bottle, leaving me alone in the wooden office with the Mars bars, Snickers, road maps, chilled Cokes, salt 'n' vinegar crisps. Not to mention the till. But my thieving was over.

I'd already walked more than 20 miles that day, plus a four-mile lift. I was determined to make the Dug Inn. Soreness, weariness, coldness – none would stop me.

The road rose towards a summit, the wind picking up. For three more miles I walked. I was oblivious to everything except one foot in front of the other, my face as impassive as a ship's masthead.

The Dug Inn stood on top of the lonely ridge. A sign outside offering food and accommodation creaked in the wind. As soon as I stopped, I knew I could travel no further that day. I tried the door. Locked. I rang the bell. No answer. I tried round the back. The same. A large 'Open' sign also flapped in the wind. At the rear were wooden tables and chairs. I sat down, felt the exhaustion take me. I was shivering, so put on my top. Despite the cold, I was drifting away. When I opened my eyes, a cat and some hens were looking at me.

I must have dozed off again. A slamming car door woke me. A Dutch family of four appeared from the front. Like me, they'd found the door shut. Could they have a cup of tea? Search me.

Another 20 minutes. I drifted in and out of sleep. I was sheltered from the wind here. My body felt taut, winched up tight. The pub's back door opened and out walked a youngish woman with a balding, middle-aged, nervous-looking man. I explained my journey, my penniless state, my need for shelter. I gave Vernon Nelson as my referee. The woman nodded. 'The owners will be back about seven. Can you hang on till then?'

I could. Where else would I go?

She led the man up the outer stone steps to the annexe. He turned. 'Writing a book about it, are you?' he asked in a high, over-loud voice.

I nodded.

'I'm going to write a book one day,' he said triumphantly.

All writers, given ten pence for every person who had said that to them, could holiday on their own luxury yacht.

The woman, called Pearl Cunningham, came back down the steps a few minutes later. 'I'm very cold and tired,' I said. 'I've been walking all day. Could I sit inside and write my diary?'

''Course,' she said, and smiled. Inside was a clutch of locals. They'd been there all the time, having gone in through their own side-door entrance. The warmth embraced me like a furry animal in this old, low-beamed pub. I found a quiet table in a corner, away from the banter. Where did these drinkers come from? The pub was perched on this ridge top, no houses to be seen.

I took out my diary, pen and ink. I couldn't pick the pen up. It fell out of my hand, which was as effective as one of those amusement arcade claws that always drop the prizes.

'Drink this.' Pearl put a steaming mug of tea down next to me, plus a plate of biscuits. I could follow, centimetre by centimetre, the journey of each hot sip through my iceberg of a body.

I simply had to sit and wait. My body would eventually come in from the cold. I'd been stupid, walked all those chilled miles in just a thin top. For half an hour I was as still as a Harrods dummy. A middle-aged couple came in and sat at one of the nearby tables set for food. I made them feel nervous. They got their own back. Gammon steak appeared for him, steak and kidney pie for her. The aroma curled up from the plate, took one look at me and heartlessly headed straight for my nostrils. Three days since my last hot meal.

My body had slowly warmed like a radiator. I concentrated on the diary, plunged into the writing. Next time I looked, the food had gone, and the couple, and 1,000 words.

The nervous middle-aged man came in and sat at an eating table. I'll call him Larry from Sheffield. He looked about him constantly. Pearl took his order. He asked her what he should do that evening. Go into the Festival? Stay here? What was on? Could he park? Would it be crowded? When she'd gone, he talked to me. What did I think? Better to stay here? Go into Edinburgh? What of the bus services?

'I'm writing this diary up,' I said. 'I'll talk to you later.'

Larry sat like a schoolboy who'd been told off for talking too much. Pearl appeared with his pint, and for me another tea, and a ham roll. She was brilliant. I was fairly sick of bread. But also starving.

All the time, I felt Larry straining for me to finish. At 6.30 I put the pen and diary away. Larry began talking immediately. He'd spent the last 15 years working abroad as an expat, employed by a foreign government. He spoke of his servants, the women he'd had cheap, the life of Riley. He'd got the sack, come back to England, enrolled on a computer course, moved back with his parents. He talked of doing this, doing that, but not doing it. Taking this and that decision, but not taking it. He talked in a loud, insistent voice. A motorbike couple sitting nearby exchanged pained looks with one another. He bought himself another pint, and one for me. So what did I think?

'Maybe moving back with your parents wasn't a good idea, Larry,' I said. 'It's going back.'

He vaguely nodded and talked on. His talking was a great juggernaut of a monologue, unstoppable, armoured against all influences. He ordered his food from Pearl. It arrived. One of those steak and kidney pies under a hot-air balloon of pastry, chips, vegetables, a huge plateful. The hot food sat inches from me.

'Heavens,' said Larry. 'I couldn't eat all this. You can have some.'

I resisted the first temptation – to scoop it all up into my mouth. The image of the two of us sitting picking off the same plate didn't appeal. 'Just leave what you don't want,' I said. 'Thanks very much.'

'There'll be loads left,' he said.

As he devoured the pie, he talked of how he'd like to be in a relationship, but it didn't happen. As the chips slowly disappeared, he spoke of all the parties in his old job, the free booze. As the vegetables were cleared from the plate, he said he didn't much like computing, but what else was there?

As he pushed the totally empty plate to one side, my ravenous eyes fixed on it, he was still talking. Pearl took the plate away. Larry dabbed his lips with a napkin. I paused, and then, 'Larry,' I said, 'you talk about absolutely nothing but yourself!'

'I suppose I do,' he replied. 'The thing is, I looked in the papers for other jobs, but then thought what could I do, and . . .'

Suddenly Larry was a symbol to me. I could no longer hear the words. Larry was all the rootless, drifting, spiritual crises in the world. Larry was all that emptiness, that bewildered sense of not knowing what it was all for, the unfocused, directionless lives. Larry was a lost soul, silently screaming his way through life. I imagined Larry some day, found slumped in a dishevelled bedsit, his wrists florid with his final futile act.

My hunger, my exhaustion, all this was as nothing at that moment. I felt suddenly stronger, more alive than I had for a long time. Like I was a tiny part of things, but massively important. It was Larry who had done this. Larry and my journey. Larry's loss had been my gain. Larry had put my month in focus.

Two hours later than planned, at nine o'clock, the landlady, Gillian Torrie, returned. I'd been in the pub three hours.

'You're the man walking the country?' she asked, busying herself behind the bar.

I nodded.

'There's a room in the annexe waiting to be decorated. Nothing in it, but you're welcome to it. Jamie will show you.' And she motioned her young son, and she was gone.

I had no time to ask about food. Jamie was already moving out of the room. I followed him. Larry followed me. We ascended the same steps. My room was on the first floor, Larry's on the second.

The room was as bare as a centrefold. A few white dust-sheets splattered with paint, the odd brush and paint pot, the fragrance of turpentine. There was also a small kitchen. I scoured the shelves for food. None.

There was hot water in the tap. I washed twice, because I liked the sensation. For the last time, I unpacked my dark-blue sleeping bag, and I folded out the dustsheets for some slight mattress. The room's door was frosted glass, and before wriggling in I turned out the landing light.

Twenty minutes later, Larry descended for the toilet. He went back up leaving the light on. It flooded into my room. I wriggled out of the bag and switched it off. Another half hour on, I was awakened again. Same operation. Again the light was left on. Again I wriggled out. It was probably another half-hour before his third visit. The sound of the toilet door jolted me awake.

Somehow I knew what Larry would do. A shadow loomed outside the frosted glass. My door clicked open and Larry walked in.

'Wrong door, Larry!' I said. There was a pause, a sort of muffled reply. Larry backed out and pulled the door shut. This time the landing light was switched off and I heard Larry's footsteps up the stairs. I never saw Larry again.

Miles travelled so far – 530

The final day
Not even the sun
Can beat me home

Downhill Racer – Return of the World – Forgotten Treasure

My final day's waking. I lay on the bare floor of the bare room for an hour after 5.30 a.m. My hunger was acute, and the first job was to empty my bag in search of remnants.

I found one tiny orange, one bourbon biscuit, the final square of Belgian chocolate and a severely squashed miniature Snickers bar all the way from West Tanfield. I laid them out in a line. Would they be sufficient fuel to reach Edinburgh? A sign outside the pub said 'Breakfasts served from 7.30', but no one had mentioned feeding me.

I shaved in the kitchen sink, using a pair of scissors for reflection. For the last time I carefully folded and packed my meagre belongings. I pulled on the faithful boots, slowly tied the purple, bedraggled laces.

I'd done no exercises for the past week. My body seemed to have taken on so many other demands. It felt tired, but good. There was a dreamlike sense to it. I was high on adrenalin, low on calorie intake.

By 7.15 my bag was packed, my diary written up. I took a last look at my depersonalised room, walked out the glass door and down the steps and went to the front of the pub. There was no sign of life. I shivered in the keen wind. It had rained heavily in the night, leaving a grey, overcast day. To the west were the Pentland Hills with their extraordinary hanging curtain of cloud. The Dug Inn, an ex-farm, was perched on top of Middleton Mains and shared its vast landscape with scarcely another building. The odd commuter whizzed past *en route* to the capital. I stamped my

249

feet, pulled the small jacket tighter around me, willed the pub to come alive. At 7.35 I decided it was a lost cause. I prepared myself for the long, unfuelled trudge.

As I turned to go, the Budweiser sign in the bar window lit up. Never had I been so grateful to see that awful US beer in lights. Another light, the drawing back of bolts, and there stood landlord John Torrie.

'Ye'll be hevin' some breakfast afore ye go?'

Well, actually, that might be quite nice, yes.

My saviour again was Pearl. I sat down in the bar while Pearl cooked the breakfast in the kitchen. The aromas drifted through, the enticing sizzles a melody in my ears. John set the table. I stared with fierce concentration at the knife, the fork, the salt pot, the pepper pot, the brown sauce, the marmalade. I picked up and fondled each one. Pearl appeared and plonked down the plate. Egg, bacon, sausage and fried bread. I paused for two seconds to take in this vision, then devoured it so rapidly it led to the almost unheard-of (for me) indigestion pains during my first hour's walking.

As a speed eater, I'd long since mastered the art of eating and speaking simultaneously. John, an ex-motor mechanic, told me he'd bought the pub the previous year. What of the name? I'd assumed it referred either to the remoteness (a need to be 'dug out' of snow each winter) or its previous life as a farm ('dug' being the Old English word for teat). It was neither. The previous owners had been Douglas and Martin and had opted for the hybrid Dugin, which John and Gillian had simply tinkered with slightly. The farming legacy persisted, though. Several ponies, goats and hens wandered about.

I was fuelled for my final leg. My journey had begun with a 15-mile trek from one large city and would end with 16 miles to another. How different the journeys would be. I had struggled from Plymouth to Tavistock all day, and had all but abandoned the whole venture. Now I was planning to make Edinburgh by lunchtime. The journey was downhill, dropping to the vast plain out of which the city rose. The breakfast had left me like a high-performance machine filled with high-performance fuel. The previous day my tank had all but run dry. Now I was revving up. Off I went.

The first break was more out of habit than need. As I closed on Edinburgh, the wild countryside fell away. I passed the magnificent 23-arch viaduct at Herdergreen roundabout. Eight miles from the centre, a flat, featureless series of long arteries stretched ahead. Each gave way to a roundabout, another stretch, another roundabout in the distance. Even at this late stage, such drabness depressed me. What lifted me was the sudden sight of the city itself. It rose as if squeezed up from the plain, as if confidently asserting its right to its unique reputation. Edinburgh had got up especially for me.

My final resting place of probably more than 100 resting places on a route of 546 miles was a grass verge at the junction of Craigmillar Castle Road and Old Dalkeith Road. I stretched out for 15 minutes and ate the final orange. I expected giddy elation. There never was at such moments. Should I leap in the air, shout 'Hurrah!'? No. I walked across the road, peed behind a wall and realised for the first time that my bag was unattended. A sneak thief at that moment, making off with diary, notes, etc., would have made for a slightly deflating finale.

It was a long haul up Dalkeith Road, with its massive tenements. And then further, and suddenly I was back in a big city. I had landed on another planet. Men in suits with mobile phones, sophisticated restaurants, traffic jams, honking horns, department stores, police-car sirens, traffic lights, petrol fumes, streets teeming with people, newspaper vendors, double-decker buses, giant office blocks.

I was swallowed up, as effortlessly as tens of thousands were swallowed up. I was just another backpacker here for the Festival, submerged in the great beating heart of the city. The lonely country roads were behind me, the long, solitary trek with all its delights, nightmares, surprises, my inner and outer journey, my month's odyssey. All another world. I was by nature an urbanite, yet felt an alien. No grass, no trees, no distant lonely horizons. Just the noise, the bustle, the ant-like teeming.

'*Big Issue?*' A young man held out a copy.

'Sorry, no money.' He smiled. He'd heard it a hundred times. Why should I be different?

Yet a part of me was childlike, bursting out. I walked into my publishers', demanded the posh lunch they'd promised me on completion. My comeuppance was still several hours away. It would arrive hours later, back on Tyneside, as I unpacked everything in the unfamiliar surroundings of my own house.

I emptied all pockets. Folded and tucked away in the top pocket of my loose jacket, secured and totally forgotten these last 25 days, was the ten pound note from Geoffrey Boucher in Tavistock.

My first task the next morning would be to return it intact.

Postscript

I was fired up when my publishers bought me a big lunch in the Magnum, next to their premises in Albany Street. I was still fired up when I got off the train in Newcastle, to be met by Kitty. We went out that evening for a celebratory pizza, and I was still fired up until nine o'clock, when it began to hit me. My body seemed to be emptying quicker than a plugless sink.

We managed to get home and I spent a feverish night. The next morning my skin hurt if you touched it. When I walked, my stomach muscles were painful. My son Dylan hurtled in to see me, and I had to tell him to handle with care. The stomach pain, I concluded, was due to eating three big meals in one day after so much deprivation. Many Auschwitz prisoners died after liberation through eating too much too soon.

Overall, messages had gone to my body. It's all over. The adrenalin could stop pumping. It did, and my body gave out. Some unnatural energy had powered me through those last days. Now the flip side. For almost a week I was physically and mentally adrift. Part of me couldn't adjust to the journey's end. Part of me couldn't believe I'd done it at all, this crazy idea dreamed up one night.

I went down to see my aged parents. My dad asked me to cut the hedge. I wasn't up to it, couldn't keep the shears up.

I couldn't see my journey in context. What was it for? A travel book? A social document? What had I been trying to do? Some people thought I'd been mimicking down-and-outs. Not so. I simply wanted to see if I could survive penniless for 500 miles. That was it.

I travelled rurally, a new experience. Whatever muddled picture of the journey emerges in my mind is mainly of rural, not urban, Britain. Some startling things. I met no black people. The countryside, in our multi-racial society, has remained exclusively white, a worrying trend. I met very few teenagers, and only one, James at Clifton Kennels, working on the land. The others seemed peripheral to the culture of the land. What did this mean for the future? I realised that the 'rural' occupied a strong position in our culture. It represented both the fiercely traditional (foxhunting, the squirearchy) and the radical (the efforts of Swampy and friends). We longed for it in a muddled kind of Habitat-kitchen way. We listened to *The Archers*. Some of us bought second homes. Few of us knew much at all about its heart-beat.

I slowly returned to normal. My trip had often scared me, forced me into confrontations with myself. Someone asked, was it like Bill Bryson's *Notes from a Small Island*? Hardly.

Apart from anything else, the trip was informed through-out not mainly by travel, but by my penniless state. Someone else joked, 'Well, I'm broke all the time!'

No, you're not, I said. Not like this. It coloured almost every act, every decision, every move. I could do little without taking into account my total lack of money.

Someone asked, were there regional differences, the north-south divide? Not at all. I was shunned in all parts, in both countries. Likewise made welcome. Stereotypes did not apply.

I began to think of the importance of walking. Few of us do it in more than a token way. I thought of a National Walking Club, its members mutually supportive. Imagine 50,000 registered members. Each member would agree to offer a maximum (say 14) number of nights' shelter per annum to other members. That member in turn would be able to claim the same number from others. Members' lists would be supplied, along with proper identification. Pre-booking your walking journey would be essential. Off you'd go, 14 nights' stops awaiting *en route*.

Most averagely fit people on a two-week walk could manage 150 miles. We would become more social, more active, more knowledgeable about our country. We would meet new people all the time, our horizons would broaden. And it would cost very little to anyone.

I'm not suggesting people travel without money. I've never been bothered about being rich, but a penniless state brings a dreadful sense of exclusion and alienation, a psychological state I found hard to deal with. My spirits sank incredibly low at times. I yearned to throw it all in.

Many people mistrusted me, as they would. I was as open and transparent as possible. What's remarkable is that in 27 nights, only once was no help forthcoming. To all those people who took a chance on me, I say a big thank you. I wrote to them all on my return. My journey would not have been possible without them.

And though I've never been interested in being rich, deprivation made me realise how lucky most of us in this country were. How much this was taken for granted.

Did I enjoy it? I'm suspicious about 'enjoyment' as the main pursuit. Fulfilment is more lasting. There was obviously a need for me to get up, confront myself, push myself to physical and mental extremes. At times the month seemed endless. I stuck it out. It now occupies a huge space in my consciousness and will always colour my behaviour, my reactions. Spending a month on a sunny beach might have been more 'enjoyable', but I'm not sure I'd have preferred it overall. How would it have shaped me as a human being?

The Indians were right. A pilgrimage at 50. Most of us are still physically active and have enough experience to fortify us against new challenges. Yet many are rushing into early retirement, pipes and slippers. What's ahead is more impor-tant than what's behind. On a 500-mile trek, or on your last day on earth.

What was the journey for? What did it achieve? Over its duration, I changed a lot. I discovered startlingly simple truths, prominent among which (for a townie) was the fact that everything we humans make or manufacture, we eventually tire of. What's made or created by nature, on the other hand, never wearies us.

Obvious? Possibly. But it explains my need each day at home to visit the sea, which is always the same, always changing. How could it ever let me down? I absorbed myself into my native land, and felt more a part of that land than ever before. And I genuinely felt that, having taken on this task, the fates were looking after me. In my darkest moments, this was a comfort.

The journey was not easy. Nor was writing the book. Early drafts seemed over-gloomy, dwelling on the depressive aspects. Who'd want to read such self-pitying whines? I tried to inject some humour. Was it too much? Did it dilute the experience? And was I merely skating across a 500-mile surface? I had no research, no statistics, no foreknowledge. I was merely one flawed human being trudging across a changing terrain and responding with a notebook.

My mental state was often strange, my mind and body fatigued. Witness how many small factual errors in the manuscript were unearthed by my excellent editor at Mainstream, Cathy Mineards. And me an ex-journalist . . .

In all of us there is a restlessness, a sense that there should be more to life, that it should be different from how it is. This restlessness will not go away. Nor will it ever be satisfied. All we have is the trying. And, after that, the trying again.